W9-BYK-814

Igniting the Sixth Sense

*The Lost Human Sensory that Holds the Key
to Spiritual Awakening and
Unlocking the Power of the Universe*

By Eric Pepin

*Higher Balance Publishing
Portland, Oregon*

This book has been transcribed and compiled from live lectures given by Eric Pepin. Some elements of the live format have been preserved.

Published by Higher Balance Institute
515 NW Saltzman Road #726, Portland, Oregon 97229
www.higherbalance.com

ISBN: 978-1-939410-03-0

Library of Congress Control Number: 2013944494
Igniting the Sixth Sense / Eric Pepin

Published 2013.

Printed in the United States of America

Other Books by Eric Pepin

The Handbook of the Navigator

Meditation within Eternity:
*The Modern Mystics Guide to Gaining Unlimited
Spiritual Energy, Accessing Higher Consciousness and
Meditation Techniques for Spiritual Growth*

Books by Higher Balance

Bending God: *A Memoir*

To discover more techniques and knowledge from
Eric Pepin, and to experience awakening yourself
beyond what is discussed in this book, visit:
www.higherbalance.com.

ADD TO YOUR EXPERIENCE
READERS ONLY FREE MATERIAL

Readers of this book receive special reader-only material that you can download for free. This extra material expands on the knowledge to be gained here.

To receive your free downloads, visit
www.ignitingthesixthsense.com
then click on the Readers-Only option. Follow the directions to enter a password from this book to login.

My sincere gratitude and thanks to the following Navigators who, without their contributions and support, this book would not have been written. Together, all things are possible.

Loretta Huinker
Vivien Fedd
Amy Provost
Joe Salvador
Penney Newman
Brady Herberle
Ray Ross
Mai Liis Sepp
Irina Isayeva
Deborah Dewet

With special thanks to Rick H, John A, Andrea D, Steve H, and Nick C.

TABLE OF CONTENTS

INTRODUCTION

IN *MEDITATION WITHIN Eternity*, you gained a new and uniquely different perspective on energy, meditation, and how it all fits into the larger concepts of spirituality. You discovered the fundamental truths of energy, how it works, why it works the way that it does, and how you can harness it through meditation to accelerate the evolution of your consciousness. You were also introduced to the sixth sense, how it relates to spirituality and what we consider God to be.

**The sixth sense is the key to understanding
and experiencing the Universe.**

Now that you have a strong foundation of understanding, it's time to probe a little deeper into the meaning of it all. It's time to discover more about you and to observe your thoughts and behaviors. You have learned how to gather Prana, but now you need to know how to use it. This is where the enigmatic sixth sense comes in.

Understand that in many ways, the sixth sense is alien to the modern thinking brain. Therefore, the first step is to re-acquaint you with it. The sixth sense is a very natural part of you that you have forgotten. In addition, it is a magnetic sensory that is also instinctual. Nature is the best way to understand how this works.

Less intelligent animals actively use this instinct on a daily basis, but they do not have the complexity of the human brain. Homing pigeons direct their flights with it. Dogs sense their owners returning home, and dairy cows sense barometric pressure changes over and above our best technology. The list goes on, and on. The sixth sense is a sense within all creatures, including humans. You need to reawaken that sense.

Beginning with the senses that you are already familiar with, the sense of touch gives you the impression of an object. The sense of sight gives you color and shading. Therefore, your five senses define your reality. If you were without one of your five senses, you would likely feel a disconnection from life. I believe that the sixth sense is that defining sense that is missing in your life. The sixth sense will identify the missing link in your *sensory* and provide the answers to the questions you have been asking your whole life. Once you identify it, you can experience it. Once you experience it, you can share it and give it to others. I want to show you how to awaken your sixth sense.

By reawakening the sixth sense, you can reconnect with the Universe and experience it with your modern mind. I believe that the Universe is capable of intellectual processes that are well beyond the complete understanding of humanity. I see evolution as the direct intent of the Universe's will. This means that the sixth sense is still a part of evolution. Evolution is waiting for the re-emergence of the sixth sense within humanity so that humanity can re-unite itself fully with God, or the Universe.

As you work with your sixth sense and master it, eventually you will start moving towards the *Planes of Light* and so much more. There is no simple way to explain these other frequencies than to say that they are other universes beyond your own understanding. They are different dimensions, whole other realities often experienced as energy although they are just as real as this universe. When you enter these frequencies, you feel and experience a sense of God's presence. The visual effects are inspiring and breathtaking. Once you have experienced these places, you are changed forever. It is unfair for me to suggest what you may encounter as each experience means something for the individual who experiences it. Your frequency is unique to you, and the Universe recognizes you by it. When you approach the Universe as a frequency, it gives or shares information that was meant exclusively for you.

An interesting effect of experiencing other dimensions is that they also teach you something new, something that you couldn't have learned otherwise. Experience is a form of knowledge; so the more you meditate, reflect, and awaken your sixth sense, the more you will evolve and progress to higher frequencies.

It is plausible to conceive that you have spent a good part of your life wandering around wondering who you are, what your purpose is, where you need to go, and how you should get there. Moreover, there are deeply hidden memories waiting to surface, if only you can approach them correctly. My point is that you will find the answers to your questions through these practices.

There is an energy that moves through all things. It moves through the world and through the Universe. Most people are not even aware of it, or don't acknowledge that it exists. But there are also a few people who constantly feel a need to reach out to it. Perhaps, if you are reading this, you are one of those people. I want to help you achieve this communion. This can only happen if you are willing to let go a little. You must accept that there are still great mysteries to discover and that inside, you hold the key to one of those.

When most people think of the sixth sense, they think of psychic abilities or things they have seen in the movies or read about. These are all misconceptions because it is not anything like that. It is the bridge from your physical self to your dimensional consciousness. We must approach the sixth sense from two places: the brain and the mind, or the physical body and the energy body. The sixth sense creates a union between the two. Your thoughts and beliefs play a strong role in how quickly your sixth sense will surface. Your thoughts determine your frequency based upon what you already understand. The more you understand or *get it*, the more your frequency will evolve to the higher spectrums. This, in turn, *tunes* you. All dimensions have a specific frequency or vibration. You must match that frequency to experience it. This is why I spend so much time on communication and analogies. It is critical that you understand in order to have success.

As you raise your frequency through your practices, you will evolve. This is the beginning of *enlightenment*. There are many misconceptions about the meaning of enlightenment, so using the word has both advantages and disadvantages. As you evolve and match your frequency with the higher dimensions, you temporarily connect with the knowledge of that vibration. As you explore the higher dimensions, it is possible to attain multi-leveled experiences all at the same time. This creates an enlightened state of mind called *Multi-Dimensional Consciousness.*

We will always have to deal with life's challenges; it is all part of change. But having the right tools to guide and assist us can make all the difference. For example, you cannot take a flower bud and force it to open. You must nurture it, give it sunlight, and water; eventually it will bloom on its own. This is what I'm doing here. I am providing tools for the person who wants to bloom and is ready to awaken.

Good journeys,
Eric Pepin

Chapter 1

THOUGHT REFLECTION

YOUR THOUGHTS MAKE a huge difference in how, or whether, you achieve a higher state of consciousness. They shape and form you. How you think defines how you perceive yourself. How you perceive yourself determines the possibilities of what you believe you can achieve. Your self-perception is pre-determined by your thoughts. It includes not only your surface thoughts, but also your internal thoughts continuously going on in the back of your mind that you're not fully aware of. Those include your feelings of being threatened by other people who may not believe or seek what you do, judging yourself, and comparing yourself to others. It also includes your preconceived ideals of having to be like others and not living your own life. Your thoughts may keep you from asking the all-important question deep inside that will lead to your liberation and spiritual awakening. You may bypass it just because of your perceived judgment from other people. That assumption comes from your inner mind. Thinking in that process confirms you are a product of the *matrix* rather than the product of self-liberation.

The matrix is the global consciousness of the planet. Matrix is a new word. The old word was *the Gaia mind*. The Gaia mind, or matrix, is the collective of hundreds of billions -- if not trillions -- of living, thinking creatures (human beings and animals) collectively pooling their intelligence. The matrix tells you how to function in life the same way those red blood cells or white blood cells in your body *know* how to function.

There is a control mechanism that keeps your thoughts and motivations in check.

How much does the matrix affect your thoughts and how much is actually free will, free thought, or free choice?

For now, let us concentrate on the thought process. The majority of spiritual teachings emphasize the importance of being aware of *how* you're thinking. A good way to do that is to be mindful. Mindfulness means to be aware of yourself, of *what* you're thinking and *how* you're thinking. If you're mindful of your thoughts, you will have a lot more spiritual breakthroughs.

That brings us to *willpower.* Willpower directs your thoughts to achieve a goal. Both willpower and mindfulness affect the thought process.

When you create an affirmation for positive things to happen in your life, you visualize objects and situations so you can manifest them. This is part of the thought process. So is self-discipline, which is creating a ritual like being at a certain place at a certain time to achieve a certain goal. Directing your will is the same thing. All of this ties together as *the thought process.*

When analyzing your thoughts, you must turn inward to reflect on how and why you think the way that you do. Dissect your thoughts; do not just look at the message, as in what you are thinking. What is the process, the dynamics, the mechanisms behind it all? Instead of simply looking at the clock, the hands and the time that it represents, learn what fundamental gears are behind it. That understanding will help to liberate something deeper within.

Thoughts are living things; thoughts are alive. When you think about your body, your thoughts govern your reactions. When you tell your arm to move, it moves. When you tell yourself to walk, you walk. When you tell your mouth to talk, it talks. It is this way with all of your senses. Thought is integrated with how you function in this dimension. And as a dimensional being, thought is how you move or propel through the ribbons of time and space to travel from point A to Z. Thought is the living mechanics of your *True Self*. Thought is the flesh of the energy body just as your physical body is the structure for what you think of as *you*.

Your thoughts design you by how you think and how you process them. Give some very serious time reflecting on that. When I say to you "thought is a living thing," it is thought that makes you what you *seem* to be. Thought is the interaction of consciousness, a representation of you expressed by how you move, talk, your facial gestures, and your body movements.

If you take an object and will your emotions into it, you create an energy program. That program has an intention. That program has thought that becomes a living thing. It's just a matter of your perception. For example, let's consider the energies of an imaginary household. A person walks into a house and they're feeling very angry. They pick up a pillow as they are talking, venting their frustrations, unconsciously twisting or hitting the pillow, totally unaware of their actions. They're programming the pillow, unconsciously with their thoughts. When they leave, that pillow still holds their intention within it. When something has an intention, it creates a forward movement. It has an agenda; a program.

Everything that's affected by thought has an agenda. The whole planet has a huge agenda and you are a byproduct of that. If you think about the consciousness of the planet, you realize that it has an agenda for all of the organic and inanimate life that's absorbed within it. You have an agenda for your own body. You have an agenda for life, for exploration, for the way you want things to appear to others. You have agendas on many different levels. Forces of thought consciousness are bombarding you and affecting you every single moment.

Do different locations affect the way we feel?

The town or city where you live holds a certain vibration and when you're there, you are impacted by it. When you leave the town you almost feel relieved. There is a thought consciousness imbued into that town that affects you. So, in terms of thought, we are no longer looking at the clock and saying we understand what time is. We understand that when we go into a town, we are affected by many different things. We also know when we go into a house we're being affected. So now, let's dissect the mechanisms that make this process work.

When we meditate, our goal is to try to get out of the matrix. The matrix is a living thing, a living program and you are part of this living thing. It expects you to function in a process that works within itself. If you bump that system, its natural inclination is to force you back into place. During meditation, we try to quiet the busy mind or the *Babbler*. The purpose of the Babbler is to try to keep you in check. So it, in itself, has a goal that is derived by intelligence with an intention. It's not just a thing that automates, and whether or not you can overcome this complex situation has nothing to do with it being there. Everything has a living consciousness. Everything has an intention and its intention is to keep you in check in a way that works for itself. If you can understand this, then liberation through meditation will make sense to you. When we say we meditate to remove ourselves from the collective consciousness so that something higher can come in, what we are trying to do is separate ourselves from the will of the matrix. This is the liberation that you're after.

We now have to look at the matrix and ask ourselves how many levels it works within. Ask yourself one thing: how many levels do you have working within you? We have many aspects inside of us that I refer to as the "I's." A very simple, quick way to describe the I's is the emotions inside of you expressed as love, hate, anger, positivity, and negativity. You have all these different emotions and consciousnesses within you. Can you imagine how complex the next level of this is for the entire planet? These I's that exist for the planet infuse you and affect you with their intention. When you are able to acknowledge this, this is the first step to true liberation. It is the first step in resolving a problem, if you can identify it and know where it is coming from.

Let's look at this in a different way. If you are being hunted, the best way to defend yourself is to be aware of it. If someone is stalking you with negative intentions they're following you, observing you, studying you, and preparing for their moment of attack. You are at a great disadvantage. It would be important to have the first initiative, the ultimate opportunity of surprise. Once you lose that you are vulnerable. The first thing you should learn when pursuing spiritual consciousness is how to recognize and acknowledge the opposition -- who or what opposes your agenda? The best thing to do is to educate yourself by studying whatever this opposing force is. And it's not that you should look at it as just an opposing force because as long as you're in a physical body, you're part of that opposing force. On a spiritual context, you are really trying to separate yourself as an energy being that co-exists in the physical body.

So now your job becomes twice as difficult because you have to work within the mechanism of the matrix. You have to be able to step outside of it. This is where things become very complicated and difficult. The matrix does not see you as an individual. Individualization is deeper within the nitty-gritty of the mechanism.

What we've done so far is to look at the bigger gears. Now, we're going to look at the smaller gears: the springs, the nuts and bolts behind the bigger gears and how all of this works together to hold time in a particular sequence. Time is an illusion, yet we know that time is something that we must deal with in our reality. When looking at Einstein's theory of relativity, we recognize time by its different aspects of distances and ratios and we understand that there are many levels beyond that.

So far, you've accepted that you are controlled by mechanisms because you see time as the accepted reality. You are also aware, on another level of consciousness, that there's something beyond all of this and you're trying to liberate yourself from it. What you need to understand is that deep in your psyche, you've kept yourself from being aware because you believe that this is where you are. You've already accepted this fact, but you just don't know that you have. So even if on the surface you tell yourself that you know there's something more and you're searching for it, internally you're locked into this zone. That's what you're trying to liberate yourself from.

What are the smaller mechanisms of the gears that you're talking about?

We know the big gear is the will of Gaia. We know it wants *red cells* to be red cells, as I've taught in other lessons. Gaia wants you to function in life, do your routine, and collect experiences. When you die, you release your experiences into the pool of consciousness that belongs to Gaia. *White cells* are constantly trying to separate from that mechanism so they can move independently. The question is, "What are these smaller mechanisms?"

We create psychic webbing every day with every person we meet. The term 'psychic webbing' is really a visual way of interpreting our connection to the collective consciousness. You pick up the vibration – their unique frequency -- of everybody that you meet, and everyone else does the same thing. The better you know someone, the stronger the connection, the stronger the psychic webbing.

When you learn *Multi-Dimensional Meditation* and you meditate, your sudden increase in vibration shakes this webbing. It sends out signals to everyone you are connected with in the present and from the past. Without knowing why, they often react. You might get a phone call from friends or people that you haven't spoken to in years. There is a way to cut this webbing that reduces your connection to the grid.

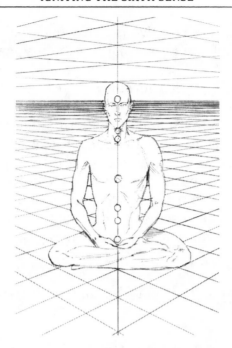

We are all connected to the collective grid through energy connections imagined as 'psychic webbing'.

Why is it important to cut the webbing?

It's important because some people frequently have you in their thought consciousness. They're the people you've cut relationships with when you wanted to move on. Maybe they weren't a very positive influence in your life, but you were sending energy to them through this psychic webbing. When you meditate, you draw in energy and shake those lines, and they become aware of you. It is important to cut those lines from the people you moved away from. Why should you do this? They're going to keep you from achieving your goal of a higher state of consciousness. They are going to do that by being your friend or even just saying hello. You know that you're trying to free your consciousness and teach it to separate from the negative patterns that you've created in your life. People represent markers in those patterns. They are the catalyst that brings you back to a method of thinking that they're used to. It's how they relate to you. Familiarity is a natural instinct that helps them relate to you in that way. So you're going to use the old pattern rather than the new, progressive way that you've learned instead.

Your thoughts and how the process of your thoughts is affecting you. The goal of this chapter is to learn how to create new thought patterns with old relationships. You're going to be able to look at someone from your past and, if you are strong enough, you will now be able to reprogram them.

How do people hold us in their patterns?

When they start to communicate with you in a playful way, like tapping you on the arm saying, "Hey, don't you remember how we used to do this?" or "Do you remember that?" You can recognize their motives. Most of the time, people refer to the past to re-establish the marker that brings you back to the past to access that state of mind. When that happens, it brings all of the old memories of your personality into the present-state of your consciousness. Do you understand what they're doing? It's a kind of a manipulation. It's not that they're doing it intentionally, but the question is, "Are they doing it unconsciously?" Unconsciously, they're bringing you into their zone to a place where you reflected at one time, but now you've outgrown that place. How you control this situation is by realizing, during the conversation, that is exactly what they're doing. You can recognize this by listening to the message behind their words or by how they're treating you.

Re-assert yourself by saying, "I really don't like it when you tap me on the arm. I don't mean to be rude. I do remember all of that, but I've moved on." You need to take control of the situation. Don't let them bring you back into the past. You have to establish the present state of who you are instead of reverting back to who you were.

Referring back to old memories can be a very dangerous thing unless you can learn to stay detached. They will become more powerful as you begin to reflect more and more on those old memories. They are like power places; they're programs that are still alive. By regurgitating old thoughts, old concepts, and other old things you've done before, you're setting up a program that goes into your computer system, your mind, and begins to play it over and over. It becomes an active program and starts to reintegrate its ways back into your personality.

Ask yourself, "What keeps me in the matrix?" It's your thought processes and the relationships that you have in life. Why is it when you want to meditate that you're often unable to do it? It's usually because other people are encroaching on the limited amount of time that you have. Or you're busy with life, which is part of the larger mechanism. But when you have free time, you often find that people infringe on your time.

We've learned to accept it. We've learned that this interference is an okay thing. It's the first step in being aware of whom your enemy could be. You can still be courteous and kind, but you have to be mindful of the decisions that you make. Be mindful when you're with other people that aren't inside the mechanism of spiritual growth that you're working so diligently for. Be mindful when you hang out with people who don't have the same goals that you do. You may be consumed by their state of consciousness, so you have to be sure that you're prepared and strong enough to avoid it.

I'm not telling you that you need to leave your family behind. You need time for self-reflection to redesign and build yourself so you can accomplish your spiritual goals. You have to realize that your family, your friends, and all of those people from the past have a predetermined state of consciousness of who they think you are and how you should act. They identify you within a program of their own personal expectations.

When you have self-realization, sometimes you will find that your family will try to bring you back into their reality. They will try to draw you into the old design that you were rather than allow you to be who you are now. If you were never an intellectual person, whenever you try to express your thoughts they will dismiss them and start speaking *over* you. They won't give your statement much credibility and the person who always was considered to be the intellectual will take over the conversation. Their opinion is suddenly more important. Everybody who's within that family or group dynamic knows the process and will face the person who they think is more knowledgeable in that particular area. It's part of being in the mechanism, and for you to bump that system takes a great deal of effort on your part. It's not that you should focus on this scenario in particular; rather you should recognize the mechanisms that are shaping and molding how you think and how you are affected.

There's an old saying that makes a lot of sense: "birds of a feather flock together." The people you hang out with reflect who you will become. If you interact with people with a low sense of achievement, likewise, you will not achieve. It's the same thing with positive achievement and a higher state of consciousness. The circles that you choose create the programming that will affect your psyche, whether you realize it or not.

Usually groups of people have a stronger collective will than a single person does. If you associate with people who don't possess a progressive goal in their lives, it's very likely you will never achieve your goals either. Even if you think that you can overcome this, how much energy will you put into swimming against the current? Even though you're making headway, how much effort are you losing in this physical life? You have a limited amount of time on the Earth, so how much of it is ineffectively wasted by choosing to swim upstream when you should simply swim to the shore and walk uphill. Why is it that you cannot see the common sense of this logic? Tiny, tiny gears are affecting you. Why is it that you insist on swimming against the current? That's what you should be asking yourself.

Reverse your way of thinking and examine what's going on in your thoughts. You need to understand why you're making the choices that you're making. Ultimately, you know what you want to do - achieve the highest state of consciousness that you can. You want to enjoy and share life. You want to be giving, caring and kind. Unfortunately, I think most people have confused kindness with foolish self-sacrifice that doesn't move you forward.

There's a truth behind the saying, "Don't throw your pearls before swine." The swine can't understand what a pearl is; so it's really you who's being foolish by throwing the pearls on the ground when the pearls could have been used for something better. Until you realize the truth behind this statement and not see it as arrogant or egotistical, you cannot progress to a higher level of consciousness. You are being held back by your own perceptions of goodness, selfishness, kindness, or graciousness. You can say that you can be kind by helping someone who always requests your help, but every time that you give advice to this person, they don't really apply it. If they don't apply it and they keep asking you for help, ask yourself this question, "Am I being kind by consciously helping them?" Simply let them go so that you can help other people who are willing to apply your help.

If the matrix, the collective Gaia mind, can affect my thoughts and actions, can I affect it also?

The matrix is a multi-level design. Everybody is affected by the matrix, the Gaia mind, or the collective consciousness. Its goal is for you to be a living organism, to procreate, to create more organisms and when you die, to collectively take your experiences and release them like raindrops into the Gaia mind. It grows in slow processes of collective consciousness, not by an individual having massive breakthroughs. Achieving this collective growth requires hundreds of people, if not thousands, to have a massive breakthrough. So your goal should be to try to step out of the mechanism and that's a very difficult thing to do. You can achieve this with multi-dimensional meditation. In meditation, you're extracting yourself from everything that attracts you.

At this point, reflect on what you've been thinking about while reading this chapter. Discovering what you've been thinking about will tell you a lot about yourself. What people have you thought about while reading this? What inspirations have come out of this chapter so far? Who did you pick as being challenges, and why did you choose them in the first place? Those are the people who have the greatest influence on you, so you better be sure that their intentions are in your best interest. Never just assume they are.

Now, I want you to keep something very important in mind. We're dealing with many integrated, deep mechanisms. It is not right to take the extreme path and remove everything in your life and have absolute selfishness in order to achieve higher consciousness. It's just not feasible. You'll only end up harming or destroying yourself and you'll never reach your true objective - finding your higher self.

This is the most intimate level of inner manipulation, inner control, and thought control. If you integrate it slowly, you can achieve a positive outcome. You should always reflect on your earlier lessons and do your daily meditations to obtain a higher level of understanding. This does not mean that you have to separate from everyone in your life. Take control of how other people affect you. It is your own fault for allowing it to happen, not theirs. You can't point a finger at them and say, "You've manipulated me! I've lost this in my life because of you." You have the power to control your own destiny. How you choose to use that power and whatever level you choose to operate from is your choice and yours alone.

Be mindful and conscious of your thoughts. What are your motivations and where do they come from? What are your motivations in manipulating someone else? What are your motivations in getting what you want from someone else? What effect do you have on other people? How much control are you trying to exert over them? What is your goal? What is your agenda? How honest are you being with yourself?

You mentioned selflessness. What does it mean to be selfless?

Selflessness is not about being aware of how you're affected by thought. It's how you affect someone else by the choices that you make. It's how you affect others with your whims and your desires, whether monetarily, sexually, or anything else. Selflessness is having self-awareness and self-consciousness that stems from a higher level of being. It's being more conscious of your intentions by keeping them in check, keeping them unselfish, or more diplomatic. But you also have to remember there's a reason to be *selfish* in the context of accomplishing your goals. If you had to be at work and you didn't have much time, is it right to ask someone else to go to the store for you because they have more time? Is it selfish to say that you would like them to go to the store instead of you, or are you really trying to manipulate them into going to the store? Do you understand there is a difference?

Being honest with yourself begins by understanding how you manipulate others to control them. If you find that you need to control someone else to get what you want, they're probably not the right person for you. You shouldn't have to manipulate the people you care about in your life just to get what you want. They should be like the yin to your yang, working with you instead of against you. If you find that someone is trying to manipulate you, it's a very, very dangerous thing. If you find that you have to manipulate them back, it's twice as dangerous because now you are caught in the mechanism.

Again, if you can only see the wheel and the distant horizon, you will never realize that the horizon nearest you is simply keeping you in the same spiral. You just think you're progressing but you're not. Once you are in that trap, it's a no win situation. You have to be able to recognize it and react quickly. Sometimes you have to separate yourself from that situation or person. That could be a very painful process depending on how rooted the other person is psychologically within your mechanism, and how rooted you are within theirs.

So, again, it all comes back to thought. Thought is the inner matrix. The inner matrix is about individual relationships with the people in your life, no matter whether they are: sexual, physical or spiritual, and even your relationship with me. All of these have their input. All of these control one another, your destination, the direction you take, and how you will unfold. The more that you can recognize this, the more liberated you will become. It's not the fact that it's happening. Rather, can you see it happening? You must understand how thought works, how thought is a living thing, and how thought will affect you.

There could be larger energies trying to control you through thought; like going into a town or a house that has a certain vibration. These are all forms of thought control. There might be individual beings with controlling desires and wants who constantly affect you on a micro level.

We're also going to talk about other forms of thought manipulation. Micro control is done through emotional broadcasting. Let's say you want somebody to care about you very badly, so you keep projecting your energy at them. They may not recognize, specifically, that it comes from you, but for some reason they feel emotionally drained. They feel a heavy weight on them and a sense of depression or anxiety. This is an example of emotional broadcasting. Usually a person who wants another person this badly will go through a heavy depression because of their neediness for that person. In my opinion, it's robbing the other person and could almost be another form of psychic attack, even though it's done without that intention.

Why is it a form of psychic attack?

It can be considered a form of psychic attack because they are willfully thrusting their spirit upon you. They are projecting their energy, their desire to be with you, to be drawn to you, and desired by you. They are literally obsessed with you. It is important for you to devise some sense of protection. If someone tries to control another person, would it be with similar methods? What if it is an act of love, is that the same thing?

Their particular reasons may have originated from a good place, but what if it's a bad person, or somebody that *you* don't want to love? What if it's a guy who feels the same way about you as a girl does? You may not be attracted to the girl, but you feel more comfortable with a female wanting you than a male. Psychologically, there is a program in your head that accepts the opposite sex more readily. If someone of the same sex is interested in you, you might see this as a bad situation. We need to re-think how we are processing this because I don't think that either case is acceptable. In the end, it's not your free will that is being expressed. Rather, it is a force of control. What happens if their energy is enough to dominate you? What if it is done to a person who does not have the knowledge to defend themselves?

What if, what if, what if? What if they say, "I don't know what's wrong with me? I'm just really feeling depressed. I don't know why. I feel like I'm being pulled on and I don't know how to deal with it." Well, that person may be so in love with you that they just want you to love them in return. The problem is they're programming you with an emotion that you may not want. So now, you have a program being forced on you that is against your will, and they're being merciless about it because somewhere deep in their mind, they're obsessed with this every waking minute. Whether you realize it or not, you're going to be affected by it.

How will I be affected by this?

How you think and how you feel is a consequence of the byproduct of their will. This happens every day. For instance, you could go to a party and someone might be attracted to you. Their attention is on you, but you don't even know who they are. You probably do this to other people without even realizing it. People do this all day long. This is a mechanism of the matrix. It's a design that keeps it stable and functioning, and it's a necessity in itself. It's a control and be controlled situation that's constantly going on every waking moment in the consciousness of the grid, in the consciousness of the planet. It is a mechanism that affects relationships, pods, electrical beings, human beings, and moving consciousness. The mechanism controls interrelationships of shared data by manipulation and direction. If someone is advancing too quickly, the collective finds a way to hold them and brings them back down again.

These are all complex systems of thought, thought control, and consciousness, and the matrix is self-sustained by them. As long as we have biochemical responses when processing our thoughts and reactions, we will be controlled by its effects. So, the most that you can do is try to limit it by acknowledging it and seeing its processes. That separates you, which is part of self-liberation, but it is not easy to accomplish. And if anyone is thinking, "I'm going to go out and do it tomorrow," well you're setting yourself up for failure.

It's better to gradually work with something than to try to do it instantaneously. Understanding thought is a critical thing. Understanding your own thought and thinking about it is called *self-observation,* which is something you're told to do often. Through self-observation you will find liberation. Self-observation begins when we think about why we're doing something or saying something. With self-observation, we can say to ourselves, "Now that I've done that, I realize that I was being manipulative. What was my motive behind it? Was it for the greater good of this person or was it for my own self-gratification?"

There's nothing wrong with wanting someone to want you, and there's nothing wrong with wanting somebody to love you. The same holds true in trying to get to know someone. It's about how truthfully you want to go about the business of doing that. Truth is a perspective of how you see things. Through self-observation, you will find inner-truth and inner-awakening. So, it's not for me to say what truth should or shouldn't be. You have to discover your own truth by listening to that inner knowing. It is aware of when you should or shouldn't be doing something and to what extent.

Where do we draw the line between selfishness for the greater good, and selfishness for self-gratification?

There are self-motivations you should utilize that will get you to a better place, and there are some things you should avoid altogether. You already know what they are. You need to have a greater will inside of yourself to release others from you. This is surrendering the ego. It's a different kind of empowerment. Empowering yourself spiritually is perfectly alright because in the end, you find the truth in your heart.

So, if you want to use ego to build yourself up spiritually, by all means please do. I encourage it. Use your ego all you want providing it leads to the blossoming of your inner spirit or your inner heart, which subdues the ego. So you can use ego to fuel yourself if you think that will get you there, but to use ego for controlling others or for self-empowerment is a very different thing. You should know the difference. This knowledge will come from self-observation.

I mentioned earlier about how people can affect you spiritually when they're in love with you but you're not in love with them. It can be a big problem because you might be feeling depressed and not understand why you're feeling drained. You might be getting images of someone in your mind, and perhaps it's that particular person. All of a sudden, in your mind, you feel this depressed person and you think that you could have been more supportive of them. You think you should feel guilty, but you don't.

Ask yourself if that is an evil, negative thing or a positive thing. Someone's in love with you and all of their energy is being forced on you. You're constantly thinking about them because it's being infused in your mind. Do you say to yourself that you don't want to bother yourself with them because you don't want to be bothered? Or do you notice that person is really depressed and that you could make them happier by giving them some of your attention because you feel guilty about them being so depressed? What is the best solution?

When you see that person again, they might still be depressed. There's even a chance they could be suicidal. But that is not something you should personally feel guilty about because they want you to love them and they cannot control their own feelings. You're going to have to think about your position on this. If you need to move on, then by visiting them and making them think they're getting your attention, you're rewarding them for their depression. They push their energy on you because it gives them the results they want.

It's better to say *it's cruel to be kind*, which is how I look at many things. It's cruel to be kind because, eventually, they'll likely outgrow you. So give them an opportunity to meet someone else and move on with their life. The longer that you give them false hope, the longer you keep feeding this energy you cannot relate to because you're not in the same place. All you see is the extremes of their suffering. What you don't realize it is you're prolonging the inevitable. Eventually, the human brain learns to shut it off and you move on.

Ask yourself if you are letting them hang on to you because you think that you're being kind. Or are you letting them hang on because you're still feeding your ego? Do you secretly want that person to want you? Is this empowering you as a backup plan as you move on through life with other things? You know the difference already in your heart. You know this with self-observation.

So what can you do about it? Are you able to let that person go and destroy themselves with their suffering? Remember the story of the phoenix? Predictably, they will come back to life and they will move on. I have certainly been in love with other people and had to let go of them. They've gone through their suffering, but they've also moved on. It might take a little bit of time, but it's a matter of doing what is best. It may seem cruel or selfish, but in the end it is the best thing to do.

You might say that you're going to gradually move away from them. That may be the truth, but the amount of energy that it will take for that to happen could be time consuming and limiting in your life's journey. There has to be a point where you say, "I've been trying to let them go, but I just never quite get there. Am I fooling myself by allowing this process to keep going on and on?" You have to realize that you need to just walk away from this situation.

So there's a very fine line between selfishness and ego, if you think about it. What is affecting you? Is your psyche, your thought process being manipulated? Ten to one, it is. Even though that person's intention isn't bad, when you begin to separate from them they can become very bitter and decide, "Well, if you don't love me, I don't want you to love anybody else either." So now they wish death on you, or ill health, or something horrible to happen to you so that you have to come crawling back to them. It is now considered an extreme level of psychic warfare. You don't have to be trained in the arts of psychic phenomena to be harmful to another human being.

So, even a red cell is capable of psychic attack?

Yes, I think one of the greatest levels of psychic attack that is done every day is from relationships that go awry. The magnitude of mental energy projected at other individuals is phenomenal. When people break up, they turn to alcoholism, suicide, anger, hate, and jealousy. It's all the worst things that you can imagine. The bottom line is that usually there's no winner in this scenario. Most of the time, people are mentally scarred forever from a breakup, no matter what kind of relationship it was. It could take a significant amount of time but eventually they do heal; that's the interesting thing.

As spiritual people attempting to evolve, we are more sensitive to thoughts and what they can do. It is good for us to learn a kind of *Tai Chi* of the mind and to use mindfulness so that we do not get pummeled by other people's consciousness. If we allow ourselves to fall asleep, we fall into the control of the matrix. The matrix pummels us, forges us, and molds us to be the byproduct of whatever it needs us to be. We cannot allow that to happen. That's what we're trying to avoid by being aware of those things when they happen. We need to have an appropriate method of mentally dealing with that kind of thought consciousness so it doesn't do harm to us. And that is the whole point of this conversation – mindfulness.

You are affected strongly by previous lovers. People that you've been intimate with know your energy best. When you are intimate with someone, you know that person's frequency. You can draw on that person's energy simply by knowing their frequency, and vice versa. Looking at it psychically, each individual has a frequency: 98.6, 104.3. You have a very specific frequency.

The people who have the most effect on your thought consciousness are the ones who know your energy frequency. The better they know your energy, the stronger the psychic connection. Ten to one, it will last forever, even when you leave this world and die. If it was strong enough, that conscious energy will still be connected. The greatest level of negative, psychic warfare is from people who have gone through relationships because there's such a mental invocation of thought coming from them as a result of it. It can be one of the most positive healing, enriching energies, or it can be a very negative, destructive, powerful, and souring energy. It has potential for either one.

Moving on to other forms of thought, you can heal someone from a distance by using thought projection. It is effective in a hospital, across the world, or at any distance. The matrix interrelates with everything using the grid of consciousness. It's a matter of whether or not you know the channel or frequency so you can connect with the person you want to connect with in your mind. You make a connection with every single person you meet in your life. Being intimate with someone creates a very powerful connection. Having a friendship, a bonding, or any personal relationship is all powerful in itself because they learn your frequency and it lasts forever. It is not something you can remove from yourself.

If you project healing energy to someone, it is a form of healing at a great distance. On the same token, if you project a negative energy at someone, you can still do it at a great distance. There might be times when you are depressed and you ask yourself, "Why am I feeling depressed?" You might not have a clue why you're feeling that way. It could be a biochemical reaction in your body, and that is always a concern. Sometimes, it's someone invoking their will on you. Someone's thinking strongly about you and they're forcing their depression on you. It's affecting you. It could be your mother or father yearning for you, or wishing to change the situations in your life. It could be people that you've met before who want you back because their life isn't as happy as it was when you were there. Maybe they're just thinking about you. When somebody thinks about you, their thoughts and information link with yours. You interpret it on the premise that you feel it and don't know where it's coming from. So you assume that it's just simply your feelings.

Thought projection is a very powerful thing, and this is why you need to meditate. This is why you need to clear your thoughts, and why you should be mindful. This is the reason you do energy movements for your body; it removes outside influences that affect your consciousness. All of it is thought-based. It originates from someone else's thoughts, and when this bulk of energy projects outward, it is a complex ribbon of life. It is a program. It has a full spectrum of intentions and desires. It is pre-designed to be input into you.

In other words, it is like a mother bird and her chicks. The mother bird goes out and eats food, and digests it in her stomach. When it's half-processed, the mother bird regurgitates it so that the babies can feed from it. The babies could not eat it normally because they don't have the enzymes to digest the food. When a person creates and evokes emotion and broadcasts it to you, you absorb it without knowing what their intention is. You just simply react to it. Your biological brain does not have the properties to decipher it unless you're trained to filter out these things or to acknowledge them. This is what makes them lethal.

Is this the reason for awareness?

If you do not know you're being preyed upon, you are a victim of unawareness. You are a victim by the sheer fact that you're not on guard. You're not thinking that you have to keep your consciousness at a level where you can check-in with yourself. You're reacting and experiencing something that may not be authentic to you. Thought is a living thing.

Do a self-study of your thoughts. Self-study means you can see: the branches of the tree, the leaves, and the branches that lead to the inner core of the tree. You can see the base of the tree and from there, you begin to study its roots and follow them down into the depths of the Earth. In the roots, you find the source where it all began. From that observation, you know whether or not it's something you want in your life and the realization it brings. Knowing the truth is self-liberation. It's why you meditate. You meditate to separate yourself from negative influences. By practicing what you've been taught, you have a better chance of finding inner truth. With inner truth comes liberation. With liberation comes enlightenment.

Most things cause a reaction in life. If you begin the "thinning out" process, you're going to find that there's not much vegetation left in the garden, but the vegetation that is left will be full of life. There will be fruitful trees that can grow if you give them the room to grow. They will give you the fruits of life, the fruits of awakening, and the fruits of enlightenment.

Once you recognize something, you instantaneously have power over it, so you have to begin to observe now. Multitasking a computer chip means that you can run several tasks at the same time. Let's say you're doing an algorithm for a particular result, and you're also going to run a Word processor. You're running different applications, such as surfing the Internet, and downloading several things. What happens to the speed of the project you're working on? The more you multitask, the slower the progress of that big project you were going to complete in five minutes.

All the other little tasks aren't necessary, but they're taking you away from achieving your goal -- to find enlightenment in this life. You're doing all these other things instead of focusing and allowing productive energy to be your ultimate goal. You need to selectively choose the right programs to isolate and leave running to complete the algorithm. All the miscellaneous things are distractions slowing you down. They feed on the same amount of energy you have to finish the project. Most of them are not really necessary at all. Through self-observation, you can remove the things that are needlessly draining you. Narrow it down to whatever is necessary for your main algorithm, which symbolically is attaining enlightenment.

There are outside influences and things that are a necessity, such as working a job, feeding yourself, and taking care of the basic things in life. But there are also a lot of things you're unaware of, the micro-programs you've forgotten about that are feeding off of you that you could be shutting down. They're drawing all your resources, like raindrops in a bucket that you had no idea you were losing. That's self-observation, self-awareness, and the reason for mindfulness.

With self-observation, you will find that you can control your thinking better. Somewhere in the recesses of your mind are the issues to be dealt with, and how much attention you give them is a whole other thing. When you sleep, there is a huge bandwidth of loss because your mind is running through all the issues you put on hold in the back of your mind. They now have bled into your dream state. So by removing them, you find true inner peace and then you can concentrate that energy into more important areas.

Every spiritual lesson and every technique that you practice helps you control your thoughts. Sit down with a notepad and write down how many ways you waste money. You already know if you're doing something wrong, but you resist thinking about it. You choose to ignore it. So start writing it all down, "I spend money on junk food. I spend money on frivolous stuff. I am a compulsive spender." Whatever your compulsion is, start writing it all down; that forces you to reflect on it and deal with it.

What is your intent now? By writing this all down, you're trying to find the answer to why you're spending so frivolously. So the next time you do that, a little alarm will go off in your head and say, "I wrote this down on my list and I shouldn't be doing it." Now, you have a decision to make. Instead of automatically reacting, which we call being asleep or in the machine, you've just awakened. You've set an alarm on that clock to help wake you up.

Now, if you hit the alarm clock and you roll back over in bed, there's not much I can do. If you hit the alarm clock and you say, "I have to get out of bed because it's my responsibility," you will put down that object and you'll walk away. You'll say, "I have to walk away; that's what I have to learn to do right now." Ten to one, you'll do it. It comes down to how much willpower you have. That's how you begin to make a change in your consciousness. First, you have to pay attention to what you don't want to be doing by being mindful.

Why write them down?
Why not just think about them?

If you don't write them down and you say, "I'm just going to think about it," you won't manifest it. *When you write something down, it has the profound ability to manifest itself in this dimension.* Everything you want to change is in this dimension; it's not just in your mind. It's how you react with this dimension. So, you're picking up the object and exchanging paper money. It's a physical reaction. If you mentally say, "I'm not going to do this," that's one thing. But if you manifest that thought into this material reality, it becomes tangible. That's the best way to change a habit - write it down on paper, to physically manifest it in paper form. It has now gone from an inner dimension of just pure electrical thought and taken on a molecular structure in this lower dimension. You've moved it from the inside out. So when you buy something, what are you really doing? You're buying something from the outside and creating self-gratification. You'll experience it through your ears, eyes, scent, taste, or through touch. It's a kind of self-gratification within your consciousness, so you need to reverse that program.

It's the same thing when I say, "Take your hands, create movements, and change your frequency instead of just letting your hands fly around during a conversation." If you write down everything you want to change in your life that is the best way to make it happen. It's the fastest way to empower yourself, but do you know why most people don't do this? Deep inside, there's a voice telling them not to worry about it. It's the *Babbler*. It's a different way of stopping you. It makes you think, "Nah, it's too much time," or, "I really don't feel like doing it. It's not going to make much difference." Test this theory yourself, and then post it up on the wall. Get a pen and every time you do that habit again, put a check mark on it, "Did it again, and again, and again." Each time you put a check mark on that list, it affects you, and you won't want to do it anymore. It's manifesting into this reality.

Can this method also be used in reverse for what we want to achieve?

Yes, this same method can be applied to whatever you want to achieve. Write it down in realistic terms. You have to manifest what's inside, outside, and what you want to change from the outside, inside. It's a simple thing -- out with the old, in with the new. It's the fastest, easiest way to change a habit. For all the things you want to change about yourself, write them down. If it's a huge list, after you write them down, number them from one to one-hundred. Then you're going to do ten at a time, or five at a time, or two at a time. Work on them for two weeks. Then work on the next two and then the next two until all of them are done. Even if the ones you've finished reappear in your life, go back and work on them again. It'll be easier to re-do them a second time. In this way, you'll master them. The second time, it might only take you one week. The third time around, maybe it'll take two days. Eventually you're going to achieve the results you want.

Eventually you're going to kick these habits, but you have to remember that the human brain is like a machine. It has a mechanism. How does it utilize its thinking process? It thinks in methods of tagging. It is a very structuralized system, not necessarily hierarchical, but a database of interpreting things. You need to project that outside of yourself so that anything you observe must be in terms of how you did it. Everything you observe is from outside of yourself. Then bring it inward. When you take an inner problem and you project it outward, the only way for you to re-analyze it is to put it outside of yourself, look at it, and re-internalize it inward again. That's how you dissect it.

Going back through the ages of Socrates and Plato, they publicly stood out for the contributions they made philosophically, not even mentioning the hundreds if not thousands of other renowned people who were never noticed. They were the pioneers in the frontier of spiritual thought. I think that you are all either a Socrates or a Plato of your time. We (white cells) all are. We've evolved to that advanced level of thinking. Everybody in our society is a Plato, a Socrates, or another great personage of higher learning. It started with only a few back then, but you can be sure there will be many more extraordinary people in another hundred years from now.

How will this happen?

It will happen through the process of self-reflection, self-awareness, and inner-truth. There are more people on Earth right now trying to find self-realization through various schools of thought than there ever has been in the history of humankind. If you look at this by factoring the numbers, what was once a few hundred, a thousand, or a few hundred thousand people, is now in the millions. So, already this progressive thinking has begun.

Gaia has a better neural system today than ever before. It's the same way your brain has evolved. As human beings, we have a better neural system with our advanced system of electrons firing in the brain, its complexities, and our biological processes that have evolved. At first we might have been clacking tree trunks to communicate information. Then maybe we would gather together once in four years, walking hundreds of miles. We would send our brightest, smartest, and greatest warriors to meet at some clan gathering. This was the beginning of our neural system collectively sending data. Well, it's the same way that the brain works.

As mankind progressed, we created a more complex means of communicating information. Not only are we saying, "Go to the river for fish," but, "If you go to the river for fish at sunset and before sunrise, when the moon is in this particular phase, you'll get a greater yield." In today's times, our communication is even more evolved. We're saying, "If you go there during the summer on a certain day at a certain time that's been recorded and documented, we know it's going to be the best time." So we're getting a lot more complex data which creates a higher evolution of shared information.

As time progressed, we developed from smoke signals to alternate forms of communication. Morse code was developed to communicate across continents, and from Morse code, we progressed to fiber optic cables for even faster communication. This tied greater synapses of information together. But how much condensed information could be written in books? Books were a huge part of this, even before fiber optic cables, because you could take complex information, compress it, send it, and re-open it like an accordion of data, which is really mimicry of modern technology.

What do we do in modern technology? We download packets of information and have them de-compressed. In a sense, it's the same way your brain works. You're taking information, compressing it, and inputting it into the brain. Your brain thinks upon it and decompresses it. When you're done with it, you forget about it. Why is this? You've stored it in the recesses of your mind somewhere, compressing it for future use. This process is how evolution of the mind is working for the Gaia consciousness. So, better usage of this system creates a well-developed form of consciousness, which comes from communicating information. The information feeds the modern neural system, which again, builds better and better systems.

As a people, we are the byproduct of that ingenuity, and our capability has improved over time. If you look at an evolved skull, you will see how the brain has adapted through time from the Reptilian era when the brain was about the size of your fist. During the Mammalian era, the brain was a little bit larger, and the Neocortex era, which is the size of the brain that you see with all the squiggly indentations. Why do they look like that? Because it's how the brain compresses data; the neurons are so long that if we spread them all out, they would be a distance of four feet from our heads. So the reason they curl in like a sponge is to hold more data. Our brains are now holding in more data, which contributes to information and intelligence, which, in turn, creates a higher frequency of consciousness.

As thought is alive, it's a way of holding our living consciousness within as we reside in the physical body. Enlightenment is a product of self-realization. When self-realization is achieved, even if you incarnate into a less intelligent vehicle, it doesn't matter. With Kirlian photography or other forms of advanced technology, you can now see a gray static electrical charge or many different colors of energy around the head. It is an expression of your true self through the activation of your thoughts, which are expressed in the reflection. The rest is held in the hyper-consciousness. It's still there, but the body that you're residing in cannot project that data.

Let's say that you have a TV that can give you 900 channels. From anyone of those 900 channels, is it possible to create a cellular phone conversation that you can communicate through? No, not yet. However, that does not mean that the information is not available; it is here. So, the brain is able to utilize whatever it can. When you die and leave the physical body, you will recollect the full totality of your consciousness to the highest level you've achieved for that lifetime. Whatever you have experienced on a lower level becomes inserted into your total consciousness; it's just another part of you.

The Universe contains an ultimate truth. If you were to observe a conch shell, cutting it open, you would see the spiral within. It is the same with a galaxy or multi-galaxies throughout the cosmos. You'd see the same unification over and over and over again. That is a method of truth for our universe. In nature, you see it again in chaos theory. It's always reproducing itself, whether it's greater or smaller. So is there an inner truth in the totality of consciousness for us? As long as you are constantly open to receive, even if you're confident that you've completed everything, the inner truth in leaving yourself open to the Universe will help you to unfold whatever you might have missed. It'll surface to the truth and you'll have a revelation.

When you refuse to let that happen or you attempt to ignore it, which everybody does, it is a problem. By controlling the Babbler, you control your inner mechanism, which is part of the Gaia mind. You are not controlling Gaia because the Babbler resides inside of you. It's like multiple channels bleeding over into each other. So you're blind to it.

When you get the inner Babbler under control and you can *think without thought*, you can think with a higher consciousness. It's a different kind of thinking. When you're inside of yourself, you have a clearer understanding. When you look outside of yourself, you can begin to separate all the static and you can see whatever truth you choose to see within the Gaia mind. Your frequency has harmonized at the same frequency.

Instead of you being one of the static channels within the multitude of static channels, you've tuned into each station individually. They all slow down. Instead of a high speed, they slow down and separate, and you can see the bands of truth within each one. Whatever one you want to access, you access. Then you see micro-bands of truth until you absorb whatever amount of information you require. Clearing your inner mind allows you to separate to see the outer side. When your frequency is just static inside, it matches the outside. You have to define your inner self before you can see what's outside of you.

There is a shortcut that clears your mind but you need the tools to recognize how to find the shortcut. Let's say you have to cross a mountain range. In order to cross it, you're going to have to drive all the way around it. Driving around the mountain range is a sure way of doing it ... or you can take the shortcut. What do you want to do? The shortcut is only good if you know where it is. You still need the proper tools to even find the shortcut. Even a shortcut needs direction.

The shortcut is on the north side of the mountain range. It's about X amount of feet up. You'll see a cave. If you go down into the cave, there are three paths. If you take the wrong one, you're going to be screwed. Take the one to the far right. Follow that all the way down and it will open to the other side and you will cut the length of your journey by one hundred percent. You know that it will take hours off your trip. It doesn't matter. You still need the directions in order to achieve your goal. With other schools of thought and numerous years of teachings, sometimes people still never get it. Every day people meditate in monasteries in complete isolation, dedicating themselves to their path, and still many are not able to reflect inwardly as deeply as you are reflecting right now, even reading this chapter. You're already taking the shortcut.

Is it selfish to always focus on yourself like that? You never give anything to anyone else. It seems very self-centered.

There is something you need to keep in mind about selfishness and selflessness. It's important that you always allow your spirituality, your inner growth, to be the dominant, most important thing in your life. If you're not careful and aware of that, you're going to allow other things to push it aside into second, third, fourth, or fifth place. That's about selfishness. It's about saying that your spirituality is the most important thing in your life. It's about not letting people who are feigning for your affection absorb your time. What I'm trying to say is that:

"You should never, ever forget that you have to build your life around your spirituality, not your spirituality around your life."

When you can achieve this, you will probably be happier in your life. Your spirituality is the doorway to your inner soul.

As difficult as this is to accept, the people in your life will always come and go. You can even marry and your marriage could end, but your spirituality is forever. The only guarantee you have is the inner development of your soul. It will reflect outward to create the best marriage or the best relationships in your life. That will be the greatest gift to long-term happiness. Therefore, if you make it the second important thing in your life and the first thing fails you, there is nothing to give life or support to you.

Selfishness means that you work on developing yourself first. It doesn't really mean that you're being selfish. In truth, you're trying to be the best person that you can be for everybody else in the world. If it means that you have to isolate yourself or make a radical change in your life, try to be as pleasant, compassionate, and understanding as you can. You will always affect other people throughout your life. Always empower yourself to make the right choices that are going to help you to awaken.

When you react to something, always check to see if you're manipulating for your ego, or if it's sincerely for the sake of your spiritual growth. An example of this would be, "I'm in a relationship that I don't want to be in right now, so I will tell everybody that I want to *find myself* instead." That's not the right answer. It would be better to say, "I'm not happy in this relationship. I want the best for you, so I've put money aside for when I leave so that you have money to support yourself. If you have problems financially, or you need somebody to talk to, feel free to call me. But I need to move on. If I feel that you're trying to make me feel guilty about this, I'm going to sever this connection." It may sound cruel, but you have to set aside a realistic amount of time to move on. You can say to yourself, "I'm going to give this person a month, two months, six months," or whatever amount of time is reasonable for them. But at the end of that time, you cannot make exceptions by extending that time. You need to move on or you're not progressing with your own life and your own destiny.

How do we determine a "reasonable amount of time?"

Youth is a wonderful thing. In youth we explore life, we explore ourselves, we explore relationships, and everything is new and wonderful. As we grow older, things that were new and interesting are no longer new and interesting because we know them well, so they become familiar things. The things that once intrigued us no longer captivate the majority of our time mentally or emotionally. It gives way to other things, and usually this reflects on the deeper meanings of life. The problem with this process is that it's not to our advantage as a white cell. It's to the advantage of a red cell organism.

The red cell organism basically wants you to proliferate, create more babies, per se. By the time you move out of the phase of procreation, you're nearing the death cycle. You know you're going to die in X amount of time and you're getting older. Your body just can't function like it once did. Procreation becomes unimportant, as well as the stuff that doesn't stimulate you anymore, and gives way to finding something deeper that will give meaning to your life. That's when you really begin to seek spiritually.

The body is aging so that directly correlates to your consciousness as long as you reside in it. For example, if you have the flu or if you're sick, it will greatly impact your thinking, your motivations, and largely your inspirations. As you age, you are also awakening to the possibilities of something beyond you, but at the same time, you've lost the ability to easily attain it. So, these are all factors that you have to consider. The sooner you realize that you need to work on your enlightenment and that you need to control certain factors that demand your time, the sooner you can assess what is the best course of action for you.

You can't put any of those other things on the back burner, but what takes priority and what doesn't is the question. Does spirituality ever take the back seat? The answer is NO. Make spirituality your first priority. Integrate the second most important thing, whether it's school, a relationship, or whatever, and then the third most important thing, and so on. To be realistic, you can only have about five things, not twenty things. You have to surrender, as they say in *Desiderata*, the things of youth, the things that really aren't serving you in your spiritual growth. You need to begin removing those things that hold you back, and you need to deal with them now. The sooner you begin devoting yourself to your spiritual growth, making it your priority, the more you're going to spiritually achieve. There's no better time than the present. No matter how old you are. So, if this is the moment you are reading this, then *now* is the moment that you understand. Now is the moment that you must put every ounce of effort into this.

Time is going to rob you of your advantages. With age, time will rob you of your motivations, your desires, your hopes, and your dreams. Right now you're seeing color but over time your eyes are going to fade and the colors will blend together. Eventually perfect sight will be gone forever. How much have you developed yourself in order to attain your spiritual awakening? Stack as much in your favor as you can. I'm not a gambling man. I don't go to Vegas to gamble because it's not to my advantage. If I'm going to invest, I want to invest as much as possible in my favor. The earlier you work on your spirituality, the better advantage you will have for achieving the enlightenment you seek.

How does this relate to thought?

So, getting back to the subject, your thought process is largely affected by your body's well-being. If your body is not in good health, your thought process is probably not in the best of health either. If you are not at peak performance, then your thought process is not going to function so well. It doesn't mean you have to be physically fit with a six pack, lifting weights. You want to be the best that you can be. So, you have to use whatever time you have at the moment of this realization. Use it, squeeze, and pull every ounce that you have left to propel yourself to that last horizon. You should never lose sight of that. You have to keep that in the front of your mind, as each day you're not getting any younger. Your birth was the first moment leading to your death in this life. There is a time limit in attaining the highest level of consciousness that you can. Never assume that you'll probably die at eighty or whatever age you assume it will be because you could die tomorrow in a car accident. You could die from who knows what. Putting all of that aside, your mind is most alert at the moment you were born, and from that moment on, even though you're learning, its ability to learn is slowing down.

Your greatest advantage to finding what you're looking for is today. That's why it's important to keep your spirituality the number one goal in your life. Never lose track of that. You'll never be happy until you learn to live your life for yourself. Don't hurt anybody else in the process. Don't willfully cause physical or psychological harm to another person. By choosing to live your life, you're going to disappoint other people. Family members always want you to live by their ideals. They want you to become a product of whatever has brought them peace or solitude. They're assuming that you will be looking for that as well, and because they love you, they want you to have it.

People who live their life making someone else happy are usually the ones who have the highest risk of depression or suicide. They end up resenting the people they lived for. You're actually doing them a greater service if you choose to live your own life. You have a right to your own happiness. You shouldn't let anybody else dictate what that happiness should be.

The first communication of consciousness exchange, thought exchange, is very biological. It's all in your eyes. It's all in your face. If you look at someone, every single thought they have goes through their mind, unless they're trained. Your face will always give you away. If you're lying, if you're telling the truth or whatever emotion you are feeling, it's always reflected by your face.

We have a natural decoder in our brain that gets that communication. So, communication isn't always just words; it's also visual and auditory. What you're hearing has certain frequencies, and what you're seeing also gives you information. Your senses are much more perceptive toward communication than you think. When you're talking, you're broadcasting whatever is going through your mind.

It seems like this can be used as a form of thought manipulation. Can you give an example?

If a person approaches you saying, "Hello," and their intention is to know who you are, there's a programming in that hello. There's a frequency that, somewhere in the back of your mind that says, "Oh, this person is asking me to tell them about my life." On the surface you hear "hello" and you're saying "hello," but on the inside you're automatically projecting random thoughts outward. It's like you unwittingly or unknowingly begin to do this. The more intellectually evolved a person is, the more difficult it is to get information from them, but the less mentally trained they are, the information naturally flows.

A salesman uses this form of communication all day long. They say hello and in five seconds you're giving them all kinds of information from your face with twitches and movements, blinking your eyes, your cheeks blushing, your chin, your lips, your eyelids, etc. Believe me, there's a thousand words being said. Your face is a reflection of every thought you have. This is the first process of exchanging information. Your mind starts going there for several reasons. Physically, their mouth said hello, but their face says, "I want to know more about you. Tell me about your whole life." You are responding in the recesses of your mind, unwittingly, by giving all those flutters of information. In exchange, they're getting information back. Maybe not exactly, but generally they're getting a sense of who you are.

By scanning you, they're seeing in their mind's eye all of those images through their own interpretations. So you might see a red house but they might see the red as a brown house. It doesn't matter how precise the information is because it comes from practice and perfection. What matters is that their brain is getting frequencies of information.

The human body has about a thirty-foot electrical field around it. Unconsciously or consciously, it shares data with everything around it, generally unconsciously. So, when someone approaches you with no particular intent, you'll find that when they say hello to you, nothing goes through your mind. They really have no intention for you. They're just saying hello and they're going to move on with their life.

How can we tell if someone has the intention of gathering more information?

If your mind starts racing when you meet a particular person, this is a tip for you to be consciously aware because this person has other motives. How you choose to handle that situation the second you become aware is another matter. So again, it goes back to self-observation. It goes back to the thought process.

How do you handle that?

It's very simple in how you handle it. You breathe in and you breathe out. Get it? So, for those of you who are reading this book, I simply manifested my heart chakra and I projected this passionate love and broadcasted it at every level. I'm still in that place, having a conversation, but it's filtering the actual information that's going out. It takes time to develop that skill and again, mindfulness is being able to juggle several things at once, so it takes practice.

You can broadcast the thought as soon as you realize what they are doing, and that's the thought that they're going to receive back. You just plugged them with this absolute love and happiness without them realizing it and they're going to think, "This person is really just a very loving, happy person." I think most people are not out to psychically scan you. It is within us, genetically, primitively speaking, to look someone in the face and read their intentions. We come from a genetic pool that was violent, aggressive, and territorial.

With animals, if you look them in the eye, it's a sign for them to attack or to fight. You can't look at another dominant one in the eye. So it's natural for us to observe the other person's eyes and read their information. It's a sense of accessing data. If there's no violence coming from you, and that person has a very strong dominant energy, you're flooded with all these different emotions or thoughts. You're also trying to feel what it is they're feeling from you. You're flipping through all this data.

It's primitive to look someone in the eye and try to pull information from them, and naturally that's the case. You need to know that you can create an emotion and broadcast it outside of yourself through your eyes. *Every emotion can be broadcast through the eyes.* When I am teaching, I'm really talking to you not only through words, but also through my eyes. When I raise my eyelids, when I bring them down, when I give you "the look," all of these things are broadcast to you and you will respond in a certain way. This is all communication.

So, there's a lot of communication going on. It's not just verbally but also psychologically through the thought process on very primitive levels that we don't always paying attention to. You should pay attention to it because it's critical. It's done every single day. It's not just the hands moving around but facial gestures, too. You can read a lot of information from someone's face. Their eyes give you away ninety-nine percent of the time. The only people that you should be careful of are professional conmen. They know how to control their eyes, so you have to use other senses with them instead.

What is the benefit of scanning someone and why do people do it? Are there different methods of scanning we should know about?

Most of the time when people scan you, there's a very primitive reason behind it. Scanning is usually sexually based; you're sizing someone up. They usually read your facial characteristics for things that attract them. When someone looks at you sexually and you look back at them, what are you doing? You're assessing them to see if they're interested or not. What's the next stage? What happens when you decide they are interested? There's something you send them that says, "I'm open for communication." Then you take it to the next level. You communicate with a nod of your head, a little smirk, or with the subtlest wink of an eye. You don't even have to wink; they just know. If they return to you right away, then one of you chooses to step forward and a conversation breaks loose.

You just broadcasted and communicated something to the other person. It's also possible to scan somebody who isn't talking to you in sexual terms. It just takes a little bit of effort and a little bit of conscious awareness to realize how to do that.

When most people are scanning you, they're trying to establish your attraction. They wonder if you could be interested in them, and if so, how can they sexually dominate you to get what they want from you. That's usually what scanning is.

Are there other motives behind scanning?

The next form of scanning is to see if you are a threat to them. It's an assessment of what your motives are, which is what you usually feel from people when they're looking at you. They're trying to size up your motives to see if you are going to take away their position of power. We deal a lot with social ranking. When you meet someone new, they feel threatened that you might want to take their position away from them.

When you approach a group of friends or even a business, most of the people there will be trying to size you up to see what threat you pose. Everyone has motives. You don't bother with a group of people without a reason, do you? If you're expecting to just be friends that is your motive. You're looking for a friend, a companionship, or you're infiltrating a group and being friendly because you've isolated someone in that group that you're attracted to. You want to get to know them. You're playing the social gamut and you're studying and sizing people up. You're projecting what you think they're going to want to hear so you can achieve your goal. All of this is thought combat. It's all social combat. It's all progressive consciousness. If you have absolutely no interest in them, ten to one, you won't approach them. If someone approaches you, right away you're wondering what they want. Right away you're thinking, "What are your intentions?" If you do that kind of thing, you need to project it as an intention to get past their radar.

You're now packaging condensed data and you're slipping it under the doorsteps, so it's a bomb. You get in and you infiltrate that person's mind to make them either like you or dislike you, but it's always a psychological, social combat. It's always a movement of thought consciousness strategizing from one person to the next. This is social programming and it can be traced back to primitive man. Animals also do this. Anybody who ever approaches you has an intention. They're not coming up to you because they want to be your friend. It's more of what has been established and why they want to be your friend. What did you do? What did they see? What do you have? There's something that is attracting their attention.

There is also the rare occasion when someone genuinely wants to be friends. Primitively speaking, the person who befriended you when you were bringing back whatever you hunted for is around the corner waiting to beat you up and take your lamb, deer or whatever. So, nine times out of ten, there are agendas hidden in their motivations. It's right for you to be skeptical because it all leads to fear, a survival mechanism. Survival tells us to be fearful of anybody's intentions because their intentions could be harmful. This is your biological sensory kicking in, so you have got to use that sensory to your best advantage.

When you use "reverse engineering" you can find ways of broadcasting information under control. For the purpose of this chapter, reverse engineering is a process of disassembling and analyzing its parts with the goal of improving upon it. Actors do this a lot. They have to create an emotion internally and broadcast it externally. Most actors can do this while performing, but in real life when they have to accomplish something, they find it a lot more difficult because they are out of their natural element.

This is all a part of consciousness. It's all communicating physically through your face, emotionally broadcasting it, and of course, verbally broadcasting with inter-fibered vibration. There are many levels of this information being exchanged, with thousands of bits of information broadcasted in a second. As soon as you meet somebody, a lot of data is being exchanged. It's about sizing up, feelings, and sensory. Is this guy after my girl? What does this person want? Think about when you meet new people and the whole exchange of the social ritual. You are establishing the pecking order. You are determining who has what to offer, if there's anything to be concerned about, and letting them know that you're not a threat.

The direct approach seems to work best, but then people think that's just a form of arrogance. I can tell when a person is sizing me up. I also know that I can say, "First of all, I'm not interested in your girlfriend. Let's clear that up right now." That is just too brutal for some people. It's too intimidating. It's like I know too much too easily. So I'm a greater threat to them so they might have to get rid of me. Otherwise, how will they know what my intention is? They might as well assume it's bad because they can't keep up with me. So, this is a disadvantage for me, and this is what most people get because I can't help it sometimes. I'm just so right on the money.

This is another form of communication. It's similar to the analogy of the airplane on the ground taking off. These are all natural elements, which are like the wheels still touching the ground. The airplane, as it begins to lift off is when you learn to go through someone's mind and get information they're not volunteering through any other physiological expressions. That's takeoff. You've learned to use your sixth sense. Instead of your hands moving around, or your eyes showing information, or your ears getting information, you've found another way to communicate.

That person does not know how to use it, so you have the advantage. If you were in a fight and the other person didn't have arms, do you think you would have the advantage? It's that big of an advantage if you can develop your sensory to that level of scanning. But remember, if someone's scanning you and they're very powerful, maybe you don't have hands but you've still got feet. Kick them. Project that happy energy at them. It's going to be enough to deal with the situation.

Each person's frequency or vibration is different. A teacher is obviously the best frequency that is approachable until you can approach the frequency of God. Whenever you acknowledge thought or the process of sharing thought, just by acknowledging this you learn from it.

It's very simple. You don't have to do anything else in your head except observe that there's a process of information being exchanged, which is thought. That's the same with everything we've talked about. As long as you can see it happening, you know what to be aware of. If you know you're being stalked, you are aware of this happening. If you can see it happening, you have the advantage. You can empower yourself. Think about when you deal with people in public and in other circumstances. You're probably going to think about it in a different way, and because you're thinking about it in a different way, you now have the advantage again. You have a power that you did not possess before.

When you are in the presence of certain eminent individuals, their vibration is another form of thought. Their consciousness resides at a place that's so refined, and just by observing them, you are learning. It also applies to a higher being versus a lesser being in everyday life. It's the same concept. You just get a different response from it. You're learning through observation; it makes you self-reflect.

One of the interesting things that I would like to point out to you (speaking to a classroom full of people) is that when I smiled earlier, what effect did that happy, heart chakra energy give you? Everybody kind of laughed and they got it, something in their head just went "HI!" Well, that was a thought that was manifested both physically and spiritually by my energy.

You sampled it through your data process and bounced it back out. I sent it out as data, you internalized it, and you re-manufactured the exact same thing you felt and broadcasted it out. You knew what it was. Thought is a living thing. You can bring it inside of you and it can affect you. Somebody could broadcast a feeling of depression at you and you would feel depressed. Someone can also think of you in a negative, hateful, spiteful way and, all of a sudden, you feel ill and depressed. When you feel positive, the health of your body increases and your immune system is strengthened. All the living organisms in your body improve. When you feel depressed and your immune system drops, you feel sickly, and you're more vulnerable to virus attack.

Can this be used as a form of psychic attack?

Yes, when someone projects negativity at you and you are experiencing it, it's an attack on your inner senses. When you have an argument with this person, it's the same thing. They're assaulting you with energy but also psychologically through every method of thought they can project. They're launching an all-out war on you because their intention is for you to submit to them. They want you to be destroyed at such a level that you are forced to submit to their will, unless they have some control and are able to walk away and cool off to find another way of communicating.

In a way, they're working on finding your bands of thought to attack to make you accept what they have to say instead of communicating with you on an equal level so that you can find the truth. Sometimes people just don't want to hear it. Sometimes a child can just throw walls up and you have to find a way to break those walls down.

What is the best way to defend against this type of attack?

How you choose your arsenal of weapons is really what's most important. You can either be strategic about it or you can blatantly strike with devastation in mind. It's better to target precisely than it is to blanket somebody with an all-out brutal assault. There is certainly a difference.

When someone from a distance is angry with you, you're going to feel that energy. You're going to feel it attacking you. You're not going to know why you feel anxious, or why something's bothering you, or why you lost your appetite. You might have a fight with somebody over the phone. Immediately afterwards you think you're just dealing with the issues psychologically, but that person is also projecting their energy at you. On the same token, you could do the same thing to someone else by pumping out that energy. If you're all wound up and thinking about them, you're evoking their frequency. If you're evoking their frequency, you've got their signal. If you've got their signal, you're broadcasting this onslaught to them.

These are things that you have to be aware of. At times you may suddenly feel anxious, but you know you haven't talked to anybody. They could have talked to someone who said, "Did you know that last week I spoke with so-and-so and they told me this and that regarding you?" That person is evoking you, your image, your vibration, your feeling. They're saying, "I can't believe they said that!" Now, they're broadcasting to you through a signal in the Gaia grid. You just don't know who it is or why it's coming at you. This is another form of psychic attack. This happens all day long and is another systematic way of keeping individuals in check within the matrix instead of helping them to get out of it. In order to reach higher consciousness, your first job is to liberate yourself mentally from things that are weighing you down by empowering the Babbler.

When other people project their consciousness at you, it's a way of keeping you from liberating yourself, from moving beyond all that. This is why you're given all these tools and methods to practice. It's not about the issues you are dealing with; there are people in your life who are constantly broadcasting their good or bad intentions to you. A person praying for you to find their religion, their God, or their belief system is still projecting their intention at you. It's another form of psychic webbing that is constantly working to keep you at a certain place. You have to understand this so you can clear away all of these things. Then you can make a clear and decisive choice from your own inner being instead of being affected by outside sources of consciousness that are forcing or molding your destination.

That's part of the matrix. That's all part of the consciousness grid moving around. Practicing your tools to clear all of that is very important, and if you don't work on it every day, you are going to fall under the will of the matrix.

What is deemed as good thoughts doesn't necessarily mean that they're thoughts that you agree with; yet, they're going to be evoked on you. And most of the time, internally, you're fully aware of what these other people's wants and desires are on you. That alone has a festering ability that absorbs your energy. All these little tiny programs are running that you don't seem to be aware of, but you *are* aware of them. If you can say, "My mother feels this way," or "My father feels this way," or "This person feels that way," just the fact that it's still happening means something is feeding on you like a little micro virus. This is why we meditate. Remove yourself from thought because it's the only time that you can shut down all of those things.

Even when you shut down most of them, there always are some programs still running. With some training, you can go into your mind and disengage those programs. You deactivate their power and disable them. Sometimes they are run by guilt, so you feel selfish if you remove yourself from those things. It's like saying, "I should care about what my mother wants. I should care about what my father wants. I don't want to hurt them." Now you've got a dilemma on your hands by choosing right from wrong.

What this will reveal to you about what's right and wrong is the real question. So all of those things steal or take energy from you that empower the main algorithm, the main path, that's working towards your enlightenment. They're all taking a little bit here, a little bit there, and when you put it all together, it's a huge amount. Your job is to isolate as much of that as is reasonably possible so that you can put most of your energy into your inner resources, your spirituality. That's where you have to get tough. That's where you have to be focused. That's where you have to say, "I'm sorry, but this is the way it is." This is why people sometimes think that I can be too tough. There are times when I say, "That's it! That's enough! Back off." I broadcast it and everybody knows enough not to bother me then because it's using my resources.

This is how thought works. Thought is imposed upon you. If you can think about it, you can acknowledge it. If you acknowledge it, you are empowering yourself because you are aware of the intentions of the stalker. It gives you the advantage. When you choose to be around certain people -- birds of a feather flock together -- if you're around people who do drugs, more than likely you will get involved with doing drugs because you begin to see life through their perspective.

So, essentially, we begin to absorb their thoughts and fit into their patterns?

Yes, we are creatures of absorption. We absorb the consciousness of the environment we choose to be in. It's no wonder that we become a byproduct of the environments we're in. It takes a lot of strength to change that environment. If there are ten people, it's unlikely that your will is going to change all ten. Usually the ten will absorb you instead. I'll give you a perfect example of this. If you moved to the south and they talked with a heavy accent, ten to one within your first year of living there, you would begin to adopt that accent and not even know that you have it. So, we are products of absorption of the environments that we are in.

If you put yourself around people who are not striving for spiritual goals, it's going to be very difficult for you to achieve your spiritual goals. It is possible, but you're stacking the odds against you. I'm not a gambling man; I stack as much in my favor as I can. Place yourself in a group of people that have the same goals as you do. More than likely, you will be helping to fuel or empower yourself to achieve your goal. Now, you have people in that boat who are stroking with you, and it's creating a much more powerful momentum.

Does this mean we'll begin to function as a collective, rather than an individual?

You're still an individual. You have to maintain your own physical energy, but you still have a group of people that are giving you more momentum and sending you in the right destination. So, where you spend your time and who you spend it with has a huge effect on what you're going to achieve. Of course, it's very important to always check the environment.

It's important to read other information outside of these lessons. It's always important to look at other spiritual information. When we lose that diversity, that's when we become like everything else. It's important that you expand your life outside of our school of thought. Do not isolate yourself. Many religions isolate; many groups isolate.

You said that we should isolate ourselves. This seems to be a contradiction.

There's a certain level of isolation that's needed, but there's also an extreme amount of flexibility. It's always important for us to think about that and reflect on it from time to time. It's always good to spend time with family and friends, but you have to feel strong enough to know what you want, and to direct the course of your life. When it's being infringed upon too closely by others, you need to know when to step back for your own self-growth, for your own inner journey.

The reason why people should have a spiritual teacher, a guru, or a mind mechanic is that you're around that person for their quality of consciousness. You're sampling, much the same way you would sample from other people, or other groups, picking up habits or things from them. You're choosing to be around a spiritual guide because it's assumed that they are more evolved than you are. You esteem them, and by being in their presence, you're absorbing that frequency.

A spiritual teacher broadcasts at a very high frequency. If you open yourself to it the same way you absorb other thoughts, you can choose to absorb it and that elevates you higher. Just being in the presence of a very spiritual person is uplifting. It's freeing, and it expands your consciousness.

This is why you should want to seek out and be in that kind of company. It will stimulate similar thought, and you're going to manifest it inside of you by reflecting on it. Of course, if you can't be in the physical *presence* of a master, the next best thing is through your studies. It's better than no stimulation, or being under the influence of other frequencies that may not be beneficial to you. You have to create that vibration through this format. Reflecting on the topics you have been reading about creates a very complex frequency, which could lead to a major breakthrough or an understanding of a higher perception.

Being in a higher frequency is always better than choosing to be in a lower frequency. Always try to be conscious of where you are and who you're with. That's called being conscious or *being in the now*. Think about the reality around you. Think about who you're with. If you don't do that, you are most likely absorbing the vibration of the people that you are around. Whether it's in your work environment, hanging out with people, your school environment, a wedding or shower, step back and think about the very moment you're in. Instead of becoming part of whatever is happening and just moving within it in non-thought, you can move in it consciously. Be as constantly aware as you can for as long as you can. That tends to be on and off, on and off, but it still keeps you in check.

Being around a spiritual teacher is like a window of opportunity for sampling and experiencing a higher vibration. This helps you to appropriately set the standards that you're trying to create in yourself by mimicking it. You can create vibrations inside of yourself by evoking them. I evoked happiness by focusing on my heart chakra and broadcasting it outward, and everybody feels it. You can do the same. *If you think that you are that person, you can feel them.* If you feel what it is to feel their face, if you shape your face into the same structure as their face, you can feel what it is that they feel in their normal everyday life.

You can do that in your everyday practice. Just close your eyes and evoke your mother, your father, or whoever comes to mind. If you do that for a few seconds, you're going to feel what it is like to be that person. After you've played around with that, invoke someone that you esteem at a much higher level than you are. This is like sneaking in the back door, but you're invoking that vibration at a certain level inside of you and you're learning from it.

So if you esteem me, you are evoking me, feeling like me, and internalizing that feeling inside of yourself. There are some things you will learn that you may not understand in ordinary thought. There are other things that you might feel, but how you choose to interpret them is what you have to be careful of. If you choose to look at things negatively and say, "It feels like this is powerful and could be very intense," that's not what you're looking for. It's more of a physical interpretation of what you sense and it's using lower energy consciousness. It works better to say, "It feels like there's a *sense of peace* and a *sense of knowing.*" You don't have to fully grasp what I know, but just a sense of knowing that it exists may open up other doors for you.

This is why spiritual people often have shrines of their gurus and other things in their homes. Most western people would judge those things as cult worshiping. The purpose of the shrines is to invoke the quality of that teacher as a memory. All of those teachers talk about God; so obviously, the student isn't worshiping that person as God. They know that the teacher is just a teacher, not God. But most western people are afraid of idolizing their teacher. However, they do it all the time. Look at all of their religious statues. Biblically, it is stated that there should be no false idols or icons, but there is. Why do people still have them? They have those things to inspire themselves. So, when you have a photograph or something personal that reminds you of your teacher when you sit down to meditate, it's not that you're praying to your teacher. It's more like you're trying to recall the memory that was evoked within you. You don't want to lose that. You want it to blossom or grow inside of you. You want to feel it inside of you. It's your way of maintaining that personal link.

Does it have to be a religious figure?

It could be any teacher or any person you aspire to. For me, it's Mahatma Gandhi. He wasn't necessarily a spiritual teacher, but he's the spiritual teacher of life, in my opinion. It's whatever you choose to inspire you. Even if the person you revere did something unscrupulous, it doesn't mean that you will act the same way. You can focus on whatever was good about that person and incorporate that quality into who you are.

Chapter 2

PRANA MINDFULNESS

EVERYTHING I TEACH is very much like a *mandala*. It grows and unfolds inside of you over time. A mandala, an ancient Sanskrit word, originates from the eastern religions of Buddhism or Hinduism. It is an integrated structure that is organized around a unifying center. Loosely translated to mean "circle," a mandala is far more than a simple shape. It represents wholeness, and can be seen as a model for the organizational structure of life itself--a cosmic diagram that reminds us of our relation to the infinite, the world that extends both beyond and within our bodies and minds. The complexities of the mandala tell a story. It's an understanding: a wheel within a wheel within a wheel. Each wheel has different corridors with interconnecting parts. It's like the combination of a safe -- you keep moving toward the center, which is like the consciousness of God.

Like the mandala, everything I teach is integrated and built in layers of understandings with different corridors and interconnecting parts. Just by discussing this, you're going to get an understanding of a *mental mandala*. The type of mandala that I am referring to is like a picture made on the ground. When creating a mandala, the Buddhist monks work together with vials of different colors of sand, and using special scraping tools, they make fine, intricate colored designs and patterns. All the designs have a particular meaning; it's very complex. It can take a week, or even a month to make a mandala depending on the subject they are trying to depict.

When they're done with the ritual, they sweep it all away. They erase the whole thing because they believe that nothing is permanent in this world.

A mandala consists of layers and interconnects, but can you give us a better understanding of a mental mandala?

A mental mandala is when you acquire knowledge and then teach it to someone else. The other person takes that knowledge, reflects on it, and it becomes a living thing inside of them. They evaluate what they've learned, and different concepts start linking together in their head. The knowledge is based on self-reflection. It suddenly connects and you say, "Wow! That makes so much sense." That is a mental mandala.

Every single thing you learn is incomplete. The reason why it's incomplete is because I'm taking something that's huge, that's extremely complex, and trying to simplify it in a minimal amount of time. It should take a year to thoroughly discuss this but it's being condensed into a moment. In that moment as you begin to understand, it begins to unfold in your mind. It's like filling a dried sponge with water and watching it expand. That's what I'm doing. *Everything I teach is like a mandala. It grows and unfolds inside of you over time.* Then you grasp something and say, "Now I understand what you're talking about." Or you look at something and think, "Now that makes more sense. Now I understand." You're finally connecting everything you're learning and it makes more sense. This creates one mandala after another and all of a sudden, there are more mandalas inside of you without me ever saying anything.

Everything I teach connects and interchanges: they're all one thing. The most fascinating and largest compilation of information is actually numbers. When a quantum physicist or a mathematician writes their formulas on a board, they are literally reading it like a book. They're seeing colors in their head. They're seeing planets forming. They see atmosphere and how that atmosphere is made, but it's all just numbers. They know that to the tenth power means it is a planet mass. They see a planet when they look at that formula. Since most people aren't mathematicians, they aren't able to handle the intricacies of numbers; so I use analogies instead.

An analogy is like saying, "Well, we can move at the same speed as a car or we can move at the speed of a jet." And you would say, "I understand that jets are very fast and a car is moving, but not as fast as a jet." We can't literally move as fast as a car or a jet, but you understand the concept of fast and slow. That's an analogy. For example: I say that the planet is a living organism. Some people go, "What?" Then I point to your body and explain that you are a living organism with millions of living creatures inside of you. Then you see the planet, red cells, and white cells, and you can understand what I am talking about. But like a car and jet, it's not exactly the same thing. The problem with using analogies is that it leaves a lot of room for contradictions. There are no contradictions in the end. I may say one thing as an analogy, but then say something completely different at another point. That is because you are looking at a different aspect of the analogy. To say that the body has red cells, white cells, and different organisms and then say that human beings, animals, and dolphins are just like that confuses you. The human body does not act or operate exactly as the planet does.

I simplified this without getting into all of the complexities to give you a basic concept to work with. It's up to you to use the mandala now to take it further.

So, there are no contradictions. Some concepts only appear to contradict each other because everything is being taught in such a manner to speed up your education. In that process, you might skip a few speed bumps, but if you back up they are there. It's going to happen. Everything is a mandala.

If everything is a mandala, how important is Prana?

Let's talk about Prana. Prana is the Force. It's the energy that's permeating the room you are sitting in. It's in the city, the whole planet, the whole universe. It's everywhere. *Prana is the breath of life.* The ancient name for the Force is Prana. When you pour a glass of water, you should think about what you are doing. You can imagine Prana filling the glass of water, imbuing it with the Force. When you think of it that way, you are creating it through thought.

Be mindful of the Force. That's what makes you spiritual. How can a spiritual person go into a house with an atheist and the spiritual person can see or feel an entity but the atheist sees nothing? Does it mean that there's nothing there or that the spiritual person is embellishing because they want to believe so much? When someone sees a spirit, it is because their tonal is higher. The reason their tonal is higher is because they are *mindful* of the Force, mindful of Prana.

When you meditate, feel spiritual, or do spiritual things you're exercising your ability, your sensory. When you don't do those things for a while, you lower your frequency. Think of it this way. Forget about being spiritual for a moment; we are electrical beings because our heart uses electricity to make a pulse. Electricity moves our arms and hands up and down. It moves our eyes and our ears. Everything is electrical. Understand that everybody is at level one in that particular moment. Level two is when you can consciously take this electricity and move it a little faster. Now ask yourself, "What is a spirit? What is it made of?" It is made of energy, only it's moving at a higher frequency. We're at a lower frequency. When the average person looks for a spirit, they see nothing because the spirit is moving too quickly for their eyes to capture. Our five senses are unable to detect it so it's inaccessible to us.

When your energy is raised, you feel like you're operating at another level. You have one foot in this dimension and the other crossing over to a higher dimension. Whenever an entity shifts down into this dimension, the average person isn't aware of it, but you can detect it because your energy is moving at a higher frequency. Occasionally, a spirit will pass through us and we'll get a chill through our body. The reason that happens is because we're electrical beings. When something speeds through our body, it's like an electrical short and the body tingles. You can relate to this world and part of the next world. That's what a spiritualist does. That's what a person who senses and feels things does. Their energy is of a higher tonal, so what is oblivious to the average person is not to them. They can feel, see, sense, and smell scents that don't seem to be there for anybody else because of their higher frequencies. So, to reiterate, when a person sees a spirit it's because their energy is of a spiritual nature. A person who can't see or feel anything is at a lower tonal. That's the difference. That's why some people can see or feel things and other people can't.

Most spiritualists are not concerned with the mechanics of how this works. They simply do what they learned to do. As a spiritualist, they may think, "It's the power of God," or "I'm psychic." But they may not realize that it's all energy. Everything needs an exchange of energy or fuel. For example: fire needs wood, oil, or coal. Cars need oil and gasoline. Fossil fuels are created from oil, and oil was created from dinosaurs. Dinosaurs ate food and vegetation, which grew from the minerals in the ground. No matter what you do, there is an exchange of energy in the Universe.

In order to do spiritual things, some people naturally go into an alternate state of mind. But we have to ask ourselves, what is that state of mind? That altered state of mind absorbs Prana. It's the feeding of energy; that's why they feel that way. They clear their mind and "go into the zone." They are collecting Prana; they just don't know it. We know that it's Prana. We know, as white cells, that we can do better than that because we know how to work with the Source.

By thinking of the Force, being mindful of It, and taking in Prana or thinking to draw this energy in, knowing what it is, we can progress from being insignificant psychics to awesome, powerful super-beings. We know now that we take this Force in and act as a conductor. Much like a T.V. harnesses the signals and converts them into an image and sound; you can take solar power from light and turn it into heat and energy. We can take in the most powerful source in the universe: Prana, God, the Force. That is a huge difference. The idea is to train one's self in all the right methods to control this energy. Without mental discipline, you can't control this energy. It's too powerful, too quirky to handle. It's like water in your hands; you have to understand how to harness it.

There is energy to be harnessed. Water is a way of taking in energy. If you are not mindful of the Force, you will diminish your source of energy and your spirituality will become weaker. Then you start to get into the mundane things of life. You can become more spiritual if you do these five things:

(1) Be mindful of the Force
(2) Think of the energy in the water
(3) Walk and breathe in Prana
(4) Think about the Prana that's coming into you
(5) See blue energy and breathe it in, exhaling the old

The more mindful you are, the more powerful you will become. You will accelerate to higher and higher levels. When your mind is distracted by human error, work, relationships, and life in general you lose your spirituality because you slowly lose your tonal by not exercising it enough. You're surrounded by a planet that has a *Doe* frequency, and that constant vibration keeps diminishing your tonal. There is one guarantee in life: If you never do anything spiritual in your life, you will be a typical human being -- part of the *machine*. To escape from the machine, you have to be mindful of the Force by thinking of the Force so your energy will be converted and the Force can accept it. But you have to think about It a lot. That's the problem.

This is why some people of faith make necklaces or jewelry with religious symbols. It's a little trick that keeps you mindful, thinking of your spirituality. That's the purpose of a cross; it's to make you think of God all the time. Symbols of religious artifacts are worn to make you mindful of your chosen path. Just the *act* of using the symbol doesn't mean you're going to take in Prana. You have to do more than *mindlessly* take action. You have to *mindfully* think about what you are doing. There's a difference. If you associate your symbol with Prana, then it reminds you to think of Prana, and by thinking of Prana you take it in. It's all about the dynamics of how the mind works and how you think. For instance, thinking of Prana as you drink water, being mindful, walking and breathing and thinking of the Force puts you into a spiritual state. It brings Prana into you. Meditating accumulates Prana into you. The more Prana you take in, the faster you become enlightened. It's really all about energy. The more mindful you are of the Force, the stronger your connection.

The room you are sitting in is filled with energy, but to a human there's nothing there but air. When you understand Prana, you'll begin to notice a blue shimmering light, which is invisible but it becomes real and starts moving into you. You accumulate it and then you can harness it. You *have* to acknowledge it. If you don't acknowledge it, it doesn't bother you. It doesn't come to you. It doesn't move towards you. It doesn't do anything. If you are aware of it, then it becomes part of your reality. It moves into you. That is how one works with the Force. That's how one becomes mindful of the Force. It's hard to do because we forget all the time. Life, in general, is very distracting. Being mindful of the Force is work, but awareness of the Force is what determines who will make it and who won't. How often do you think of the Force? How often do you implement it into your life without distracting yourself too much, creating that balance? When you do anything spiritual, you must always be mindful of the Force. Whenever you do something or take action, you should be mindful of the Force.

Being mindful of the Force also means you have to check your feelings and emotions sometimes. Are your emotions true or are they fouled slightly? If you take the Force in and you're in a bad place, will you cause a negative reaction? Say you're angry at a friend because you had an argument, so they left. Then you decide to breathe in Prana. You sit down and the Prana moves through you. You're aware of it, but you start thinking about how angry you are at your friend.

Now, let me explain something first: everything is a hologram. The room you are in is a hologram. It's just moving energy. The only reason reality is solid for us is because we are all moving at the same frequency. Using cars as an example, one car moves at 75 mph. The other one moves at 25 mph, so there's no connection between them. The first car can see what is going on in the second car at the same speed. So, I'm talking about higher tonal versus lower tonal in moving the energies. If you're both moving at the same speed, you could reach out and touch the other car.

This whole *dimension* is all moving at the same speed. You're moving at the same speed as the chair you're sitting in, as the wall in the room, and as the book you are reading. Everything is moving at the same tonal. That's what makes it solid for us. Even though, in retrospect, we know that this is just a hologram. It's light; that is virtually what it is. Light -- none of this is real. That's what this is about, teaching you concepts so when that right moment comes, you'll be able to interact with another dimension.

In any case, when you take in enough Prana, you can affect time and space when your mind becomes skilled enough. Now, it's always easier to do something negative than it is to do something positive. That's because negativity is driven by instinct. It is how the brain works. It's going to be harder for you to do good things than it will be to do bad things, unfortunately. When you take in Prana and you feel negative toward someone, you're willing it on them. You can make somebody get in a car accident. You can make someone ill.

Horrible things can happen if you're not careful, if you're not mindful.

The Force doesn't say, "I'm going to let you use me as a form of energy, but I'm only going to let you do good things." There are different levels of thought for the Force and for us. The Force sees everything in the same concept as Shiva. If you break a glass, one person believes the glass is ruined – just throw it away. An artist walks in to the room, sees the broken glass and is amazed at its beauty. It's the greatest thing they have ever seen! Look how it captures the light! Look at the rainbows emanating from it! It's a new creation! If you, in retrospect, harm a friend because you're angry, the Force doesn't think to slap you on the hand. God does not think the same way we think. That's humanity's idea of God. God doesn't rationalize the same as we do. God doesn't care about computers. God doesn't care about what shoes or clothing to wear. God is more like a giant organism that's existing. It has a sense of life and a sense of protection, just like an animal would protect itself. Now, that's not to say that God is not intelligent. The intelligence of God is *exceedingly* beyond us, so different than our capabilities. For us to biologically conceive it is impossible.

You are a thinking being and you are directly attached to your body. Are you aware of your lungs right at this very moment? Can you feel how long they are? How wide they are? How thick the tissue is in them? Can you feel the rounded edges in the globular sections inside of it and the moisture? Can you feel your kidney right now? You probably don't even know where your kidney is. You probably don't even know what size it is. You can't feel the shape of it. You can't feel any of it: your liver, intestines, none of it. You're unaware and yet, you're directly connected to all of it. If it has a problem, it sends a signal to you. It conveys that it's in pain and you react to it. You react to it by not eating certain things, if it is your stomach. If it's on your skin, your skin burns or throbs. Your mind now is attentive to that specific area for that moment of time. The only reason you're giving it your attention at that very moment is because it cried out to you. Once you've tended to it, it stops crying out to you and your mindfulness now is completely gone from there.

The Universe, or God, isn't coming down to Earth telling everyone what we're going to do today. It doesn't work that way. I'd like it to work that way. What a great relationship we could have! All the religions would finally wake up. God is a Force of energy. It has awareness, like you are aware of your body. You're not specific to any particular cell. There are billions of cells. There are more people and living creatures on the planet than there are cells in your body. Think about how vast that is. And yet, you are aware of every single cell, but not personally.

When you do something wrong, God does not stop and judge it to be evil. God doesn't cry out, "You shouldn't be doing that!" If one white cell attacks another white cell, you don't even know about it, but it happens. Things happen; mistakes happen. Prana can come into you, and if you have the wrong intention and you think of it as a negative action, you can accidentally harm someone. You can mistakenly cause them to have an accident. You can make them sick. You can do psychic attack or psychic defense.

So, you have to be mindful of where your thoughts are when you do things. You have to clear your mind. You have to be in a positive state of mind when you're going to act on something. It's like a ritual. In magic, you sit down, set up your altar, light candles, and burn incense. You do this because you are putting yourselves into a trained state of mind. We don't actually need all those props, but we need enough mental discipline to put ourselves in the right state of mind, regardless of what is going on with us in life. That's mindfulness.

Your mind knows you're going to deal with your situation, and anger has nothing to do with Prana. It has nothing to do with energy. You always have to exercise your responsibilities. You have to be aware of them. Now, many people wonder how they can be aware all the time. They assume it is impossible but it isn't. You drive a car. When you get mad you don't run somebody down, but you could. You could be mentally lazy, stop paying attention, lose control of the wheel and hit another car. Sometimes you do mess up and go over in another lane but you straighten the car out. It happens. But you're *mindful*. Being responsible and aware is no different. The only difference is that we are not used to exercising that kind of control over our thoughts and emotions. We have the ability to do it, but we have learned to let our emotions do whatever they want. It's very simple; you just have to be conscious of what you are doing.

If you're angry with someone when you sit down to meditate, do you have to consciously be aware of your intention to harm them or can it happen unconsciously? How would you prevent that?

It's going to happen. You're not going to be able to control it. If I never mentioned this, there would be nothing governing your unconscious thoughts. Do you know how psychotherapy works? Let's say you have an issue about something or your mind wanders when you hear somebody talking and you're not mentally there. If it's pointed out to you and you can catch it, it removes the problem just by realizing it or thinking about it. By the sheer fact of me explaining to you what you could do, even though you're angry, you'll remember it. In the back of your head, you will know that you're not supposed to harm someone. You can be angry now and thinking of Prana, but you know in the back of your mind what you should and shouldn't be doing. You don't really have to think about it anymore. It's already implanted there.

Energy is everything. With Prana you can heal people. You can let your mind go into the Akashic records. Do you remember what the Akashic records are?

It's all the knowledge in the Universe.

Yes. It is the accumulated collective consciousness of everything in the world. It's the Gaia Mind. Then there's something higher than that, the solar system. The solar system collectively gives to the galaxy. And the galaxies give to the Universe. So it's like a database. A database on a computer is when you have one program that you type in people's name and address. Another program has their name and social security number, and another program has their name and license plate on their car. A database lets you look up information, say on John Doe. It takes the driver's license from one place. It takes the social security number from another. It takes the address from another place and puts it all together. This gives you the information you requested.

That's what the Universe does. The Universe has specific places that do a specific thing. A specific kind of knowledge is developed there and it inputs and combines everything until, eventually, it becomes one consciousness -- God. It's like your body. Your foot has one job, your arms have jobs, your eyes have a specific job, your ears have a specific job and your body combines the information into one result. All of this data pools into one consciousness. We are a micro system that is similar to a much *grander* and much more complex system. It's hard for us to perceive how it all works because you can't imagine eyes and ears in a cosmic database, but you can use the analogy that solar systems would be like the ear of God. A galaxy might be the nose for God. Whatever is going on there for that Universe, collectively, this data is sent up to a higher consciousness. Then it all pools together.

The Akashic Records is a total collection of *all* the knowledge from all the whales and dolphins on the planet. It's a collective consciousness of all the human races that have lived for thousands of years. It's all the information that is collected and pooled for the planet. When the planet dies, maybe in a billion years from now, all that energy is released to the solar system. Energy cannot be destroyed. It can only be recreated. The solar system collects information from the Earth and from all of those other little planets that have lived and died over billions of years. Everything that was collected is released to culminate again. It just keeps going on and on and on. So, the perspective of time, in this case, is usually based on size. A mountain's lifetime could be several million years. We are smaller, so our lifetime would be about one hundred years. An ant that feels like it has lived one hundred years has lived for maybe two weeks. It *feels* like it's lived one hundred years. For the Universe, time is very different.

There's going to come a time when you're going to go through several phases. As you learn, you're going to understand things way beyond you in size and scope. You're going to feel very miniscule in size. Very insignificant compared to the Universe now that you understand it in different ways. This feeling will come, but it will pass. You may go through different periods that your spirituality will go through highs and lows because you're learning *so much*. For weeks, you're going to be thinking about this. You may not realize that; it's just going to move through you and it will be like a roller coaster. But that's the work. It's about refining yourself spiritually.

Remember, your body is a vast universe, but most of your cells will travel less than a few inches. This measurement of "time" will be like one hundred years for that cell. But think about this: *one cell* in your entire universe can create cancer and can cause you to die. It will kill the entire universe of your body. And so it is that one single white cell can affect numerous amounts of negative or evil cells that intend to destroy your universe, changing the whole path of your entire life. It's just hard to perceive because you feel so insignificant in size. That's what you have to remember. *One single white cell, one person, can change everything!*

Chapter 3

MIND TOUCH

PSYCHOMETRY IS THE ability to discover facts and information by touching inanimate objects associated with a person or event. It is an important exercise for the sixth sense that can be applied to more than just objects once you are good at this skill. Scanning is the ability to systematically observe and analyze information about a person that's physically in front of you. You can scan their consciousness, desires, emotions, hidden agendas, and know certain things that are going to happen to them in the future. Scanning and psychometry are similar in that you are tapping into the frequency of the object or person by using your sixth sense to pull out information.

Human beings emanate a specific frequency which is different for every person. A radio station utilizes a specific signal or frequency that you can tune into. Your clothes pick up the frequency of your energy that feels like you. The same goes for jewelry and any other object when you infuse it with your energy. In psychometry, you need a solid object to work with because it holds energy that contains information. I have found that metal is the best substance for psychometry. The second best is solid, hard plastic, and then clothing or other personal items. The reason that metal is better is because it holds a stronger charge, a better imprint of energy. With clothing, the energy signature slips away in a short period of time.

When you hold an object and tune into it, you take the frequency of that person from the piece of jewelry and you transfer it from your hand to your brain. Then you can tune into that person's frequency under the right conditions. Your energy field is connected to your brain, your mind. Through clairvoyance or clairaudience, your thoughts draw images from the object. Like audio visual, you can hear and see things in your head. You simply describe what you are seeing. Either it makes sense to you or it doesn't because it could be a future event.

Some people have asked me how it is possible to see the future. I don't think anybody knows how to undeniably explain it, but let's look at the facts. In the past, people have accurately predicted the future. If it had happened once or twice, that would be amazing. If it had happened a few times, that would be miraculous. But it has been done millions of times throughout history by reputable people. Let's say you do a psychic reading, you predict somebody's future and then get into an argument about knowing that information. Is the future predetermined? Partially, it is predetermined because parts of it are predictable. It just depends on the psychic's filtering the criteria and how accurate and reliable they are. This conversation is not predictable because it is minor information, or something that is not very important. But car accidents, critical points in your life, or anything noteworthy are written in time and space. You can psychically pick up on it.

Einstein said that everything that has ever happened will happen again. To me, that is like saying time is a giant film strip. We are in the part of the movie where the light is going through the projector and the director says, "*Action!*" This is the big moment. It begins with an outline and the images become more concrete as it approaches every inch or tenth of an inch to the moment of '*action*'. This very minute, every conversation we've had and everything we've done is already happening repetitiously over and over somewhere in time. We don't know what *time* is exactly, only that it makes it possible to see the future. The more spiritual and enlightened a person is, the more energy they have. They are almost impossible to psychically read. They have no future. They truly live in this moment and create or embrace destiny on a much higher scale than most people do. The red cells that basically function for this planet have a very high level of predictability.

As a spiritual person beginning to awaken, do I start using my own will to guide my life?

Yes, the higher your will, the truer it is. It's mindfulness or mind versus brain.

Is that making me more unpredictable?

Yes. You are no longer prodded and moved along as a function of the machine or an organism of the planet. You are a free, living individual because you have awareness. You are awakening to who you truly are. That's what these classes are all about.

So you're saying I can create my destiny and write my own future?

You can literally will your own destiny. As you evolve through classes in the future, you will better understand what I mean. For now, we are talking about average reasoning. I have to give you the basics so that you will have a better understanding of what I am talking about.

The article we are looking for when doing psychometry is a piece of jewelry. It's something that belongs to the other person that they have had for a while. It has their energy imbued into it. Energy is very interesting because someone else could wear your ring just for a day, and even though you wear it 99.9% of the time, the psychic may pick up on the small amount of energy from the other person. I don't know how the energy lives in there, but I have seen it happen. You never know what you are going to get when doing psychometry.

Is that because their tonal or frequency was stronger?

Psychometry is not about being stronger. A frequency is recorded and manages to stay in the object. Metal objects are very capable of holding recordings of all sorts of things for a very long time. Let's say a psychic sees something from your past. So, are they using a form of telepathy and reading your mind? I don't believe that is the case.

Let's look at this from a different perspective. You see with your eyes but your eyes aren't touching anything. Your eyes record all the information in your brain electrically. Your ears record all the sound electrically. Your senses of smell, taste, touch, and your feelings and emotions are all recorded in your brain electrically. They are recorded electrically and they are also stored electrically. Like a video, isn't it possible to be recorded on "a tenth of a pin"? An entire year of life can be recorded in a hair line portion of a solid metal object. Who is to say how it is possible for that to happen or what mechanisms allow it? What I do know is that it is recorded there as an imprint.

Psychometry can be used for finding missing people, which I have done in the past. When I was searching for someone, I was given a piece of jewelry that belonged to the missing person. When I found the energy trace from that person, I started to get images of them. It may be things they saw before they died or where they are currently because they aren't necessarily dead. You get bits and pieces of information. You have to separate the Hollywood version of a psychic versus reality. Don't expect it to happen like in the movies. Let's say someone is missing. When you get an image of that person in your mind, you probably don't see the town, street, exact corner, or get an address at the same time. It doesn't work like that. You get bits and pieces of information. You see different circumstances that might have happened. In one case, I saw a dirt road. It was actually an oiled road. In Connecticut, a lot of the older roads are oiled and coated with sand. It restores the consistency of the tar so that it lasts longer and saves the cost of re-tarring the entire road. This is quite common, so it wasn't a big deal. It was not a "good hit," but all information is useful. It took three days of work to come up with all the material by piecing together all the individual bits of information into a full picture, like a jigsaw puzzle. Don't think you will just walk in, solve it, and walk out. The second thing I saw was a stone wall. The wall was pushed over on someone's body. Originally, the wall was standing on the other side of the oiled road. I saw the shoes, the sneakers. I saw the person's body. None of that told me specifically where the body was. There are a million stone walls in New England. It could have been anywhere. It was like a needle in the middle of a haystack.

The next thing I saw was a field and a silo. The silo was tilting awkwardly, like it was falling over. That was good but there are a lot of old silos that are falling over. Again, it wasn't really a good hit because nobody could say exactly where it was. Then I saw something that was very strange. There were big stones overlooking a giant field. I saw a picture of Charlie Brown and Snoopy painted on a stone structure. There was a stone that stuck out and they made a dog's face out of it, painted it, and it looked like Snoopy. One of the people with me during the reading turned around, jumped up and said he knew where it was. He knew the town. It was the pumpkin field by such and such farmer. The theme there is *The Great Pumpkin*, Charlie Brown, and it's been that way for years. They drove out to this area and sure enough, there was the road that had been oiled. On one side was the field, and on the other side of the road was the stone wall. As they were walking, they looked around and there was the stone wall that had been pushed over. It all lined up, so there was a connection.

This is a good example of how psychometry ordinarily works and could work for you. Maybe you won't know all of the detailed information at the snap of your fingers. You have to work with logic and rationalize as you find good descriptions of the pieces you collect. This type of work can also be called *remote viewing* when you do this at a distance.

One of my greatest assets in doing psychic work is the ability to express myself very well because I can describe things in great detail. For example, a typical psychic might say, "I see a blue house," when they need to be more specific. What kind of blue are they talking about? Is it baby blue, royal blue, sky blue, or grey metallic blue? If they say, "I see a two-story house," it could be a Victorian or a typical two-story house. It could be any type of house. Description is everything. The more you can describe something, the more accurate you will be. Most pseudo psychics won't even give you a detailed description because they aren't able to.

One might say, "I see a blond haired woman. She lives in a two-story house and she looks like she is in her thirties."

"Oh well, that's my sister or it could be my aunt," you say.

"No, it's your sister and I see her having a good time," the psychic assures you.

"Oh my God, you are such a good psychic!"

I get very angry and frustrated when I hear of people who falsely claim to be psychics. The idea is not to just see the blond hair but also describe the style of hair, the clothing they're wearing, and the build of their body. There are some obvious disadvantages in doing this. It's difficult to describe people's body height, width, and weight from just a picture in your head. However, there are some things that you can do to help you. If they are not standing next to somebody that you know, you can't accurately judge their height. You can give it a try, but you have to use your own mind to compare other objects. Is there a mail box near them? You already know how big an average mail box is because you have seen all different types. You see the one you are familiar with, how big it is, and you get an idea of height. That's what I learned to do. Compare different objects to give a better description of height, body weight, and size.

Sometimes when you do readings, you don't see crisp, clear pictures. Often they are very faint, like a faded picture. Imagine putting silly putty on a picture in the newspaper, pressing it down, pulling it off, and trying to see the image in detail. It is a fair copy of the picture. The reason for the lack of quality of the image is fear. Fear is the number one destroyer of any psychic's ability. No one wants to be wrong. No psychic wants to be wrong when doing a reading. They don't want to be told, "No, that's not what my sister looks like." How do you know that's their sister? You don't, so why even say you think it's their sister. You're just opening yourself up for an attack. What if they told you they don't even have a sister after you saw a woman you thought was their sister? Already, bad feelings are created and doubt slowly creeps in. You start to second-guess the quality of what you see. This causes you to stop the flow of information. You're paralyzed. If you say nothing, you can't be ridiculed. You can't be wrong. That's how a lot of psychics are destroyed in the process of becoming better psychics. They give up too quickly because they think they are not good enough. They don't realize that it's a skill that needs to be refined.

The most important thing to do is have faith in what you are seeing. You have to trust what you see. You cannot stop to think about it or second-guess yourself. When you stop to think about what you are seeing in your head, it stops the psychic connection and you start using the brain to describe instead. When doing a reading, you can't stop to think, "How can this possibly have anything to do with this person?" I'll give you another example of what I am talking about.

I remember doing a very interesting reading when I lived in Connecticut. There was a lady who I did psychic work for. She was always pleased with the readings I did for her, and a lot of the predictions came true. Some psychics make predictions that take years for them to come true. By that time, most people do not remember what was said. Sometimes their predictions would never happen, but there was no way to check the information. The predictions I made happened within hours. They would go home and things would start to happen right away.

I have saved people's lives. One lady came to me and I told her, "Your husband, I am getting fluid in his lungs. I see him all swollen. He has a lot of medical problems."

She said, "Well, when do you see this happening?"

I said, "It feels very strong -- right at this very moment."

She got up, went to her car and drove home where she found her husband in shock. His whole body was enlarged and there was fluid in his lungs. The reading saved his life. Of course, she came back, gave me a great tip and said she would be forever grateful. I can't tell you how many things like that happened to me.

One time, out of the clear blue, someone came to me and said he had been looking for his father for almost thirty years. He didn't know where his father was. He heard about me and drove down from New York for an appointment. I went ahead and did the reading. The first thing I saw was a road, and by chance I happened to see a street sign, so I described it. It was an area that I knew well -- Foster, Rhode Island. I had been there before. That's when I saw the graveyard. I apologized to the man and told him that I thought his father was in the graveyard. He took it very well. He listened to everything I said and left to go check it out. He came back a week later and brought me photographs of the grave. He found his father in that specific graveyard that I picked out. His father had passed away about two years before.

When you do psychic readings, sometimes you wonder, "Am I being accurate? Am I correct or is this my imagination?" When you start to think it's your imagination, you create with your imagination. This is why it is so important to meditate to quiet the Babbler as much as you can. When I tell you to meditate using the Multi-Dimensional Meditation method, you learn every skill there is to develop psychically and spiritually. It's the entire work out, like *Bally's Total Fitness*. You are covering everything, not just becoming relaxed. When you shut off the Babbler, the pictures become fluidic in your mind. You want to receive the images clearly, describe what you see, and not second-guess them. You start to screw up the entire image the second that doubt enters your mind. Then you are scared to tell the other person because you think you are going to be way off and they are going to come back and say you are wrong.

One time a lady wanted me to do a reading for her neighbor. He seemed like a typical guy. Then he came over and I warned him about dealing drugs. I said he was doing these things and if he didn't stop, he was going to get caught. I described everything as I saw it and he was shocked that I knew. He really didn't want a reading because he thought it was phony. He even told me he thought readings were just for women, but it wasn't his money so he didn't care. He said, "She gave the money to me to pay you. She dragged me down here. I don't believe in any of this. This is a bunch of bull, but I'm going to make her happy. She has been bugging me for two months." He was a biker-type guy.

So, now I'm thinking, "Oh, great." As I'm doing the reading, I see different things that I tell him about and all he says is, "Uh huh." Nothing I saw was spectacular, but you can't make up things about people's lives. Some people don't have anything special happen to them their entire life. They live and die, boring. They don't even have a car accident. So there's nothing to talk about. I'll tell those people, "Sorry, but I can't do it." There's nothing to tell because I don't get any highlights on them.

Anyway, with this biker guy, I started to see something that shocked me -- pink pigs in this guy's kitchen. I saw him at a kitchen table, his head was down, and I saw three pink pigs running around. BIG PIGS, not little ones. They were a brilliant pink. They knocked over the kitchen table and he fell over.

I thought, "If I tell this guy what I'm seeing, he'll think I'm crazy and just out to take his money." I had to decide if this was my own imagination or something I was really seeing. I decided to tell him anyway. I told him the whole thing. He looked me in the eye and said, "You make a hell of a good living for a guy who sits on his ass telling all of these ridiculous stories." Then he got up and he left. He didn't even pay me.

My motto was, "If I see it, I say it." That's the rule I've always lived by. A month later, I got a letter in the mail. It was an apology letter with $300 in it. It said, "You may not remember me. You told me the story about the pink pigs. Would you please call me?" I figured there's $300 in here, so something must have happened. I called him and he told me his friends threw a birthday party for him. They were from out of town, a farming type town. This happened in New England where there are a lot of farms. They brought some pigs with them to play a joke on him when they knew he was smashed. They painted the pigs pink. When he got drunk in the kitchen and put his head down to rest, they let the pigs into the kitchen and shut the doors. The pigs ran around in this little room and knocked the kitchen table over. He thought he was freaking out because he saw pink pigs everywhere. The reading now made perfect sense to him. Everything fit into the picture and was definitely one to remember because it was so strange. You have to say what comes to mind. You have to take that chance. If it looks really bizarre, you don't have to say it. You can skip over it and stick with the normal stuff until you build confidence in what you're doing.

As far as a psychometry reading goes, let's say someone gives me a ring. When I hold an object, in this case a ring, I rotate it in my hands a few times. This creates some kind of an electrical field. This is purely instinctual from my childhood. Then I take the ring and I hold it in different ways. I slide my fingers through it. It's not that I am pay attention to the contours of the ring; I look at the person I'm reading, the person who gave me the object. If I'm picking up an object without an owner or I don't know who they are, I will just stare off. I play around, holding the object, moving it around, but internally I am searching to find a frequency. I am waiting for my mind to slip into the right pitch. I am looking to electrically synchronize my mind with the frequency of the object. It's a matter of decoding it.

Make casual contact with an item, such as a ring, for Psychometry. Let your mind tune into the object's frequency.

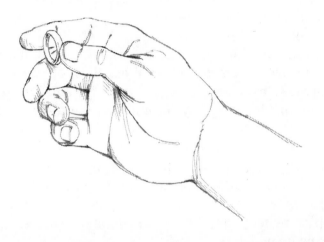

There are millions of codes going through my brain until I break the code or the energy of the ring. Once I start to get into it, I feel a sense of relaxation going through me. I just relax. Then I allow different things to go through my head. The first thing I see is a boating community. Maybe the owner of the ring told me about the boating community before, so my first thought is that he told me this already. Why even go there? Now I am already analyzing what I am going to tell him and what I am not going to tell him. I am already deciding what kind of pertinent information he is going to be privy to. I am *filtering* and I don't want to do that. He should be the one who decides that. Maybe it means nothing to me, but it might make a lot of sense to him.

So, is this what you mean by non-thought?

Just let your thoughts flow. Don't even think about it because you really see in pictures. If you start to rationalize what you are seeing, you'll lose the connection. You'll start thinking to yourself, analyzing it in your brain. Let it come to you and describe what you see.

Once I start to pick up activity, I notice one thing right away. I feel the energy kick in and my mind shifts. At that point, I start to perspire. This almost always happens and is one of the signs that my energy is ardently tuning in. As I start to wind-up, I build my psychic energy. I see zillions of things, but I tend to be selective.

In this case, right away I see a girl. She is kind of short, thin. She looks young but she is not too young. She has short hair. She's a blond, a reddish-blond. This is somebody the person will probably meet. I assume this is where the brother is and this is somebody they already know or they are going to be hooking up with later.

It's a good idea to move away from other people who might be around you because if you look at them in this state of mind, you will start picking up on their energy instead. You're working with the owner of the ring. You've got his frequency, so you have to shut out the other distractions. Human eyes have recordings in them. When you scan people, look at them right in the eye so you can get their information. Divert your eyes so that you can focus more on what you are getting because you're now going into a psychic state where you are trying to retrieve information about the owner. Once you wind-up and start talking about a few things, you might ask those questions to narrow the reading. What kind of things do you want to talk about? What are you interested in? What would you like to know about? Pick a subject, love, marriage, money, business, school, education, or vehicle. It could be anything.

Before you get together to do a reading, tell people to write a list of questions down. If they are put on the spot to have a reading, their minds often go blank and they can't think of any questions. Sometimes you need to focus your mind on a subject in order to pull information. I can tell the owner of the ring is going to have his truck hit in the rear end of the parking lot at the local Vons. He can prevent it if he knows it, so I tell him it is going to get hit. Somebody is going to be backing up. They're going to hit it at the Vons near their house. I know the parking lot because I have been there. The truck is angled towards the bank that shares the parking lot.

A long time from now, there's a hot air balloon and a lot of land masses below. It's a little vacation for this person. Here's something to keep in mind: you can't control what you see. Sometimes, it's just random pictures and then it comes fast. Earlier, I kept seeing a pine forest like the kind you see in Arizona or Big Bear in California. I give out random information until something more detailed comes in.

Once the flood gates are open, the data starts to come easily. Of course, those are not big things but they seem to be pertinent. He seems to be having a revelation in his mind. Maybe he is thinking, "This is incredible. I am so glad I am doing this. This is beautiful." An incredible moment happens in the balloon that explains it further.

At some point, you reach a flow that's hard to stop. It all starts flooding in. The first few times you use psychometry, it can be difficult to control and shut off. As long as you stay tuned in, your mind will keep feeding you data. You can literally reel out tons and tons of information. After a few minutes, it begins building up. You create a link to the person you are tuning in to, especially if they are there with you. When you are ready to stop, clear your mind and take some deep breaths.

It has been a long time since I have done psychometry, but you can pick it back up quickly if you get good enough at it, even if you stop for a while. It's like riding a bike. I gave up psychometry in 1990, but it comes back so fast for me. Trust what you see in the description; that's the key. Allow yourself to go into deep description, but then hold yourself back until you build the confidence. Some stuff is irrelevant. That's psychometry. That's basically how it's done.

It doesn't have to be a metal object. You can hold somebody's wallet. Go after a driver's license and things like that because some people don't wear jewelry. Anything that is more stationary, that they would carry with them is good to use. If they don't have any jewelry, usually they will have a wallet. If they don't, the next best thing is a shoe because of the rubber. Also, they always have it on.

What is the key to mastering psychometry? It seems intimidating to even begin.

Practice makes perfect. If you practice, you will get better and better. It comes down to trusting yourself, clearing your mind, and preparing yourself for the job.

Scanning is the same thing. You are tuning into the energy frequency except you do it with a photograph or a real person. There are some definite tricks for doing this. In the beginning, use stereotyping to your advantage. There are only about twenty different types of people so you can figure out their particular pattern. Once you figure out what they all are, you will *know* a lot about a person. Use your rational mind. Look at somebody and stereotype them. As you begin to scan, your brain does not discern where to stop. You start to know more about this person as you are drawn into studying them. Then you start to know something about the person that, logically, you shouldn't know. You are using something to figure out this information. Then you start getting more and more information. If you just looked at them and said, "This is what you do for a living," you would probably be way off as a beginner. Let your mind study them and take that person in. Studying the person is really the first level of scanning. It's like a plane moving down the runway, building up momentum and starting to pick up speed. Your brain starts to know things as it is processing.

Assimilation is when you become an object or another person. Here is an exercise for you to practice when assimilating a person:

Look at a person near you. Stare at them and feel what it is like to be them. Look across at each other and feel what it is like to feel their face, see through their eyes, their body, their clothing. Become them for a moment. As you are studying them, you will find that the more you look and stare at them, the more you start to realize how they think and how they feel. You start to pick up little nuances that aren't yours and you know the difference. Think about what you would do or what would interest you if you were them. Feel their clothing, the way they wear their hair, their particular look, and the quality of their eyes. You know if they are intelligent or uneducated just by looking at their eyes. The muscles in their face tell you a whole lot about how they carry themselves, how they feel, how they think. That is the beginning of assimilation.

Another form of assimilation involves objects.

Clear your mind, sit back, and stare at an object. Don't cross your legs or arms; everything has to be flat out. Never cross anything when you do something like this. Take three really deep breaths in through your nose. Relax and have non-thought. Exhale out through your mouth. Take one more breath and let everything in your body sink. Focus on your toes right now, on the arch of your feet. Don't move. Lay really still, almost motionless, and let yourself sink into where you are. Everything is relaxed: your lips, your cheeks, your chin is sinking, the sides of your face are like putty that's starting to run off the sides. The muscles are relaxing; your whole face is collapsing inward. Your eyes are relaxed, your scalp, your earlobes, everything is just letting go. Everything is very, very heavy, hanging off the bones, just sinking into the floor. Now become whatever you are laying on. If you are on the carpet, become the carpet. If you are on the couch, become the couch. If you are the couch, feel the texture, what it is like to be the couch. You are the couch.

You are the floor, if you are on the floor. Feel all the hairs, the space in-between the carpet fibers, the mesh underneath the carpet, the pad underneath for cushioning, and the floorboards. You are those things. They are your new body. You can even feel the things that are touching you, the feet of the chairs, the table, the computer racks, the bodies lying on you. You can feel everything that is touching you.

If you are the couch, you can feel the springs, the cushions, the fabric, inside the couch, the coolness of your skin and the warmth of the body touching you, your springs bowing down to the pressure, conformity, and shape of the body lying on it. Become the object of whatever you are laying on. You can feel everything that it would feel. Think about all the things it would feel.

Become anything you choose, any object. Start exploring. Feel what it is like to be that object: the coolness, the tightness of wood, the cold, smooth texture of steel. Become a machine, like a CD player. Feel the mechanisms, pulleys, needle, magnetism, the turning. You can become anything you want. Assimilation is when your energy connects to any object, allowing you to experience what it is to be the contour and shape of that object.

That is assimilation. You can do the same thing with human beings.

Choose a person. Think of someone randomly; your mother, your father, or somebody you know. Feel what it is like to be in their body; become them. Feel what it is like to feel their face on your face, the clothing on their body, the way their body moves, the way they talk, their habits. Pretend you are them. Think about the things that go through their minds. Become that person. When you become that person, you know things about them that you normally wouldn't know. Feel what it is like to feel their body, their knees, their stomach, the shape of their body, their chest area, their groin area, their hands, their feet, their clothing, everything. Become that person and just walk. You become that person. You know and feel what that person feels like and how they would deal with any given situation because that is how you would deal with it. Take a deep breath. Open your eyes and sit up when you are done.

You can do assimilation, even with nature. Sometimes, I become an entire forest that I am sitting in. I can literally feel the wind blowing through the trees and grass that I am. I can feel the insects on the grounds that are walking through the body of me. I can feel every stone, everything. The power and sense of knowledge that comes with that is incredible.

Sometimes, when you assimilate people and become them, you can transfer thoughts to them. If you do a really good job becoming them, you can introduce thoughts and they start thinking what you were thinking, even if they are far away. You can *will* a feeling. Don't specifically give them a direct order. The brain works with desire. You can't make the mind do anything, especially if it is a trained mind, but the brain can be affected. Because all of us are interconnected right now to the grid, you can make someone feel or taste something right now from wherever you are, without even looking at him. You can make somebody desire chocolate, have nausea, feel like they have to go to the bathroom, or have an itch on their body. You can do all sorts of things but you have to become them for a minute.

By becoming them, you are synchronizing with their energy. You're cloning, becoming a chameleon and their body doesn't know the difference. All of a sudden, you start feeling something. They connectively start to feel it also. If you think about what you are doing, it collapses. If you think about yourself, it collapses. You must have a very disciplined mind.

By becoming other things, you teach your body that you are not really a body, that you are a soul. The goal is to become more aware of your energy body rather than your physical body. By becoming other objects and realizing that you can experience what they are, you realize that you are more than just a physical body because a physical body couldn't do that.

Assimilation is very important. If you can let yourself go, it's amazing what you can learn. Try to experience different things; there are no limits. I have experienced what it's like to be my cat and other animals. I've experienced what it is like to fly. I've been a condor flying over a giant valley feeling its wings, the air pressure against them, the stiffness of the wind, and the cutting of the air being pushed by thermal energy. It's an incredible experience to see through their eyes; their vision is completely different. I've experienced what it is like to be different animals and different objects. It's fascinating and it really adds to the depth of my experiences and my knowledge. I suggest that you all try to experience that.

You can have an effect or will your desire on animals. If you keep thinking the same thought repeatedly and you project it towards an animal, as long as it is a basic thought, they will start to do or react to it. Nevertheless, you have to be consistent for it to get through to them. You can literally send a vibration to animals. You only have to believe, have trust, and a certain state of mind. It's a state of mind that's passive, humble, yet willful, but with no thought.

Can you do the same thing for people?

Whenever I heal somebody and I scan them, I assimilate them. I become them so I can feel all their wounds and all of their inner problems. Then, I just study myself to see what I feel, and then I know what they feel. If you don't utilize something, it's not even worth having. If you don't exercise or practice what you've learned, what good is it? Practice makes perfect.

To assimilate someone, you have to become that person. Then you can make them feel or do something, whatever you want. Some people will fight it off if it feels foreign. You have to feel the desire and make them feel it by becoming them. Then will them to do or feel it. Then they will have that reaction. When you have cravings for no reason, sometimes those are pockets of mental thought from other people nearby. You can't understand why you are having that desire, that feeling or emotion that you know you shouldn't be feeling. It's like you are picking up on something. You could help somebody heal their body if they are ill. You can make somebody feel better if they're on a lot of drugs, 'wigging out', and having a bad trip. You can help them this way by becoming them, designing an emotion for them to feel, and then putting it into them. There are all sorts of things you can do with this. It's a very powerful tool.

Are there limits to how we can use psychic abilities? You say we can make them do certain things, or put our desire in them, but it seems like that can be abused. Are there certain people we should not use them on?

There are *house rules*. We are not allowed to use our psychic ability on anybody who doesn't have this ability. We are spiritual people who are awakened on a planet that should not be awakened. We are not supposed to exist. We are the fictional realm. We are the unreality of reality. Red cells are the majority of the world, and we are the exception to the rule. We're supposed to be the hidden secret. We're supposed to walk between the lines. If we use our ability on people who don't have this ability, we not only have an effect on them but also on the chain of life. Red cells are psychically all connected to hundreds of thousands of other people. There is a certain amount of responsibility that you must have. There are always three levels of play. If you take one to foul up the other one, it's like taking a rod and putting it in the wheel of a tire.

Everything has a specific mechanism. We are a giant watch with different turning mechanisms. You can't take one mechanism and cut into the other one as it will jam. We have our purpose. We are helping the little one and the little one is helping us. But if we cross paths, it's a problem. The house rules are: *you are not supposed to use your abilities on someone who does not have abilities.* If you have faith in the Force, you don't have to worry about energy beings. You must have faith in a Higher Power and surrender yourself to the Force. Then it will take care of you. You know it's in your heart. It's humility. It's love.

There are four days a week that I get down on my hands and knees, bow, and say I am totally submissive to the Force and that I wish to be more with the Force. It's the feeling. When you get caught up in life, you think only about your bills, your money, the house, life, everything. At some point, you have to realize that there is something beyond all of this. This is only a moment in time. This is simply a moment of material existence. It's a moment in time but you have to commune with The Force. It's here forever and it never changes. Life changes, but the Force doesn't change. IT is always here for you. By allowing yourself to forget all of this and everything else, you are simply humbling yourself.

There are times when I am overcome with tears in my eyes as I think about the amount of love I get back from the Force, and I am submissive. I have been this way since my childhood. I let go of everything and anything and let that energy become one with me. This is my choice. This is what I choose. Whatever It decides for me, whatever It wants me to do, I will do it. I don't question it. I moved across the country because of the Force. That's faith. I left my friends, family, and everything behind. If the Force tells me to do something but I don't agree, It says this is going to help make my awareness higher, better, and stronger in energy, so this is what I do. I don't question the Force's logic. It knows better than I do. You do need faith. You have to say, "The Force knows something more than I do and I am just going to have to trust It." I trust the Force with my whole life. It has never failed me once.

What is the Force? It's something you can feel, see, and breathe. If you look around the room you are in, shut off the light, relax, and feel comfortable, you really can't see anything. You start to see a silhouette, but what is in the room? The room is filled with the Force. You can think about the darkness and all the dark evil things that could be in the room. If we can't see anything in the room, we tend to think it must be bad.

The Force is here in full force so calm yourself. Clear your mind and let your ears listen to nothing. Feel the weight of the Force, as if it was a hefty weight on your body. Then just take it in, inhaling through your nose and feeling it coming into your chest, like something going right into you. If you look around the room, you can see static electricity and energy. At your level, you can see as well. In the past, I saw it the same way as you do. I believe that I see even more than you do now because I've become *one with the Force*. You have to find peace in the darkness because it's not the darkness of evil. It's the darkness of solitude.

Because you are an energy being, this matter doesn't exist. If this matter didn't exist, there wouldn't be darkness but there would be brilliance of energy that is light. That's the Force of God. When you think about that, there is a level of peace that comes over you. When I am home alone, I sit in the dark, clear my mind, and emotionally express how I feel about the Force, and It expresses back to me. I am at the point where I can feel It come into me. I can feel the Force living inside of me. It's not a power. In this state, you know the feeling of being calm and humble.

Every plant life feels the Force. All life feels the Force, but you have to be without thought. You have to be without desire. You have to be without anything. You have to simply succumb to this beauty and let it become one with you. Don't try to define what you are supposed to be feeling, what you are thinking, or anything else. Just let it happen and all of a sudden, you will feel this emotion that's happy, but sad. You almost want to cry, but you don't cry. There's a part of you that feels like it is part of something or somebody else that's empty. That's the duality because there are two of you. There is your soul and there is your physical body. That is the beginning. That is your communion with the Force because you are recognizing It. If you teach yourself to recognize the Force, then you accept It as being real. When you accept something as real, it starts to correspond with you, and as a result, a special relationship ensues.

Chapter 4

HIGH GUARD: THE ART OF ENERGY DEFENSE

HIGH GUARD IS something that I've been developing over the past twenty years. When I was younger, I experienced attacks from entities that were very negative, very aggressive, and in rare cases, they physically attacked me. A lot of what I experienced back then was emotional and psychological with different variations of that. In the beginning, I really had no idea how to handle a psychic attack, although I was often asked to investigate hauntings or paranormal activities. I would put myself in a position that made me very vulnerable.

Are there different levels or forms of High Guard?

There are different forms of High Guard because there are different forms of attack so there are different strategies to deal with those attacks. As humans, we think that every form of attack is going to be something physical, and we don't often take psychological attacks into consideration. These psychological attacks are a form of abuse in our physical reality.

Entities are energy, and most entities do *not* have the ability to physically attack you. That only happens in rare cases with unique beings. The majority of entities will attack you emotionally. You may suddenly feel overwhelmed with depression or sadness. You may even feel nauseated to the point where you can hardly function and want to throw up. You may receive very sharp pains in your temple area. It feels like a needle pulsating in your temples. It can be very painful.

There are many ways of being attacked. If you are being attacked psychologically, you need to recognize that what you are experiencing is not a normal experience; it is unusual. You might sense that you are not alone or that there is another presence in the house with you. Or you might sense that something is there when you're investigating a place that is holding negative energies. So, there are a variety of different types of High Guard: one for psychic attack, spiritual attack, and physical attack.

What is the most common form of psychic attack?

Whenever something happens that feels like negative energy, it's not always a psychic attack. People always jump to the wrong conclusion, that it's a psychic attack. Sometimes a house can hold energies that feel like depression. If you're not aware of those energies, or if you can't control those energies, how do you defend yourself against that kind of threat? This is considered a form of attack even though no one is consciously willing it upon you.

One type of attack can come from someone who isn't purposely doing psychic warfare or willfully attacking you, but mentally despises you. For example, in a divorce case one person suddenly becomes ill or something negative or unusual happens to them. This is because the other person is willfully throwing some very negative, hateful, and aggressive energy at them with their thoughts. They don't realize their thoughts can have an effect on others. On a subconscious level, they are drawing a map of your energy in their mind by thinking of you and focusing negative energy on you. They literally are attacking your energy field. So, these are a few forms of psychic attack. Most people are not consciously aware that they are able to do this. It's unconsciously done on their part. This is the most common type of psychic attack.

Studies have been done using Kirlian photography. One particular study showed two fingers almost touching and how their energy was battling each other. The energy was sparking at one another. The conclusion was that when two people become aggressive, one person will dominate the other. The energy from one person will cross over and start to control the other person. An additional study showed that when two people were loving or passionate towards one another and they kissed, the photographs changed color, becoming a beautiful violet, or a pinkish neon color, which is a very positive response.

It is possible that someone can be a long distance away and affect you energetically. We believe that there is a grid work of consciousness. We have to stop thinking that we have to be physically near someone to affect them. This is a concept that we think of when we see ourselves as physical beings. Energy is all-inclusive, and it's all connected. So when one person, at any distance, invokes a negative energy at you, it's going to travel to wherever you are and you will receive it. It's going to affect you. You may not understand why it's affecting you, but suddenly you will become depressed, suicidal, anxious, or have pains in your body. Even your nervous system can be affected. You think it's just a natural, biological reaction when it's actually something completely the opposite because somebody is invoking negative energy upon you. That's the most common type of psychic attack.

As you move into the realms of the paranormal, it gets rarer and rarer. It's not usual for somebody to want to attack you, or to have the knowledge of how to do it. There are a variety of other levels beyond this that are a little rarer still. You may meet people who just want to dominate you. It's part of their personality to dominate you. This is another form of psychic attack. Whenever a person consciously or willfully has this intention, their energy is all over you.

Let's consider a typical male/female scenario that takes place at a bar when a male is very interested in a female. A female will often say that she can feel him on her because she has a higher sensory for this kind of feeling. She can literally feel his presence on her and she's aware of that. She just wants to get away from that person. Well, what is that feeling? That's a sensory, but it's really that other person's energy that's touching her. His mind is on her, and his energy field is now approaching her and attempting to seduce her or trying to get her to submit. This is another form of psychic attack even though it's not perceived as aggressive. There are other methods where people just want to dominate others, and it has nothing to do with sexuality. It's just their nature.

As you move up the spiritual ladder, you're in a state of consciousness where you can assist other people who have negative energy, affecting them or someone psychically or spiritually attacking them. Even religious situations can become negative. People think that if you are 'religious,' you pray for only good things to happen, but sometimes people pray for God to smite you, thinking that you're the enemy. They invoke spiritual energy saying, "This person's trying to harm me. Please, remove them from my life. I want them gone." Regardless of what they say, their intention is to get rid of you. In their perception, you're the villain. They're mentally willing you to be banished, or for God to remove you. That is a psychic attack.

Now let's talk about mediums, or psychics – people who have developed paranormal abilities and are willfully choosing to do harm. The vast majority of them are good people with good intentions, but I'm speaking about those who have studied a formula of ritual magic, or similar techniques, and knowingly use it on others. People of the *dark arts* will use objects or a photograph of the person they wish to attack. An object holds the one thing they want – your energy, your vibration. Objects are saturated with your vibration. The person attacking you is able to tune into that energy and use it to reach out dimensionally to you, to have an effect. This is a powerful form of a psychic attack.

Other people are true psychics who don't require any mechanism to harness this power. They're just very developed in the mind. They can invoke you by trance and attack your energy to deteriorate it, or willfully do harm to you. This is another direct and very potent level of psychic attack.

The last one is an entity that is extremely negative or aggressive, usually angry. They're in a mental loop, usually in a dream state. Their anger hits extreme peaks which gives them the energy to physically attack you, throw you across a room, or do harm to the energy field of your body, which will affect you biologically. *This is a very extreme and rare case of psychic attack.*

Say it's not an entity; how can you differentiate a psychic attack from a physical condition, like you are simply sick or just have a headache?

You have to sit down. Clear your mind, and use your intention. You know what you want to know without using words in your head. That is your intent. You've decided, "I'm sitting down and clearing my mind because I have issues right now. I don't know if I'm being affected in a psychic, or paranormal way, or if this is just naturally biological. Sit down, clear your mind, and let that answer surface in you. You have to be careful. You don't want hysteria allowing the Babbler to create ideas like, "It's your wife," or, "It's your mother-in-law," or "It's your neighbor." You have to be very careful of that. There's no real way of knowing if you're going to be able to have an absolutely clear answer. Recheck yourself several times and then make a decision. Don't just jump to conclusions.

Your intention is to know if you're being attacked or not so that you can find out where it is coming from. Let your mind clear and with that intention, your energy field will allow information to come into you. If you are aware, you will see a picture of someone in your mind. Or you may sense that it is entities or spirits but you will know what it is. Just clear your mind and be open to receive. Whatever has been sent to you, whatever you feel, you are going to know if it is something unusual. Your sensory will tell you that. We're so used to ignoring the sixth sense that we usually block it out by talking over that information. Internally we know something's wrong. We know something unusual is going on. We know if our space is being invaded. It's a matter of sitting down and studying this feeling. Where is it coming from? What does it mean? Let yourself internalize that sense to convert it into something you can understand in this reality. Whether it's a person, a thing, or a being, the answer is there. If it comes from a source, that source can be followed instantly by tracing the energy. You will get that information if you just open your mind to it.

Sometimes it can be from something that you would never imagine. I was recently contacted by an old friend. Something happened years ago and there was a disagreement between me and this person. This person talked to their mother and miscommunicated what had happened or she misunderstood the facts of the information. The mother took it upon herself to throw all of this negative energy at me. This person told me that for two years she threw hateful energy at me. Then, when she found out what the facts were, she realized she shouldn't have done that. It didn't really affect me, but you never really know where it's coming from. You have to open your mind and see what the intent is. Don't get too concerned about the source. Be more concerned that you release it and that you create energy around you that's impenetrable. That is more important.

In life, you are always going to be psychically attacked. We are all interlinked. It is thoughts. People don't realize their thoughts have power. It's human nature to be aggressive and territorial. Look at all the different forms that it can take:

1. *You could become interested in a girl and somebody who is already interested in her, senses that. Without telling you of their interest, they befriend you. In the meantime, they're throwing hateful energy at you.*

2. *There's competition for work, or a better position with people you work with.*

3. *You could have an issue with a neighbor over property.*

4. *There is a bombardment of aggressive energy that's constantly going on, so there are always these different things. It just goes on and on.*

Create an energy barrier around you that will remove all these energies that are attacking you. Do it daily, weekly, or however often you feel is necessary. When you do use these techniques from *High Guard*, you will see a dramatic difference in your life; literally within minutes, maybe hours, maybe days, depending on the circumstances. They are absolutely the most powerful techniques you can use, and they're going to have a dramatic effect. I don't care what kind of energy is coming at you, no matter how bad, how dark, how powerful, how intense, or how many people, it does not matter. These techniques are foolproof. They are absolutely the most powerful methods of handling these circumstances.

There is one thing I have concerns about. My intention is not to teach people how to do psychic attack. Unfortunately, by learning how to protect yourself, it's pretty easy to figure out ways of attacking someone. I hope that does not happen. I hope this knowledge is not abused in that way.

How can you keep yourself from subconsciously, or psychically, attacking someone else? If you have negative feelings for them, how can you prevent it from turning into a psychic attack?

There is always going to be an exchange of energies. As you develop spiritually, your intensity is going to get stronger. But one of the beautiful things about developing is that as you grow and become psychically stronger, you can also develop an intentional "on/off" switch. You'll almost have to will yourself, intentionally, to do something to someone, rather than simply getting mad or angry at them.

It is possible that in the normal realms of everyday energy, you may affect someone. If you realize you have done so, you may feel a little bit of guilt. I wouldn't worry about it too much. If you're meditating already and you're using the program, your energy's going to be pretty balanced. There shouldn't be a reason for that to happen. In the rare case that it does, simply use different techniques that you've learned from this program and invoke a positive energy on them. Don't create a festering of negative energy; simply release it. Surrender it.

If you did psychically attack someone, is re-affirming a forgiving vibration the best way to reverse the effect?

Tell yourself that you forgive them; use whatever comes to mind. Everybody has a sense of *knowing* within them and you already know what you need to do. Acknowledge verbally that you won't hold any anger towards them. That releases any kind of negative energy you're sending to them. It is not very easy to unconsciously do a significant amount of harm to people that isn't already done in normal circumstances. People have a natural ability to filter out a lot of energy that comes towards them already. So to directly have an effect on someone, you will have to flip that on/off switch.

What are the repercussions of using this knowledge for personal gain? Where do you draw the line?

You know the difference between right and wrong. You're creating your frequency and that's how the Universe is going to recognize you, by the vibration or frequency you emanate. That will determine your entrance into the higher levels of dimensions that you want to experience. If you are aggressive, that is what I call the 'truest sin.' It's the suppression of human life; controlling life by doing harm to it, and turning your energy into a negative octave. The Universe is going to respond that way to you. It's going to see you as a mechanism that has the intention of doing harm to the whole living organism. If you are doing a lot of harm to someone else, it's going to reflect back on you. That energy's going to push back at you and there will be repercussions. It isn't something to take lightly because psychic attacks, while they may not seem real, can cause physical harm.

If someone wants to willfully do harm to you, it can come in a number of ways, depending on how strong and well refined this person's intention. Most people are able to energetically send sharp pain to your head. Sometimes it's delayed; it might hit you a day after it was sent out and there's a number of reasons for that. Other people, who are more skilled, can throw energy at you and you could end up having muscle spasms. You might, all of a sudden, have a case of asthma that you've never had before, or it can affect the nervous system. Everything about your body is electrical; your muscles expand and retract by electrical currents. Generally, the muscles in your body carry a lot of emotion. It's as if your brain reserves a place to hold certain information that may not be good. Your body reacts to psychic attacks in different ways.

I remember a case many, many years ago, where a lady had psychically attacked a student of mine. His body reacted in such a way that he broke out into, what looked like, the measles. He had red bumps everywhere all over his body. Immediately he came to me and told me about a confrontation he had with this woman. He said she threw a lot of negative energy at him and he could feel it. He was aware she was doing it. However, he felt it was too strong for him and he didn't know how to handle it. I shifted his energy and in a matter of hours the red bumps disappeared. I was rather amused at the effect she had on my student and later went to meet with her. She obviously respected me and was a bit intimidated by me. She, of course, did not know what effect she had on my student. It was only a reaction caused by her throwing her energy out at my student. It was how his body reacted, probably in an effort to purge the energy in a physical way. It was very interesting.

Different people can be affected in different ways. I've seen cases where someone's physical mobility was affected; someone else lost their hearing, and another person was blinded temporarily. It depends on how willful or how strong the person is that projects the energy. With any form of attack, from any person, even the simplest techniques from High Guard can stop or remove them.

If High Guard can teach you psychic defense for yourself, can you also use it to defend others?

Yes, absolutely. It takes a great deal of concentration; you have to know the formula. You can change your formula if you like, but for me, this method has been refined all these years to become the best, most universal way of teaching people psychic defense. Absolutely, you can create your own style, but you can definitely protect other people. Using it for others is rare. Most people use this skill because of their fear of entities. Most of these fears are baseless, but there is a little truth to some of it.

Why would an entity choose to go out of its way to attack you?

There is some truth in every 'wives tale.' You won't necessarily find a negative entity or a demon. I don't believe in demons, but I believe in extremely negative entities that could be called a demon. They tend to be angry at life, and how life has dealt them their hand. They are extremely angry, but they are also spiritually developed, which led to their creation, as an entity, when they turned. I hate to use the 'Darth Vader' concept, but it's like that. They develop to a certain point, but something in their life turns them psychologically. Perhaps they lost someone they really loved and they couldn't accept letting that person go; so in their mind they became very spiteful.

Remember the story of "Dracula?" He was a warrior who lost his lover and was spurned by God, or felt he was. He then turned all of this anger towards God and became a dark, vile creature. The reason why we come up with these stories is because our inner knowing tells us there's a higher truth to these things. If someone wants to grow spiritually to become very powerful, it is possible that they can turn dark. It may be due to circumstances they refuse to accept or understand, or they want to change the greater will of the Universe. When they can't do that, they become spiteful.

Most dark entities have harnessed this ability by their anger and their frustrations. Then they seclude themselves. They stay in the physical plane because anger tends to be a very physical energy. It doesn't let you move into the higher planes. So, they stay in our physical plane, but as intense energy beings. They don't have our sense of time because they are made of energy. A hundred years of our time does not feel like a hundred years to them. When their space is infringed upon, or human beings go into their space, they are angry. They want to be isolated, so they become spiteful. Often dark entities don't even react to you. They could be there, but they just don't care. A spiritual person might sense them, or detect them, and try to communicate not knowing what it is they're really communicating with. Then there's a backlash of anger; hence, all the stories about Ouija boards, and spirit contacts, and all of those things. It's innocent enough but this is where the stories about possessions, attacks, and demons come from. These entities are more or less reacting in a negative way, and this is where you get the intensity from.

Is there a particular attribute that makes someone more prone to other people's or entities' psychic attacks?

Most spiritual people have empathic abilities. Empathic abilities are a sensory or a form of telepathy where you can pick up the other person's emotions. You feel people. If they are depressed, you feel their depression. You internalize it as if it's your own but, deeper within, you know it's from somewhere else. Your biological brain, if it's not trained, accepts it as your own depression and reacts to it. The same thing goes for happiness, negativity, anger, or anything else. You pick this up from other people. This is *selective energy*.

If you remotely give your mind to someone, you'll start to feel them. A lot of people don't realize they're doing this. They just think something is going on with them; they become mentally confused or emotional. They don't know why they always seem to be on an emotional roller coaster. It's not them; it's because they are sampling from all of these other people's issues. When empathetic people go into a house where an entity might be residing, a graveyard, or any place where entities might be trying to find some seclusion, they're going to pick up on the entities and they may not realize what the intensity is really about.

Empathic people are very healing and nurturing. In other words, they want to help. They feel an instinct to assist others. In the process of wanting to be of assistance, their good intentions invoke a negative response back to them because they don't really know what they're getting into. They're feeling it and they sense there is trouble and they want to help. Of course, there are different levels of empathic people. It's not so much about their ability; it's how well they are aware of their ability and what they're doing with it that determines what kind of trouble they're going to get into.

What does a psychic attack affect? Does it affect you physically or energetically? The brain or the mind?

It's probably going to affect both. Your physical body is combined with your energy body. Your energy reacts with your physical body so you can move, touch, smell, and do all these things. It's a two way system. If your energy is affected, then your physical body is going to react. Sometimes, when you go into a house with paranormal activity, or you go into a haunted place, you get a chill through your body. Sometimes that is an energy being moving through you. It moves through you, and your physical field, your nervous system, reacts to the change in energy. It communicates through a chill up your spine, as they say, or your back. A psychic attack, or spiritual attack, is energy-based. Your physical body is tied into your energy, to work with it, much like how your hands move, or your mind works. It is going to relay messages through the brain. Not only will it affect you physically, but there can be serious damage to the energy fields of your body as well.

This goes both ways. If you can be impacted physically and energetically by a psychic attack, then you can affect physical things, like people, as well as energy beings, like entities. Most people feel helpless against entities defensibly, but I don't like teaching people how to attack an entity. I don't want somebody to go around now, looking to pick a fight with an entity. My whole purpose here is really about self-defense. It's like martial arts. In the process of defending yourself, you may have to suppress the problem. That is the intention but for the sake of learning, know that you can go on the offensive or defensive with an entity if you choose.

What about something completely different? Can you also attack physical objects or materials like your TV, house, car, or something similar?

It's absolutely possible to program objects; an object can take in energy. We are physical but energy-based beings. When you hold an object and you will an emotion into it, you've literally programmed this object. When another person takes it, and holds it, if they're unaware of how energy works, their energy field is going to feel different. They're going to react to what they're feeling. If it is a very negative effect, it's going to affect that person. There are many stories of electrical items constantly being shorted in paranormal places. Once you start to deal on levels of energy, the possibilities are endless. It's only as limited as your beliefs.

What is psychic vampirism?

Psychic vampirism is when another person or entity taps your energy field, or your manna; your life energy. Your life energy is the energy that's between your physical energy, or your physical organic body; which would be your lower energy that makes your body function, and your higher energy; which is your dimensional body. It's this fuel that keeps all things alive. It communicates with the cells of your body. It's an interactive form of energy, and it's highly important. This energy comes from trees, nature, life, and from God. It's Prana-like; it's what you've collected through meditation and spiritual practices.

A person who has very low energy, instead of finding energy in life and in nature, unconsciously, will come over to visit you and drain that energy from you. Most people are not aware that they are doing this. I'll give you an example. Let's say you're feeling good and have a lot of energy. You're ready to go out for the day; you're looking forward to it; putting your clothes on, you want to get out. Then a friend stops by and they have very low energy. They sit down and talk to you for a while. It's small talk, nothing important, but all of a sudden, they start getting more energized. They're getting all pumped up talking to you, and feeling good. You are probably unconsciously aware of it, but you start to sink into the couch. You start feeling a little bit drained. They leave, but you seem to have lost all of your ambition to get up and go on with your own day. In other words, they've taken your life force energy, or they've diminished it.

Now you are being affected in a physical way. Your body doesn't know the difference between your physical energy from food and spiritual energy. There is a connection of the two, especially for those of us who are more spiritually evolved. It affects us even more than the average person. We react to the loss of spiritual energy in a physical way. The brain starts to impress on us that it must be one and the same. This makes us feel tired.

This is how it looks to me observing this energy. It is like a mist going over vegetables in a grocery store. You can see this energy moving across an area, and it gathers around the other person into their lower chi area. They're drawing it to them, sapping it from you. If they hold you, or are very close to you, that's even more powerful. There are different ways this can happen, although there is a very simple method of preventing this from happening.

Think about your lower chakra point, just below your navel, your chi chakra. You don't even have to touch it. The second that you think about it, just by being aware of it, actually pulls your energy in. It tells it, "Don't flow out to other people." You're countering any effect that may be happening to you by drawing in energy to this center. You're reversing the energy from flowing out, to staying within you.

Energy being drained looks like a fine mist gathering around the lower chi area.

Mentally focus on the chi chakra to pull your energy in. This reverses energy that may be flowing out, breaking the connection.

If you intensify it long enough with the intention to take it from someone else, you can literally take that person's energy from them. That now becomes a form of psychic attack on your part. Or you could call it defense, depending on their intention. If they take energy from you, and you take it back, call it even. You'll focus on the chi chakra, with the intention in your mind of drawing energy from other people. You will see them getting tired, and you're going to start feeling stronger, feeling like you've got more energy. You can watch this happening.

Are most people that are psychic vampires aware of their actions?

Most psychic vampires are not even aware of their actions; they do it unconsciously. But we all know psychic vampires. We refer to them as draining. Something about them is tiring. You feel like they are too much and you just want to get away from them, not always for logical reasons. It is that internal knowing. Your sixth sense already knows about them. Stay conscious, awake, sense what you're feeling, and understand why. Most people's energy is pretty good. They either respond to nature very well, or they have a natural flow with pranic energy in life. There's not a switch there. It begins psychologically with most psychic vampires; they feel a sense of despair. I don't want to say that they're needy people, but that is often the case. They emotionally need support every waking moment. It could be because biologically, or biochemically in their brain, there's a lot of depression built up. Instead of centering it inside of themselves and coping with it, without realizing what they are doing, they've learned to sap other people instead. Initially their intent is to get emotional support, or feel loved, or wanted, or acknowledged, or feel that somebody cares about them. They go to seek that out from another person. They want those positive emotions and to receive comfort from them, but in their neediness, they tap in on a subconscious level, draining that person's energy.

They often start out going from household to household, visitation to visitation. A common factor of the psychic vampire is they don't like group settings. They prefer to visit, or be alone with that person, perhaps unconsciously. They prefer to visit one on one. It's as if they are self-conscious about being with a lot of people. I suspect that they are aware of what they're doing and they know it's not a good thing. They're doing it anyway and ignoring the fact that they're doing it because they need the lift. They don't know how to get it any other way. They are afraid of other people being around observing them because they can only concentrate on one or two people at a time when this happens. It's not something that you can do in a crowd because people would react to it and know there's something wrong.

You don't want to be near that type of person. There's something internally inside of you that says there's a danger there. Then there are some people who just cannot be vamped at all. It's their psychological nature that programs their energy. They feel the psychic vampire trying to drain them; they sense the energy loss and mentally react to it. They will cut the person off and leave. They can feel that energy drain going on, and immediately, they naturally pull away. They don't know why, but they take the steps to avoid it.

Does non-thought play a role in psychic defense or attack?

One of the key factors in psychic defense is non-thought. When you have non-thought, you are at a much higher level of protection. It's like when you meditate. It doesn't matter if the hordes of hell are coming in; it isn't going to affect you if you're in non-thought. You don't need a perfect meditation to have this affect. When you have non-thought, you have peace inside of you. You remove yourself from distracting emotional states. You have a balance inside of you, and you have clarity. When you have those three things, you have one definite thing that's happening - a communion with God, the Force, and the Ultimate Being of the Universe.

When you have that level of clarity, there's nothing that can come near you. You are a beacon of light; you're a beacon of vibration. When you can maintain that state of consciousness, it will be like a giant ocean wave washing away everything that's dark and negative around you. You're going to flush it with pure light, pure energy, pure God-ness. Nothing, nothing, nothing can approach you if you remain in that state of mind. You are a doorway for God to be present; for the light to come out. You become this center point of beauty.

When you are psychically attacked, it affects your energy field. It has to cycle through the brain. If the brain is being controlled to keep you from babbling, the attack doesn't have a regular way to process and to affect you physically. If it tries to affect your energy, it can't do much to you because you have a movement of energy coming from the inside of you out because you're harmonizing with God. That is obviously the absolute most dominant energy.

Let me give you an example: if red dye was seeping into a sponge with little drops of red color and you are pouring milk from the other side into it, what's going to happen to the sponge? As long as you have a huge flow of milk to counteract the red drops, it's going to be overpowered. They're going to eventually stop. The milk is going to keep flushing it away. The red dye just cannot grab hold of the sponge, and even if it does, it's purged, literally purged.

Does mindfulness play a role in psychic defense or attack and is it the same thing as non-thought?

Mindfulness absolutely plays a big role in it because mindfulness keeps you more aware of what's going on. It keeps you aware of the subtle energies around you, so you know why you're feeling tired talking to someone. You can feel this person pulling your energy. You can feel it; you can sense it; then you can take action. As soon as you realize what's going on, the opposite effect instinctually happens. It's self-preservation; like how you protect yourself from falling off of a cliff, or you pull your hand back from something hot. If you recognize the danger, it doesn't really take a lot of effort to protect yourself. It's only a matter of whether you can recognize it. If you're mindful, you're as aware or as conscious as possible.

If you're not mindful, that means you're automated in the Gaia mind, or the matrix, doing your job and reacting to people in a set mannerism that you know is appropriate, such as:

"How are you doing?"

"I'm fine; thank you for asking." It's the traditional format for communicating: saying what's expected of you in a social circle.

Most people operate without awareness. They're not really conscious of the moment; only in rare cases. If somebody says something that's interesting, you might give them more attention just to communicate what's going on, and then eventually settle back into your remote-controlled process.

If you're mindful, you are attempting to remain very conscious of everything that's happening in your environment, and the intentions of other people. It's not that you're specifically focused on anything. It's just that if anything out of the ordinary happens, that usually would get under your radar; your radar's so intense now; you're very aware of it.

What about other people's psychic attacks? Can you use them against the person attacking you?

I believe that what is good for the goose is good for the gander. When somebody throws negative energy at me, I reverse it and send it back to them. I take the energy in, and I just deflect it back. But there is a cynical part of me. Usually, when someone sends energy, it comes in a stream. So it hits you, and hits you, and hits you. I take it all, condense it into one wallop, and then throw it back.

Of course, it's more intense when I send it back that way than how they sent it to me. I'm still only sending all of their intentions, just in one shot. It's going to be more devastating. I feel that if you're negative enough to do this to me, then it's your just deserts. It's not that I really want to make them sick, or ill, or do real harm. What their intentions were for me is just as fair that they should have those intentions for themselves. I don't always serve it that way because I want to be more intense. I'll be very honest with you, and it may sound arrogant, but I don't want to spend thirty minutes focusing on this person, sitting there throwing their negative energy back at them. I have the capability to wrap it up in a thirty-second thought, or a ten-second thought, and just compile it back at them. Let them deal with it. If they want to put that much time and energy into doing it to me this way, that doesn't mean I have to give them the same time. It is what it is.

Does psychically attacking someone or attacking in defense affect karma?

Yes, but karma is not exactly what it looks like. You could say to me, "Well, Eric, obviously you choose to send back what's sent to you, so you stay within the guidelines of reasonability." Of course, what I really feel is: "Who are you to do this to me? I'll just zap you!" But I also believe in the preservation of life. People make errors. They make mistakes and they act upon incorrect information. I may be needlessly reacting to something, so I need to stay within a more compassionate state of mind, a more forgiving state, instead of attacking them, for attacking me, with more intensity. This is why I say it's fair to send back what they deserve. All I'm doing (catch the important message of this statement) is simply sending back what they sent to me. That's all I'm doing, no more. I'm sending it back to the source. Now, I might be condensing it into a little wallop to send back to them, but that is what they get for doing this to me. The Universe views it as an exchange of energy. The energy was simply returned. It doesn't matter how it came back. Yes, I'm intensifying it, but I'm intensifying it with a very strong sense of reserve. I certainly could do a lot more damage, if I intended to.

Is there a difference in your intention of sending it back as opposed to somebody that wanted to get revenge?

There are two circumstances. The first: the reason why you get attacked is because you're not on guard. You're not using your skills from *High Guard*. If that were the case, you wouldn't be able to be attacked. You wouldn't even be aware of it. Your energy field would be too strong. It's like rain on a big rooftop; you don't even know it's raining out. It's nothing. It's like pebbles.

The second: if you're not aware of it and you haven't been practicing your shielding, and clearing out your energy fields, then you're a lot more vulnerable. In that particular case, you may react as it's dealt out to you. You wouldn't be doing it consistently. If you do it once, then you should expect something else to happen. Logic would dictate that you set up your structure, get on with life, and forget about it. Why should you dwell on this and let it consume you negatively when you can say they need to deal with that situation? Whatever their issues are, you move on knowing that it can't affect you.

In anything I teach, whatever you learn really boils down to one thing – consistency. As long as we are in a physical world, time is established by deterioration. Everything is affected by time in this reality. A mountain will become a desert; hills will rise to mountains; we start off young; we grow old. There is a cycle of change. All things, even spirituality, need a maintenance schedule. If you tune yourself up and maintain things at a reasonable level, you'll never have a problem. The same thing goes for a car, a house, or anything. You're constantly taking in information through your six senses. Because this information comes in, it's constantly affecting you psychologically, affecting your brain, your mind, which then reacts to your personal energy. You may have something devastating happen in your life that makes you very depressed. Your energy fields are dropping because, internally, you're affecting it. Hence, meditating or rebooting the system gives you a very good, clear, energy field. It purges you. Now you need to set up some structures of energy, and check them every few days to make sure they're working. Then rework them.

If a beginner is sending energy back, could they accidentally do it with negative intentions? Is it important to do this with a compassionate intention?

With some people, I send back the energy that they've dealt to me. They have bad intention. My rule is if you're at least a reasonable level, or if you know what's going on, you react to the person based upon what their capabilities are. If they are evolved spiritually, and energy-wise, then they deserve what they get. They know intentionally, what the deal is, and sent it out to you to do harm. I send it back.

If the energy comes from someone who is reacting emotionally but unconsciously, I can sense that it is not from someone who is psychically developed. People get upset and throw energy with their thoughts, not understanding that it can affect someone. It's a different kind of energy that you'll recognize by your intuition. I don't send back their energy as intensely; I usually try to create positive energy and reflect it back to them. This might cause them to stop and think, "Well, maybe this person isn't as bad as I thought; maybe I'm overreacting, or now that I'm calm, maybe I should forgive them." They feel a sense of love from you that will change them. I certainly encourage sending positive energy over negative, but different circumstances require different actions. Compassion is always the best way, yet sometimes, although I hate to say this, being compassionate gets you killed. You want good intention, but if somebody's so intent on doing you harm, your energy and health are going to take a beating while you're trying to send them positive energy. They are doing damage to the physical cells of your body and you're being passive. They may not notice any positive energy, or be so intent on harming you that they don't care. You have to rationalize what kind of response is reasonable.

If you are sending energy and taking care of the situation, is it unnecessary to put in more of your own energy while returning theirs?

I don't put a lot of effort into it. I take the energy they sent and return it. I'll give you a little High Guard trick using the Pyramid, which you will learn. I feel that any unnecessary energy is food for me. I call this the *great converter*. When people throw negative energy at me, I have my energy fields set up in such a way that it's like a water filter. Imagine pouring Coca-Cola in one side of the water filter. Now, I'm not interested in the Coca-Cola – it's dark, sweet caramel sugar, but Coca-Cola is mostly water. When it goes through the whole filtration system, pure water is what comes out the other side. I usually let energy hit me if it's negative, but it's really juicing me up. I convert it over to positive energy that I can use. It filters the negative out, leaving the pure energy. To me it's the greatest thing. I let them continue throwing negative energy, and in the meantime, I don't have to search for other resources or tap into Prana as often. It's just naturally cycling through me.

Be clever about how you do things. Do it the easy way. Negative energy can be a great resource of energy; it's just your perception. You can look at garbage, and say, "It's garbage." Or you can recycle it and find lots of useful material. I don't really spend a lot of time throwing negativity out. This is only for certain circumstances because it's a way of teaching.

Can you briefly explain scanning? A person with an active sixth sense can feel it. You can feel the energy move into you, but is this a psychic attack?

No, scanning is not a psychic attack. Scanning is meant to acquire information about an individual or an environment. It uses your sensory to collect data; it's a form of telepathy. It's not a form of psychic attack. Attack would be simply that – attack. It means to have an intention of suppressing or damaging, or to have an effect that's going to be negative to the other person, something undesirable. If you are scanning someone, or being scanned, certainly the intention is not to damage or harm them. You can use *High Guard* to block scanning, even though it is not an attack, but it certainly doesn't warrant reacting in a hostile way.

Can you use High Guard while mind projecting, like astral projection?

It would call for some unique consideration and a slight adaptation to the circumstances, but it can be used. There are many ways to adapt the techniques you are about to learn.

Can you use more than one kind of High Guard at the same time?

Yes, you can combine different systems at the same time. It needs to be layered. You do one thing, then the next, and the next if you want to combine things. I wouldn't do two things at the same time if they have been taught as separate techniques. Usually, most of the High Guard techniques encompass several different formulas that create the whole process. There is a reason for the quality of the outcome; it is not diminished in any way by combining several techniques into one.

Let us begin and learn the first *High Guard* technique. We will start with the Pyramid. The Pyramid is one of the most useful psychic defense systems available. In my youth, it definitely protected me from some very intense, negative beings. The Pyramid is a technique that you use to program your energy and, like all *High Guard* techniques, it's semi-visually based. The methods are energy-based, so you're invoking certain emotions or thoughts by visualizing that energy. It programs your energy, or at least tells it what it needs to do.

There's nothing elaborate about doing defensive energy techniques. Nobody thinks about doing them, and that's what makes you vulnerable. If there's no response when being spiritually attacked, you will take the beating. You take the punches, or you deal with it and cope because you don't know what's happening to you. If you don't know how to defend yourself, or what the process is, then you really can't stop it.

To do the Pyramid technique, first clear your mind. You may sit down into the meditative position that you learned from the book *Meditation within Eternity*, an earlier course. Begin by clearing your mind, having as much non-thought as possible. Next, focus on breathing slowly in through your nose and then out your mouth. Visualize Prana in the environment, meaning energy. Give it a texture or color. See it as silver bits of energy. It's not important what you visualize; it's more important that your *intention* is to see and feel Prana all around you. Recognize this as a very good and positive energy.

What is taking place here is that you're *reverse engineering* your thinking. So instead of trying to take something dimensional and bring it in physically, you're trying to take something physical into the dimensional. This is to make your brain and mind bridge together to achieve the desired result.

Begin to visualize Prana moving into you; little beads of light streaking into you very quickly from all over. It's an infinite amount. Now, with your mind focused in the center of your physical body, imagine silver light is being built; as if a bar of light inside of you is developing and it's made of light. Slowly now, as you breathe in, see it expanding as it's filling you.

See it expanding, expanding, and expanding even more until it reaches the outside of your body. It's coming out of every pore of your skin, out of every molecule in your body. It's all pure energy now. See your entire body as a molecular structure. All of the organic bodies are made out of molecular structure, and become pure energy.

This white light begins to fill your whole body. It begins to look like it's a white being of light. Now you're going to expand it beyond you. It starts expanding outward, above and below you. Let this energy take the shape of a pyramid. When most people think of a pyramid, they envision three triangles and a bottom. A pyramid has a bottom and four sides.

Let this energy drop down as if it was a glass-shaped structure that you're sitting in, floating in the center. You will be in the middle of it. See this energy moving down and expanding to the four corners of the base of the Pyramid. It's filling outward, towards the four edges, and then rising above your head by several feet. It's going to fill that space until it's a perfect triangle.

Fill it now with this absolutely pure, white energy. Take that energy and give it one final touch. Switch to your heart chakra and feel an intense amount of love and happiness permeate that energy all around you. Say, "So it is." By saying, "So it is," or something similar, this tells you it is done. It is complete. It's solid. My work is done. It's that simple. Of course, the process should take about fifteen minutes or so.

See the energy expanding out and filling the pyramid.

Remember what I said to you about meditating and it being the highest state you could possibly be in to defend your energy? Nothing can hit or attack you; it just moves right through you? Now you're taking a quality of that energy to use. You're building it up around yourself. You are telling, or programming, this energy to stay around you as a protective barrier. Once the Pyramid is complete, get up, walk through life and deal with your situation. The Pyramid prevents negative energies from being able to affect you. Literally, you have all of these energy barriers preventing those energies from being able to affect you, just as if you were sitting and meditating all day long. That will require some maintenance. The better job that you do with focusing, setting your intention, and clearing your mind; the better your pyramid field is going to be.

The pyramid field is also self-expanding and retractable. If you're sitting and doing your meditation, when you stand up it will expand to always be 'X' amount of feet over your head and 'X' amount of feet into the ground. When you walk, and move through a room, if there are negative beings standing by the couch and you walk past it, your pyramid is going to be like a plow. It's going to push them out of the way. It will move through objects like an energy static field. It's always around you and all you have to do is feed it once or twice a day or week or whatever the circumstances may demand. You cannot think in terms of physically how we perceive ourselves. You've got to think in terms of energy being able to permeate every environment.

Now, I'll tell you one of the things that I do when I meditate. I purge my home of negative energy when I move into a new house or apartment because I don't know what kind of energy is already there, what the intentions were, and I don't want to be concerned about it. Meditating and focusing on this energy, I take the pyramid and instead of just expanding it around my body, I create one around my entire home that takes up the entire property. It will go deep into the ground, high above the house, and deep within the barriers of the home. Then, I permeate it with positive energy, intention, and vibration. It prevents negative energy from coming into my house, especially when there are guests in my home.

But, it needs to be maintained. Sometimes I forget about it and get some interesting energy coming around me because of things that go on in my home. Other times I know I've got to re-strengthen it, and then I'll check back with it in another month to see how it's doing.

What do you feel about the people who build pyramid structures and hang them above their beds and such?

Inevitably, whenever we are talking about using a pyramid as an energy defense mechanism, someone asks about physical pyramids, which are popular in some New Age circles. These are pyramid frames that you hang above your bed, or pyramid tents, and similar things like that. What you're really asking me is, "Do I think they have a positive effect?" Yes, I believe there are some good results from using them. However, most of the results have been over-exaggerated. Pyramids affect subtle energies. Therefore, on an energy level, they certainly are effective. If you're going to use a pyramid for other purposes, it is a whole different thing. If there were physics in spirituality, pyramids would be effective on spiritual energies, or conscious energy, or mind energies more than they would be on a physical level for this dimension.

**So those pyramids serve mostly as a reminder
of a person's intention or goal?**

Right, it's more about how you're manipulating the energies around your body.

**Is there a difference between creating a pyramid
with energy that's cultivated internally as opposed
to collecting energy from an external source?**

Yes, there absolutely is a reason why you internalize your energy from taking Prana in. Then you build from this thin thread. The mind is very psychological; therefore, what works for the mind can also have an effect on you. Some people might wonder if they put a pyramid around them, what if this negative energy is inside with them? Now it's encased inside of them. By creating a thin level of energy and working your way out you're purging everything from the *inside out*. It's foolproof and that's what you want. You want a guarantee you have done the best job you can at the moment; that's what you're after. By internalizing it from the very center and creating a thin line and expanding it, you remove any thoughts of something else being contained within you. If there was a presence around you, or in the room, you don't want to think you've encased something inside with you. You also want to create the best quality of energy that you can. So, forget about having something inside with you. Make sure you're surrounded with the best energy possible.

Why a pyramid? Why not a cube or a sphere?

This is a *knowing* on my part. Now, in certain circumstances an orb will be the most universal structure. But, because we are in a physical reality and we're dealing with creating ourselves dimensionally as pyramid structures, there is some significance to pyramids harnessing energy. It's an internal knowing inside of us.

When you see an orb, you don't really feel the same thing. When you see a square box, you might feel a sense of security, but a pyramid structure seems to give all the effects of a squared box plus it gives the effect of the circular. It gives the effect of energy; it has everything in it. There's a reason – because it's very copacetic, very understandable of our physical nature and our spiritual energy. It's as if it's able to work with both fields. That's what it does. On a physical level, there's a structural security to it, like the box offers, but a pyramid gives you a sense of being able to move through dimensions. Or if another dimension tries to affect you, it's able to respond in that dimension.

The Pyramid serves a very universal and defined purpose. If we were purely in our dimensional body, and we were no longer on the Earth, then I would say don't utilize the pyramid structure. Use an orb.

Do you have to be in a specific posture when creating the pyramid?

In the beginning, create this field of energy the best you can. That means being as relaxed as you can, but there's no limit to the possibilities. You can do it standing up; you can do it walking, and you can do it at the snap of a finger. If you're mentally disciplined enough, it's really the details that count. You don't want to be disturbed. You don't want to have someone talking to you in the process. You want to be able to develop this as perfectly as you can. The more detail that you give the process as you slowly develop it, the higher the quality it will be. If you do something quickly, what is the quality you have achieved? It's probably not very good. If you take your time and put your energy into it, you have something that's perfectly made. Let's say you're in a situation where you're walking in a place with all sorts of negative energy going on. You can instantly, with just a thought, zip your pyramid out and it's up. But that comes from practice. That comes from practicing this method and putting time into it.

Can your pyramid interfere with someone else's pyramid?

They're both made out of the same material; they are both energy. They're not going to sap or drain off one another. It's an intermingling of two very friendly energies, unless someone's pyramid is made of something very negative. Then there would definitely be something that feels like two magnets repelling each other.

Can you include other people inside your pyramid?

Absolutely, you're as limited as your consciousness allows.

What about creating a pyramid around a place that you're not in; for instance, a family member or friend's house?

You are the center of the expansion. So, you would go to your mother's house, sit down, meditate, build this pyramid, and you would leave. You can come and go -- the Pyramid is programmable, and you can have this intention without saying it. You're obviously setting out to leave the pyramid. You're not going to take it with you. It knows to remain there. You've programmed that environment; if you build the pyramid around you, you know that it's supposed to stay around you wherever you go. It's not something you really have to give constant thought to. It's already preprogrammed by your intention. There is a way to do it remotely without actually being there, but that is more involved. For now, work with the basics but know that it is possible.

Most energy in life has no intention; there's no set program behind it. It's usually human beings that unwittingly end up programming their feelings or emotions. It's like someone's clothing; you wear it and then you feel like it's their energy on you until your energy saturates it. Or when you go into someone's house and you can feel a certain vibe or feeling about their house. Energy has no intention, but it's constantly developing and building. Light, sound, heat and cold are saturating objects. In essence, you're taking objects that feel like water inside the sponge and are swelling, but your intention is, "Blue dye will have this blue effect," and it takes the energy and converts it. It's not that there's more blue dye; it converts the water to become blue with it. It tints it, and that becomes the intention – the program.

This goes for everything. A house is filled with energy, but it takes very little intention to fill it and consume it. A little drop of blue dye might make a whole gallon tinted with blue. When you build a pyramid, you intensely program it to shield. Your intention, in the back of your head, is that this is for protection. This is going to prevent any psychic information or attacks or negativity from getting in. Although, you have also internalized that if it is positive energy, it's welcome.

So, you're doing more than you realize you're doing. You set the premise by sitting down and building this energy. You're literally doing a technique that we'll go into later, but you're programming your environment on a very intense level.

Does it matter what color or texture you visualize the Pyramid to be?

When visualizing the pyramid, I always suggest seeing it as white. White signifies a sense of holiness, purity, and clarity. It's something that cannot be tainted, something that doesn't have any intentions. It is pure. When we think of heaven, we think of something white all the time. When we think about absolute emptiness, it's usually white, or sometimes black. White signifies purity or clarity to us. Work with the simplest and most powerful concepts. When I say white light, I mean literally white. Like a white wall.

We think of light as being bright, but see-through. Imagine it then like sunlight, as if you were looking into the sun. It's white light, but it fills where you can't permeate. That's the kind of light I'm talking about. It's so intense you can't see through it.

When you're building your pyramid, should you pick a spot like you do when you meditate?

If you're building your own energy, that's fine. Work in your own spot like your mediation place, but you want to have diversity and different challenges, so always up your game. If you're ever in a situation that's unusual, you've given yourself some endurance training so that you can react to a negative situation, whether you're in the mall, at someone's house, or out in the forest. Sometimes these energies can come upon you without you even knowing it. You have to be able to do what you need to do, so I would say to go to different areas and practice.

Is there a benefit to focusing on a specific chakra when building your pyramid?

There is a benefit to focusing on your lower chakra, and your heart chakra at the end. It's not so much an intellectual thing as it is something for the physical and dimensional energies. So right away, it's also about constructing, so use the constructive energy from your lower chakra. The final, most intense programming should be the heart chakra. When other people feel this energy, all they're going to feel is this very positive energy from you.

Is your personal pyramid an extension of your aura?

It can be combined with your aura because your energy field is going to be more prone to working with it, but it's not necessarily part of your auric field. You could say it is, because they're definitely interwoven.

If someone moves through your pyramid, would they be affected, or would it affect the pyramid?

Yes, they could be affected. Usually, it won't affect them unless they have a bad intention for you. The pyramid is designed to protect you. As long as it doesn't feel that there's any threat, it's not going to deal with it. They can walk through it, but if they're immersed in it and suddenly they have a negative thought or feeling, that person's going to be purged out. They're going to get a bad headache, or feel nauseated, or definitely feel like there's something propelling them away from you. Sometimes people don't show that they're reacting to it. They don't realize what's going on. They know that something's happened that doesn't feel good, but they don't quite know how to react to it. If they have no ill intent for you and they're just people in the store, or coworkers, it's not going to be a problem. Their field is going to go; but the second it senses a frequency that is negative, it instantaneously will begin repelling.

What are other circumstances that you could use a pyramid for?

Use it if you're going into a place that you're not sure of what you're getting into. It doesn't have to be a place that's haunted or anything like that. You could be going into a dance club and you don't know what kind of people are going to be there, or you're going into a hostile environment where people are fighting, or you're going to separate two people from fighting and don't want them to turn on you.

It does have an effect on people's psyche. People react to people. There's a lot of visual communication that goes on with body language. It could be a particular look in your eye, the movement of your mouth, or a muscle. When someone wants to take offense, they'll react. We react physically on a subconscious level to many things. They could feel an intention from someone's energy field. If you're going in there to separate them, you have intention for them, which is to physically remove them, not that you want to do them harm, and they may react to that. They may also react to whatever subliminal things are going on, or even your own fear of what's going to happen as you're interacting. You might go into a mall and interact with people where they sense your fear because you're not very social. By having a pyramid of energy up, it really filters a vast majority of this sensory field between people. They can only gather information physically. Anything that could have tipped them off is going to be energy reoriented. The Pyramid will block most of that from being sensed, if at all.

How often and how long should you keep your pyramid up?

When you build it, one of the things you're wondering is how long it is going to last. Once you set the Pyramid up, it's basically good for twenty-four to seventy-two hours, rule of thumb. You've just internalized a clock in that energy field without realizing it. The better job you do, the longer it's going to last. You will know when you need to build it again, because you will feel it and your inner knowing will tell you. There will be a time, maybe a day or maybe a week, when all of a sudden you will feel that you need to do your pyramid. It's going to occur to you because you set a timer to alert you when your pyramid is resonating at a lower field of energy. It is time for you to reconstruct it and power it up again.

You will internalize it with your intuition, or you can do it the other way and just create a regimented system of energizing it once a day in the beginning, or once a week.

Once you do it, you're going to feel the benefits of it. As it becomes stronger and better, it's going to be as familiar to you as anything else in life. If you weren't wearing a shirt, you might feel uncomfortable. If you had a lot of hair and then you got a haircut, you feel the vulnerability of the change; until you adapt, you would fix it to feel more comfortable. It's very much that same feeling; you'll know as you progress.

Is there ever a point where you're focusing or expending too much energy in the creation of a pyramid?

Don't worry about using energy for your pyramid. It doesn't take a lot for Prana to fill this energy. Prana is an absolutely universal, never-ending flow of energy. You build this energy up intensely for fifteen minutes. After that, you're draining your mental faculties with something you've already done. Something in your head is saying, "I've got to make it bigger, better, more powerful," and it's going to get bigger. There's only so much you can put into it that's going to permanently make it what it is. The rest is maintenance. It's like filling up a gas tank. You can only put so much in there. If you keep pumping, it's just going to overflow. In this case, you'll become exhausted by trying to continue reprogramming something that you've already programmed well enough.

What are some examples of other things you could program your pyramid for?

You could program a pyramid around a family pet. You can program that energy around your car. It is only as limited as your imagination. We're talking energy here. We're talking about programming subtle energies to have a particular purpose. So it's really about what you want to affix that onto.

Let's say you wanted to put a pyramid around the earth. There are so many other consciousnesses affecting the Earth, so it's almost impossible to accomplish that for the average person. You have to look at programming something within reason; something without 10,000 people unconsciously trying to affect it. So, you can affect things that don't have everybody working on it, like your car, a pet, or other similar things.

You can even use it to help people that are ill. Instead of filling it with your heart energy when you're done, fill it with your heart energy, but also program it to see a healthier cellular structure. Now, when you are using this on another human being, you have to keep in mind that because you're affecting them, they have to be very sympathetic or accepting of this program. If they're not, you can't invoke that on somebody else. It's such a personal energy.

Prana energy doesn't work as an aggressive energy. If this person doesn't want it, their energy's going to push it away. You can invoke it on them, but now you're getting dominating and aggressive. You may believe you're attempting something positive, but that is what's happening. You're just putting your own spin on it.

Are there ever times or places when using the pyramid has a limited or ineffective result?

There are times that I would normally use a pyramid but then purposely don't. Let's say you want to have a paranormal encounter with entities. If you're going out to investigate or put yourself in a situation where you want to communicate with potentially disturbed beings, you may not want to reinforce your pyramid. Remember that you're putting yourself at a level of vulnerability though.

It's so powerful that most entities will feel it, because it emits a light. If they're negative energy, the closer they get to it, it's like a wild fire. They really know to stay away from it, because it's going to affect their energy field. So you might want to tone that down a bit because it is a bit unapproachable to entities. Here you come in with this intense energy field about you. It can be very intimidating to an entity because they're not used to seeing that. When they see you, there is this very dim energy that's very transparent. It's like how we see them, only in reverse. They're going to see this intense illuminated body. They're going to see this very transparent, rotating pyramid energy field. If there was a person like that coming near you, you wouldn't know what to make of it.

Does the Pyramid raise a flag for people who are more inclined towards an awareness of energy?

If an entity can see a pyramid like that, a person who has some level of awareness may also notice it. They're not going to be intimidated unless that was your intention. If they have positive energy, they are definitely going to be receptive. It's something that's desirable or at least inoffensive, because your intentions are good. But it's not going to affect them as if it were saying, "Hey, look at me!" It's not saying that. It's saying, "If you have a negative intention towards me, there's going to be a response, and you may not like it." That's really what the Pyramid is saying.

You said that this is really for defense, and that the limitations are set by your own consciousness, your own awareness, and your own imagination?

Right, but don't take it to an extreme. The more you kick something up, or the more you try to add bells and whistles, you're going to thin the program because you overcomplicate it. For everything that you do, there is an equal and opposite reaction. If you take a very simple structure and complicate it with extra features, then each one of those features may also have a hole in it, or an opposition that you hadn't thought about before. In this particular case, simple is best.

Food is wonderful. It's good for you, but what happens when you eat too much? You put on weight. Sometimes too much of a good thing is not good at all. In this particular case, you've already programmed the pyramid with positive, loving energy. You don't want to be plugged into God every single minute. It's certainly a feasible process, but you're going to burn yourself out.

Remember that you're using an organic brain as your central format to interpret this dimension. Not only that, but as long as you are within this body, it's a two-way street. Anything that you experience spiritually is going to go from your mind and reverse engineer into the brain, because this is where you've chosen to centralize right now. Too much data or too much energy for the brain to process is going to make you nauseous. It will feel like you're under psychic attack, because your brain can't process this information all day long.

If you build up your threshold slowly over time for taking in this kind of data and energy, can it help you retain that spiritual state of mind longer?

It's going to help you become more spiritual, and to become more balanced. It will do all of these things by assisting you. You're preparing yourself to hold higher levels of God-consciousness for longer periods of time. When you meditate, you can say you're trying to find this spiritual atonement inside of you; that's what you're looking for. Don't do this all of the time. Like working out, you have to build your endurance up.

When you meditate, you're taking brief moments to raise your tonal. You can only raise your tonal as much as your body and your brain are ready to receive. By making this a constant flow, it will be too excessive; unless, of course, you are a super athlete spiritually. You're not prepared to funnel that much intense energy within you all the time. When you meditate, and you go to that place and come back, you carry a certain vibe with you. But I don't recommend that you try to pipe that vibe in from wherever it's coming from and forcing it into you non-stop. I recommend intensifying yourself. Do it, and then move on with your day. You will glow with the remnants of that. It's like a glow stick. You break it, you shake it, and it glows. It's good for a certain amount of hours and then begins to softly fade. Then you have to reinvigorate it. But to have it constantly run, it's just too much. It's going to exhaust the brain so it won't want to do anything. It's going to want to withdraw.

That should be enough for the Pyramid, so let's move on to the Sword.

To explain the Sword, I think it's more important for me to first explain its purpose. Psychically, we are meeting with people, developing relationships, and interacting with them on an everyday basis. We're creating *psychic webbing*. Psychic webbing is really an interpretation for something: For everybody you meet, you store a vibration for them. You get a feel of their energy, their vibration. With some people, it's very quick and you don't build much of a connection. With other people, you build a very strong connection.

When you learn Multi-Dimensional Meditation and you meditate, you're jingling these webbings of other people in your life. Sometimes, they're people you haven't seen for five years, ten years, twenty years, or longer. You may not even be interested in seeing these people again. Perhaps you had a bad relationship with them or they were very draining on you and you're glad to be free of them, but there's still this connection to other people. When you meditate, and you build up all of this energy from the meditation, you send pulses of energy through these pathways. Then, the people on the receiving end start thinking about you.

Suddenly, for no reason, you might get a phone call from an old friend or a relative that you haven't heard from in a while. You're going to have mixed feelings of whether or not you really want to meet these people again and have them back in your life. That's one aspect of psychic webbing.

Now, the other part of psychic webbing is that some people build a connection to you, which is very effective. It may be damaging, draining, or attacking your energy field constantly.

Rather than just using the Pyramid, you might want to also utilize the *Sword*. This is really an energy that you develop inside of your body and then bring forward out of your body to create a sword.

The reason why I chose a sword versus a stick or a broom, for that matter, is because a sword represents sharpness, nobility, and strength. It has deep-routed psychological concepts connected to it. The brain works very well with it so that the mind can actually utilize it. There's a very positive kind of connection between the two states of being.

To begin this process, we clear our mind, sitting in a chair or on the floor in half lotus, hands and back in the meditative position. With your mind clear, start to see energy in the room, pure, white light. Then see it moving into you and filling you. Take a nice deep breath in. Now position your hands as if you're handling a real sword. Take this energy and extend it out as if an energy sword is being made in your hands. You are holding the handle. It doesn't matter what kind of sword it is. It could be a machete; it could be a katana; it could be Luke Skywalker's Jedi light saber. It's whatever you want to make it; it doesn't matter. Take that sword now, as you're making it come from your internal energy, your chi chakra, extending it outward and growing to four feet in length, give or take.

Move it outward, and visualize the webbing that is attached to you. Take your Sword and swing it up over your head. See it cutting these webs that are like rubber; see them slingshot away from you as you're cutting them. Then cut them from the front; cut from the side, and behind your back. Go through the process of cutting webs with this energy. You constantly want to see this sword effect.

Focus on the detail of your imagination and try to visualize this as a very real effect happening to you. After you've finished cutting all of these webbings that are connected to you, you will feel a sense of release. It's a detachment, as if other people's neediness or energy, which may not be agreeable to you, is released. You're cutting away their connection to you.

That is the purpose of the sword and how it is utilized. Make sure to use your hands, as if you are really holding something.

Visualize a sword extending out of your Chi chakra. Move the sword all around you and cut all the connecting energy webbing. Bring the sword back to center and see it disappear; its energy returning to you.

Do you always have to move the Sword around with your hands?

Yes. The reason why you do this is because you're helping to confirm a physical reaction that affects your body from being drained or mistreated. By simulating this concept in your mind of the sword in your hands, getting your hands to move around, it helps to reinforce the mental connection so the brain can assist the mind by releasing those energies.

Can the Sword affect physical matter?

It's energy-based. The reality is that there may not be any energy coming from your hands, depending on how well you have control over your energy. It's a ritual, more or less. It's a concept that is so clearly defined that your energy knows to let go of those connections. It knows that you're seeking out something that should not be there, or at least it's there without your permission. It's more of a process of communicating with your inner energy and your biological self to react to that. You're giving it a name, a structure. You're giving it a very defined purpose. That's what it's reacting to.

Is there a benefit to focusing on a specific chakra?

Most energy defense is associated with your lower chakra, your chi area. There are seven chakra points, but using martial arts as an example, it only uses chi as an energy source. That's because chi is connected to the physical as well as the spiritual. Instead of your heart, which is a very high vibration, or your mind, which is also a very high vibration; you want something that is still going to affect you physically, but also energy-wise. This is why almost all defense mechanisms for doing these kinds of exercises are chi-oriented.

Is the Sword limited to any particular physical distance?

Don't get theatrical with the kind of sword you visualize. Some people want to have the biggest and greatest so they create a ten-foot glowing, massive sword. Keep it as real as possible, because in your mind there is a sense of reality. Think of a real sword that you can reach out and grab; it could be about three or four feet long. The more you can create a realistic sword in your mind, the more your brain will accept it. If you create a glowing ethereal sword made of thousands of rubies or other gems, the brain will see that as animation. You're not helping to reinforce the process.

Work with this process with as much reality as you can. Your mind, or your brain, finds it easier to evoke a clear image if it can accept it as being tangible. It's even better to use something that is tactile, that your hands have touched and felt, and you have a data pool of past experience to create that concept. Work with stuff that's very similar. If you have an old sword or collector's sword around, you may want to practice with it very carefully. It's not really a necessity, but it may help. The goal is to focus on the concept as much as you can. If you do use a physical sword or item to practice with, limit how often or long you use it. You don't want to focus on physical things too much.

Would you discourage someone from actually going out and buying a sword?

It's better to work visually; this is more of a visual process. But if you want to get familiar with it, go to the store and examine one; feel one. Use your standard sensory of touch to become very familiar with it, and then close your eyes while you're doing it. This way you're building up the information in your brain. When you practice, try to remember to invoke that feeling, that structure that you felt with the physical sword. Then place it into your energy sword. You may want to get some ropes or feel some thick rubber, or a bungee cord. Just feel it. You're adding to your imagination. The more that you can visually create it with your imagination, focusing on that process, the better the results will be.

If the Sword can be used to cut my own webbing, can it also be used to cut someone else's webbing?

The answer is both yes and no. That person has their own intentions, their own vibrations, and their own energies. They would almost consider that to be an attack, especially if that person does not accept your intentions or is not aware of your intentions. This is part of their misunderstood reality. It is just the way things are.

Here you are chopping away at their webbing, and they're feeling a sense of relief, but they don't know why they feel that way. It may not be interpreted as a good thing for them, without understanding your intentions. The best thing to do is to communicate with them that you're going to be doing something to help relieve the negative energy around them. You don't have to give them the full process, but it becomes more complicated because now you have to assimilate their energy. Just like we did earlier assimilating objects, you will use it here. You should now begin to see how much of this knowledge connects together. You will need to clear your mind, focus, and then feel that person. Try to remember as much as you can about what that person feels like so that you can create this through assimilation.

Your loved one has a certain smell; your mother or your father have a certain feel to them, a certain presence. Create as much of a realistic feeling of that person's vibration as you possibly can. That's what tunes you into their particular frequency. It doesn't matter if they're an inch away or a thousand miles away. To energy, it's all the same.

You're tuning into their frequency, so envision yourself as them. You're both yourself and their vibration at the same time. Then you begin to cut whatever you visualize as their personal webbings, as if you were them. In essence, you're projecting that process to happen around them, and it will have a given effect when focused with clarity. The better you can maintain what you're doing without having any babbling going on in your head, or any mental distractions, the better results you're going to achieve.

Visualizing this webbing, how long would you say it takes for the webbing to reconnect?

It depends on the intentions of other people and the situations in your life. If it's the first time you've ever done it, you're going to drop a lot of stuff that's been accumulating for years. So, you may only feel the results. It might take you a week to feel the results of all those releases, because it's not always instantaneous. It slowly fades, deteriorating away.

In Oregon, they have a type of ivy that grows all over the trees, but it's foreign. It's not natural to the area. There are groups of people that are trying to take the forest back to its natural habitat, so they cut all the roots of the ivy and then they leave it. The ivy chokes all of the other plants because it's become so overgrown that it prevents light and nourishment from reaching the trees, which flourished before the ivy's existence. Now that there's no more life feeding the ivy, it will take time but the ivy will slowly wither away and disintegrate. The ivy's purpose is disconnected, but their effect is still radiating there. So it will take time for it to diminish and fade away.

It's similar with webbing. Some stuff is going to react much faster, while other stuff may take a longer amount of time before you really see the effects of it. The structure of all those connections is still there. After you've cleared this and you've controlled a lot of the energy that was attached to you, you need to maintain it at least once a week. Generally, I wouldn't do it on a daily basis; that's more often than you need. In some cases, once a day is good; it depends what is happening in your life.

Does this webbing only connect around your head?

No, this is why you need to swing the sword around your sides and back. It could attach to your hip, your back, or other parts of the body. Try standing up while you're doing it. It's all about holding your consciousness and feeling it. Don't let your mind wander. Wax on, wax off. Practice makes perfect. Your training from previous books will really help you maintain your focus and concentration. Stay fixated on your visualization, what you are doing, and the purpose of it. Create the details of what's happening.

Is the Sword technique meant to be done in combination with the Pyramid? If so, should you do them in any particular order?

Some people prefer to cut their webbing before they actually go into creating the dimensional energy of their pyramid. Others feel it's not necessary to use the Sword if you've got your pyramid active and working. It doesn't really matter. But, there is the rare case that you feel it's a necessity.

Let's look at this a little differently. Much of what goes on in your brain is psychological: how you perceive things happening in your life, your relationship to other people, and how they affect you emotionally. Maybe there is anxiety because of a relationship separation. When you do these rituals, your psyche is very energy-oriented. Your brain works with electricity and energy. By doing these rituals, it will relieve your brain and teach it to let go of things that no longer are prevalent. It's not just spiritual; it's also biochemical.

It's also ingrained in you as an organism, as much as it is reflected in a duality as energy. So, you're working with your energy, but it also affects your biological brain and vice versa. Some of these cords could also represent mental states that are burned into your psyche from things you've experienced, things you want to let go of like a bad relationship. Perhaps you need to release your emotions from someone when you need to move on. It doesn't necessarily represent something that somebody's doing to you.

It could also be that you're holding onto the webbing when you know you need to let go, but you can't bring yourself to do it. The brain is designed to hang on to certain things. We imprint images of other people's faces in our brain, and when they're not around, we release certain endorphins that cause depression and make us anxious to seek them out. When we see their face in front of us again, or hear the sound of their voice, we change the chemistry in the brain that makes us feel relaxed and stabilized again. Well, this is a horrible thing to have to go through, especially if you know somebody's just not right for you, or not healthy for you, like an abusive relationship. So, by seeing your connection to them as these cords, you're really telling the brain biochemically to start letting go.

It's not really a standardized tool or concept that you may see in traditional psychological therapy, but it's very effective. Nonetheless, you don't necessarily need to understand how it works. It's just like healing with the body. There are people that claim to be great healers in different places of the world when they're totally fraudulent in what they're doing. But, because the recipient believes so much in what they're doing, they actually change their dimensional self and they're healed. Their brain is so convinced that it somehow starts to heal on a cellular and molecular level. It's not that the 'healer' is curing them, but the body is able to heal itself under the right conditions.

If it would help you to think this way, you can see it as an illness you're cutting out. It could be a psychological situation you're cutting out. You're teaching the brain, instead of accepting that illness is your reality and that you're helpless. You are communicating with your brain by using reverse engineering to let go of something. You're saying, "This is how you're going to let go."

The Sword cutting is more psychological than spiritual, whereas using the Pyramid is more for spiritual energy. You may be connected to other people's energies that aren't good for you in a spiritual way, because it's so ingrained in you biologically. It's giving you a second tool to help with the healing process that's profoundly powerful to work with.

When you're cutting the webbing, is it important to look for or visualize negative connections specifically?

Look at this in several ways: You can look at it as a general intent. Obviously, you're looking at negative stuff; you're never going to cut positive stuff. The positive energy that affects you uses more of an ethereal energy; it's more of a light. You can't really cut it and you don't want to either because you're receptive to it. You want to see it. The connections that you want to cut are the undesirable things that you're manifesting in your mind. You're actually defining its pitch, or its tone as something that you want to remove.

You're making it come forward and solidify as a frequency that you now are tuning into, like tuning into a radio station; once you're locked onto it, you can experience it. You're choosing to find the negative versus the positive. In so doing, that's what your reaction's going to be.

How long should you spend doing this technique?

The length of time spent cutting the webbing should really be no more than thirty minutes, maybe forty-five minutes; that's the maximum amount of time. It's really up to you to internally sense. Usually, ten to fifteen minutes is enough. It's how clearly you focus. I cannot stress this enough. The *clarity* of what you're focusing on is *critical*. Give it detail; give it a sense of emotion. Give yourself a follow-up emotion of release. If you spend too much time focusing on it, and if you haven't worked up your mental skill of being able to hold non-thought, you can end up reversing the work you're doing. You are visualizing cutting the webbing, but then time passes and you start to think that the webbing is coming back, or you missed some, and now your intention is reconnecting them. Stay focused, keep your mind clear, and you'll be the most effective.

Communicate with your brain through emotions, and it will understand. Not words, but emotions. Don't tell it what it's supposed to feel. Create a fictitious sense of feeling and accept it as being real, and the brain will accept that. This is something that's very good for many different issues. If you want to let go of somebody, cut the cord of that relationship. Say to yourself, "This is somebody who I need to let go of. This is somebody who's harming me. This is somebody that's bad for me," and see that cord being cut. See it snap. See it flinging away and now it's gone! "No more will this attach to me. I have the power now to defend myself. I will protect myself. I have the ultimate tool of defense right now, and I will no longer allow myself to be harmed." You're telling yourself. You're letting the brain feel those emotions symbolically. And it's able to purge those things that are embedded biochemically into the brain. It sends the right receptors to help release that programming.

There really aren't any set limitations. If something is connected to you, then you can cut that connection.

So, you're saying that this could even be used to cut negative connections that are influences from past lives?

Past lives, childhood or anything and everything that you want to let go. There are no limitations that you can possibly think of. Just choose and discover what needs to be cleared. It could be anything, such as abuse or memories. You're ready to move on. You've digested it but you need to let go. You don't have to forget the memory of it; rather let go of any negative programming that's affecting you in your current state of mind, how you were carrying around that luggage, and how it's surfacing now in your personality. Work on removing those. Give it time. Don't expect it to be instantaneous with this technique. Actually, it is instantaneous because it could take weeks, months, or years with other forms of therapy.

When a cord is snapped, will there be some sort of feeling or relief associated with it?

You will probably feel a sense of release, or a noticeable sensation. In some occasions, you don't feel relief immediately because internally you're not really willing to let go yet. You might have to work on it once a week, once a day, or whatever time it takes to let go of it. But, eventually, you'll feel it give. Sometimes after you cut it and go back to it, you're still feeling it. So you need to keep checking because there's some part of you that's not willing to let it go. But if you keep hacking away at it, it will snap. It will dissipate. But you have to be consistent! *Consistency* is the biggest problem for anybody with any of the techniques. Without *consistency*, you cannot achieve much. With *consistency*, hammering away at it, you will achieve this without a doubt.

Does this affect the person on the other side of the cord that has the connection with you?

It depends on the person, if they even notice, and what kind of relationship they have with you. If that person's connected to you, they will feel that you've gained some kind of strength, especially if they are trying to control you. It's that inner knowing with dominant people. They can feel that they have power over you. And when they lose it, they also can feel that they've lost something. They feel like they don't have that control anymore. Once you remove it, and you have the correct tools, you definitely have the strength to keep them from gaining it again. But, again, you have to listen to that inner knowing. They'll know; they'll definitely feel it. You don't have to be there; they'll feel that something has changed.

Now, whether or not they consciously can say, "Oh, this is exactly what's going on," maybe they will, maybe not. Sometimes they just feel like they lost the connection with this person. Or that it's diminishing rapidly, but, they will sense it as an inner knowing.

In the event that you encounter an entity, will the Sword ever come into play as a mode of defense?

This goes into another level of *High Guard*. It's not necessarily that it's a sword, but it gets back to the fundamentals of what the Sword is. The Sword is an extension of your life energy; it's an extension of Prana. It's an extension of you. It's an extension of you mixed with the God-Force: your consciousness, your organic energy, and it's a combination of all of it. When you deal with entities in a form of defense, you will be using *your own energy frequency against their energy frequency,* rather than your organic, physical body. This means if you can use the sword to cut energy webbing, there isn't much difference using it against an energy being, such as an entity. But we'll discuss that topic more as we enter into some other material *on High Guard.*

Almost all forms of psychic defense are going to be oriented through the chi area of your energy, much like martial arts. This is why there is a connection between physical attacks: using the energy in that area, meditating on it, breathing through it, and developing that kind of energy because it's the one that's closest to our physical realm. So, whenever someone is drawing energy from you, thinking about your lower chakra holds your energy in. If you want to push someone's energy away, draw energy in and then push mentally out. Always breathe in from your chakra and see your energy extending out as you breathe out.

A simple technique to use if you feel there are bad vibrations in a room, or entities, or whatever, is just to clear yourself, breathing in through your chi chakra. Around your chi chakra, you instantly will feel a shift, which is going to be a very faint tingling almost, if you're in the right state of mind. It's very empowering, and you'll feel that sense. You'll create that sense of power. Breathe in. Then release and see that push. Visualize that push coming out of you. It's very much a form of psychic defense, psychic attack, but it's how you handle negative entities in a room. They're going to feel that wave of energy push out from you.

For us being clothed in our physical body, we don't really feel a lot; but to an entity's energy field, it's like a ton of bricks hitting them. It depends on how much you can create that energy and move it out. You don't have to be a martial arts expert to understand that. It's the same energy as martial arts in combat when somebody uses their chi to affect another person by throwing them across the room, or prevent them from physically moving. A person, who's significantly developed in that skill, can touch their chi center. The opponent can push with all their strength, but they can't move the other person. People, or even groups of people, will try to push over someone who's focusing on their chi, and they can't do it.

Now, I will explain what's going on. Energetically, the chi is so close to the physical energy of your muscles expanding and contracting and the physical nature of your body being able to move that it literally cancels the signals between the brain and the muscles in your body. You are trying to tell your body to push, but your muscles are getting a different signal that's telling it not to expand or contract. It's saying to cease or to lock up.

This is what's happening with that chi energy on a physical level, if you can harness enough of it. To deal with entities, you don't need that much. You're dealing with a very subtle energy. You just have to understand that you're able to create this energy and move it out from you. You're not throwing it out. It's like a ball that has a rubber band on it. You are throwing it; it's snapping back, and you're catching it. When you breathe into your chi and send it out, it's like a wave that goes out and comes back in. So you're pushing with your hands, pulling back in. You breathe again, and you do the same thing. It's like an extension of yourself, but an energy vibration coming from your body. Because it's so oriented with being part of your physical body and your energy field, it's easy for your body, your mind, and your brain to adapt to this concept to make it effective. If you were to use this on any other chakra point, it would not have the same effect. So using chi energy is a great way to deal with negative entities.

If you feel there is a presence in your room and you don't want it there, just push it out with your breath. See the energy moving out and make the muscles in your hands tighten as you expand outward. Just push with your body. Feel the muscle tension, but visualize this outburst of energy pushing out. It's going to have a devastating effect on the entity or any spirit that you want to affect. Trust me; this is how you should handle something aggressive. If you want to deal with it, you're matching it energy for energy.

If an entity wants to attack you, it's going to be an energy-based attack, which is a very specific frequency. That frequency can't really affect anything physically. So, if an entity passes through us, the most we'll feel is a tingling sensation. Now if they harmonize their energy well enough, they can manipulate us to make it feel like we've been hit. It's very similar to people who can create wounds on their body because they psychologically believe that is the case. There's documented evidence of people who get lumps on their body, or they bleed or create open wounds, yet they were never touched except for their brain. It is so real to them that the cells of their body reacted, as if to mimic the creation of what the thought was.

If an entity can stimulate your energy enough, it's not going to create an open wound or something; you'll almost feel the attack like a punch to your muscles. That area will lock up just like a charley horse, swelling and tightening up. It's the same process in the brain. It's just doing the opposite and the body will react to it. When you connect with your chi your energy changes, it is a dimensional force field to entities. They cannot penetrate it. They just cannot. It's impossible.

By breathing in through your chi chakra, you're really taking energy in, and much like you learned in Multi-Dimensional Meditation, you're going to convert it into a very specific energy. It's designed to become half physical and half energy; your body really works with it. It's like an extension of armor, or something out of Japanese animation where you're in this robot body. As you move your hand, the whole powerful robot's body moves that way, but it moves with the power of twenty tons. See yourself in this energy field, and you can move your body in such a way. If you just think about it and you hold your concentration, you can walk through and they cannot permeate you. The reason why you are intensely powerful in thinking this is because they are trying to affect you in the physical realm. They are incredibly weaker when trying to manipulate this level of reality. You are geared for this dimension because you are contained in a vessel that's designed to keep you here. You have the biggest advantage; you just don't realize it.

Once you begin to focus on this energy, and you push your energy out; you can move your hand and a burst of energy, maybe five or six feet, extends out with just a wave. It would be very hard for you to maintain it that way because your mind would feel like it needs to breathe back in. It's like holding your breath. You can do pushes of energy and see it expand out. You don't have to feel the retraction; it happens instantly. You don't even need to think about it. Just work at it. Even as I'm doing this, I'm developing my energy. That is why I'm breaking out in a psychic sweat; this is what chi does. People who practice Tai Chi are doing something very similar, but they're internalizing it as a workable energy. If you are dealing with an entity or any negative energy, you want to disperse it. Then, you are dealing with that lower energy, your chi. You breathe in from it and project the energy outward as you are breathing outward.

Is this more of a mental pushing or does the result depend on the actual physical motion of the push?

When you reinforce your mental pushing with a physical motion of pushing, it helps to strengthen your belief and it allows the energy to extend out from that. You have to visualize that you're reaching across the room or it won't happen. Don't just visualize -- believe it! Believe that you are, and you will be that much more powerful. If you can only see yourself reaching out as far as your hands go, it is not going to have the same effect. It's a combination of balancing the reality of what you can do, and combining it with your imagination to extend the possibility. But it becomes a reality because you're dealing with energy. It becomes a real thing, and your energy reacts to it.

People have to study how to see auras. When you look at your hand, you can see the aura around it. I teach people how to see my aura and then I alter it. I will expand it and I'll say, "Let me know that you are seeing it." Then I'll expand that aura and then bring it back down. It is not just me who can expand the aura. It's just a matter of breathing in, expanding different chakra points, visualizing, and feeling. You can feel it happening! But you have to also believe that it is possible, otherwise your brain will restrain you from making it happen. Your brain is the *Governor* – it tries to limit you. You've got to push the limits of the *Governor*, by fooling it a little. After you fool it a few times, it accepts it as a reality, and then you have all these extended abilities.

You said before that you can use this technique to pull an entity into you. How do you do that, and why would you do that?

I do not recommend this for most people and, in some ways; I'm reluctant to even explain it. It's possible to use this technique to pull an entity towards you. There are occasions where I will consume an entity. It sounds much more dramatic than it really is. One of the things that I design my energy to do is almost act like a filter when negative energy hits it. The energy is filtered through. I get all the real core of the pure energy, but all the programming looks like sludge on the outside of my Pyramid wall, and it just slides down. Self-washing, call it whatever you want, but I gain all that energy from it.

For a negative entity to function in this reality, it must do much like us. We have to see the armor expanding, the energy field that we have to breathe through our chakras. Just go into that zone and be conscious of it. It empowers us so that we can affect them. They are virtually doing the same thing in order for them to move into this dimension to affect you. Their normal energy can't affect anything here. It just moves through, the same way that radio or television signals do. They are here, but they're not really something that can easily be affected without tools. They consume a certain kind of energy which acts very similar to chi for us, in order to build something that's more of a physical energy, so that it can affect this dimension. It takes a lot of skill and, for this reason, I don't recommend this to most people. When there is a very negative entity, I may decide to pull it into me. You can literally take all of its coating, its armor, and take it into you and spit out the remains of the frequency. I call it a spiritual tough-guy move.

Possession is not possible. You have a very specific frequency. That's an algorithm number that is so vastly unique to any other living thing, it's unbelievable. If you're going to pull something into you, the first fear you have is, "What if it possesses me?" Well I don't believe in that. I don't believe it's possible. I can debate that all day long if you want to. So what really does happen? You can take in energy. You are going to suck it in and spit out the remains. The only thing you have to be worried about is its programming. If it programmed that energy, it's like a virus attacking a computer. You don't want to take that program in because then you get a lot of physiological damage. This is why I do not recommend this for the majority of people. My energy is so well developed and controlled that, even if I were to take in a virus or energy program, my body knows to eject it. It happens very rapidly for me. Most people don't have that kind of awareness yet, so they should stick with the traditional methods. They're awesome. They're powerful, and they are all you really need.

For me, doing something like that with an entity is an extremely rare thing. But if you practice enough, and you get skilled enough, you'll know when you can do it. It's an inner knowing, and it's not about ego. If you are dealing with a lot of negative entities, sometimes it's the best way to cut down the odds so that you can appropriately deal with it without them all distracting you. So there are certain cases where it's a necessity. Doing this to an entity is about as close to killing something as you can get. It's now going to have to spend a great deal of time rebuilding its energy. Rebuilding is going to have a traumatic effect on an entity. You really have traumatized it if you do this to it. But again, "What's good for the goose is good for the gander." It doesn't have good intentions for me. I didn't destroy it. I didn't kill it, but I certainly taught it a lesson.

What is the difference between focusing on the chakras for psychic defense as opposed to meditating on them?

It really comes down to intention. Meditating has a defined purpose; you're training yourself to take in pure energy, and that energy can be used for defense. You're really building up a reserve, a reservoir of energy to call on at a moment's notice. It's like a battery pack. Let's say you have a computer and the computer power goes down, but you don't go down because you have an hour of reserve. So you have a reserve energy that is being built, that is really powering other psychic abilities, or whatever you are developing. You're feeding that sixth sense. It's like an arm, leg, or other body part that needs to be exercised. That's a form of building it up, so that you can be prepared to deal with circumstances, or to meet them. The sixth sense needs subtle energies in order to function well, so you're building up a reserve of those energies. The lower energy isn't just used for combat. It's used for a variety of things. So you have this reserve building up, slowly empowering other divisions of your energy fields and consciousness. If you wanted, you could probably react with a push of energy without even having to draw it in, which, in essence, makes you more prepared for dealing with situations. Because you have these reserves of energy built up, you really become something to reckon with at any given time.

Are the other chakras useful for defense?

The lower chakra is the main chakra that is used and, while you can use other chakras, it's not really necessary. Yes, you can get very creative. You can take a really nasty being and put a virus into it the same way you can pull a virus into yourself. You can program that virus by going to your heart chakra and finding absolute love. The intention is to permeate the entity like a knife going inside of it, and then blossoming like flowers and other plants, growing life within it. Now, to you that may sound ridiculous, but you've got to understand that energy works in terms of emotion and you've just sent this spear of absolute love into a hateful, negative energy. All of a sudden now, it is going to start reflecting. You will feel the emotion that is put into you, and that is how you internalize it. Your brain then takes this emotion and creates a concept for it that it can relate to, and then you're affected by that.

So, you are doing just the opposite to a negative entity. Instead of them just dwelling on all this hate and wanting to destroy life, they've now internalized life. There's a chance, depending on how strong the virus is that you thrust into them, that they're going to have the opposite effect. It's going to calm them down. It's going to help them to surrender and feel peaceful, and maybe a sense of clarity to reflect on. They may say, "Wow, I've just not been myself. I've been reacting chaotically." It gives them a moment of clarity to make their middle pillar, their true consciousness, step forward, and maybe change their tonal, or their vibration.

When I say vibration, I mean frequency of energy, not a sound vibration. It is possible to use sound as a technique that's utilized by your consciousness. Certain sounds and vibrations make our mind feel a certain way, or project a certain way because sound is a projectile when we use it. We're as familiar with it as a form of communication that, unconsciously in our brain or our mind, we also utilize it for projecting. For instance, we could do Aums. When you practice Aums, you can feel right away that it permeates an environment. You are projecting a vibration into an object; it's just another method of programming energy. So, if I was to go, "Aaaaauummm," there is a projection of a certain feeling that's coming out of me with that sound. Although you would think that because it's vibration, it's not going to affect something dimensional, which is probably true. The feeling that I internalized is also projecting at the same time as energy. It's combining these two, so that it affects those who are experiencing on a physical level. Those dimensionally are feeling it on another level in the same manner. I'm permeating the walls. I'm permeating the furniture with my intention, and that intention is, of course, a sense of balance, a sense of peace, and a sense of clarity.

Much like when you meditate, and you try to have clarity of mind, you're achieving the same thing by doing this particular Aum. The secret to this is intention. What is your intention when doing this? If your intention is to go, "Aum," and it's to put people to sleep, then you'll probably have an effect in making them sleepy. It's whatever your intent has designed. Now some intentions just don't work at all with sound because it's how we perceive them. You're trying to magnify the sense of vibration you're throwing out energy-wise by manifesting what you already have confirmed in your mind.

If I clap my hands together, it's a sound vibration. Let's say there are a lot of negative vibrations that I want to clear from the room. I could pull in energy and as I clap my hands together, have the intention that the clap is a shock wave to remove, permeate, or disturb the negative energy that's around me. If you are in the room to hear it, it's almost like a shock wave. I'm aware of this. That's the effect I'm going to have on entities. I want them to know, "I'm here and you better be scared. Here I come!" In essence, I'm commanding with intent inter-fibered with this sound, on a dimensional frequency, that's emanating from me at the same time. It's a broadcast; it's like a big speaker going, "Hey!" It's sending out this reflection that's going to affect entities as much as it affects people. So sound, in certain ways, can affect dimensional entities.

Bass-rhythm is very disturbing to entities. In Africa, they deal with spirits and entities a lot in that culture. They want to keep their families near them, but because of the culture, they have entities that are doing a lot of negative things. So the Africans do a lot of rhythm bass stuff, enforced by their psychological belief, and the rhythms emanate out on a dimensional frequency. Rhythm has a pulsating, cleansing, programming effect that clears objects, much like pouring milk and dye theory. The rhythms of the drum have a certain vibration that seems to cross over into dimensional frequencies. This is the same reason that Buddhist monks have those big horn instruments that they'll blow. They believe it clears out the entities if they make lots of noise.

In this particular case, rhythm, or these particular sounds, certainly can have an effect on a place. If you've got an actively haunted house, then hook up the big bass speakers and play some deep bass music for a day or two. Maybe you'll clean out the place. It's just another method of utilizing the tools as a defense system. High Guard offers you many options. Shock waves of a booming sound break down built-up energies. So, in a house that has a lot of negative vibration, or feeling, if you play this type of music, it weakens the vibration and makes the programming deteriorate. It's a way of cleansing, much like using salt, but a different method.

Storms, which are a combination of electrically charged particles and the booming sound of thunder, have a cleansing effect on mass areas of land. Because the planet is a biological organism, it develops certain methods of balancing itself. As far as the collective consciousness goes, one of the interesting things I've noticed is that when telemarketers call certain areas of town, they have a very bad response. Nobody buys anything. The overall feeling seems to be, "Leave me alone. I don't want to be bothered." So they drop the campaign instead of continuing to call that town. Then they'll switch to another area and they'll get a lot of sales. It's almost as if the neural synapses of the human beings of the planet create a collective consciousness in each area that moves and changes.

There's a wave of consciousness that moves from place to place that affects thousands, or hundreds of thousands, of people in each community. It can change, so it's interesting to observe how people react to it. What does the reaction of the collective consciousness have to do with the booming sounds? Emotions are all programmed, not just in households, or in a piece of clothing from somebody else, but there are different levels of this that affect things. So, entire states or counties that have accumulated a very negative vibration can be cleansed from the booming thunder. It is nature's way of taking care of those areas. It's nature's way of breaking it up, and moving it so it doesn't become like a log jam in a river.

So the sound doesn't have to originate from you, but if you want to program the sound then it should originate from you right?

Yes, if you are going to program it, it should originate from you.

Can you program sound for other things besides defense?

There are other ways or uses you can program sound for. You can be creative. Anything is possible. It depends on how creative you want to be. When you think about beautiful music or a person singing you a beautiful song, what does it do to you? It affects you. You may just think it's what you're hearing, but you're really experiencing this. Now, music from a radio may not capture the full effect of it, but regardless, there's communication going on in the music that is reciprocated into the brain. The brain unpacks it, and we experience whatever it is. It is not quite as effective as the real thing, and you're not getting that same intention, but I do believe on psychological levels it's communicating with us, more than it's saying in the words.

Sometimes, I listen to music I love, and then out of the blue I'll sit down and listen to what they're actually saying in the song. It never occurred to me what they were talking about before that, so it's almost like two different things going on. There's something that's talking to me emotionally, and that's usually how my mind works, because I consider it a higher level of communicating. Then when the words come in, they sometimes don't quite fit what is being said because they could be saying one thing, but there's a whole other meaning in the octaves of their voice. This is not just spiritual. It can affect your brain, and that becomes spiritual, because it moves into your higher levels of consciousness.

Is there any benefit to focusing on a specific chakra when programming a sound?

Yes, I definitely would say there is. You can really build up a feeling of love before you project it out. You can create a push by feeling the buildup of that energy and then projecting it out. So by combining those, you make it that much more intense, but it's that much harder to do.

Is the sound necessary or is it really more about the intention?

Why do we use sound? Energy is energy, right? Why couldn't we program energy for the same effect without any sound at all? The sound is simply a bouncing board for you. You're reinforcing it with your brain to cross over dimensionally. The more your brain is accustomed to the concept, symbolically, the more you can attach to it, the better effect it's going to be, because you're going to have less filtering going on from the brain. The *Governor* isn't going to filter the strength of it so much. Using sound improves the effect. It allows you to believe it more.

How much you believe what you program is also an issue. If it gets too complicated, even if something is possible, it's not practical. Programming sounds around your house, like if someone turns a door knob and that sound releases a programming intention, is creative but too complicated. Yes, it's possible. Anything is possible. But if you start to make things too complicated, you're going to become discouraged with your effects. Don't try flying a jet until you've at least tried to ride a bicycle. Build yourself up. Encourage yourself, because you're dealing with your brain, which is saying, "This is not possible," or "this is not how reality is designed for us to accept." So you start doing too much, which is what everybody tends to do, particularly youth, and this is why you don't get the results you're looking for. Then you throw the towel in and you go back into the *Doe*. There is nothing to encourage you. Take small steps and work yourself up. Be consistent. Don't rush. Then you will have a more profound and amazing effect if you just take simple steps instead of making it so complicated.

What are the most useful applications of this technique?

Imagine walking into a home that you're visiting or even a rental house for a holiday weekend and you feel negative energy. Maybe the last people there were extremely negative or had a big fight and now you're feeling it. You might want to disperse this energy. You need to say, "Whoa, stop." You've got to defend yourself. You've got to push all this negative energy out before it overwhelms you. Then, when you've destabilized it, you can regroup. Now it's time to start programming better energy. This is a good time for using sound techniques; it's very therapeutic. It's very natural for us to work with sound, if people could just get over their embarrassment or their shyness. Fear and social pressure keep the *Doe* very powerful. So, we are embarrassed and ashamed to release our inner feelings to project them out. We think we have to sing well, be charismatic, or have a beautiful voice. You don't have to sing beautifully; just to do hums, or certain emotions that you can express. It may sound odd, but in the privacy of your own home, you can release different feelings from inside of you.

You can also use that to project a vibration into your house. Sound, emotionally coming out without any verbiage is more spiritual than just singing a song, or saying words. Words connect in our brain as a form of communication, formatted for us to communicate with, but sounds can release emotions better. That is ideally what you want to do. Maybe you could release some tones in the privacy of your own home - sounds that are beautiful to you. Everybody naturally has a sound to release; it's a beauty from within. It's a choice if you want to release it, and it comes from inside. It's just something that comes out. I think it's a marriage between your soul and your physical body. It is an expression of both parts that you want to release. Paint the whole house with it! Just let it go. Many people can't dance, but secretly when no one's looking everybody will do their little dance thing. Doesn't it feel wonderful?

In society we are taught, "No, you can't do that." We control ourselves, and we set limitations for ourselves. Most people are pretenders; they show other people only what they want them to see or know about themselves. I would say all people are really false to some degree, so if you can't be real in the world, then try to be as real as you can by yourself, as often as you can. You will discover more things about yourself than you could possibly imagine. You will discover more things spiritually than you would think possible. That's what I'm trying to say. Instead of just dancing, sit down and let some tones out. Let some hums out. Find an emotion and just urrrrrrrrraaaa! Just let it roll out and watch how wonderful it feels. It really will speak to you internally, physically, and mentally if you release it by sound. Let it come out of you. Purge it through an emotion. Emotion and making tones somehow resonates with your cellular body more than words. The only reason why we use spoken words is because we've learned that is a way to communicate from one person to another. We've lost the ability to internalize and release, and that is what you want to take into consideration with the sound techniques in *High Guard*.

I have heard something called The Hand of Hands is the most powerful High Guard technique. What is it and what does it do?

I remember seeing a picture of Jesus many years ago, and later a picture of Buddha; then other pictures and diagrams of other deities or enlightened beings. I began to notice that in these paintings, or drawings, they often held their hands in certain positions. At first, being younger, it really didn't mean that much to me. But internally with that inner knowing, I knew that there had to be a deeper meaning to the gesture. I am sure the artists did not know all of the people they depicted in their art, how to draw their hands. It may just be something they felt or a description they read somewhere. I do know that to be the case. I'm talking about the "Hand of Hands" in particular.

Your hands are a *secondary communicator*. If you could be aware of your hands while you are talking, you would notice that there's a whole different way of communicating as they're moving around. If you put your hands a certain way, it means stop. Psychologically, I'm saying, "STOP." If I motion to you, "Why don't you come this way?" I'm telling you to come over here. If I say, "Well, why don't you think this way?" I'm telling you to agree with me, to come over to my side.

There's a whole different language going on with your hands that is very subliminal; you might not even be aware of it. Your mind is really reflecting through your hands, and communicating to people, even though people may not be paying attention to them. It's a way to reinforce what you are communicating. If you pay attention to a good speaker who really gets their point across to people, you'll find them using their hands all the time. When I say, "Getting across to you," I'm looking you in the eye, and I'm taking my hands and moving them around with expression. It's an impulse of a thought to make you say, "Yes," or to pay attention.

Our hands are constantly mimicking our mind, our real intention, if you can just follow what they're saying. Now, when I said, "Follow what they're saying," my hands did a rotation, meaning there's a lot to it. You know, follow it. But in my mind, I'm thinking, "Well, there's a lot to cover," again a secondary form of communication.

Now, having said that, what I began to realize is that if you take your hands and you put them out in front of you, just think about them for a few seconds, just be aware of them. Feel what it feels like to feel your hands and their weight without touching anything. Then simply bring your pinky to your thumb, and then inhale, feeling that touch, and try to be aware of how you feel for a second. Notice any very subtle energy. You're reversing the outward effect by turning your hands; your communication is going *inward to your mind* or *to your brain* rather than *your mind to your brain outward* as an expression. You're reversing it.

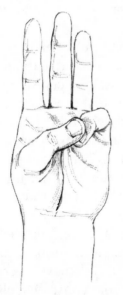

Bring your pinky to your thumb, and inhale, feeling the touch. Be aware of how you feel, noticing any very subtle energy.

It's essentially giving you a key to work with your mind to strengthen it without the brain realizing you're doing it. It's a back door; that's what I'm saying. It's a door that the brain doesn't realize it left open and it has no defenses to control it. It's so natural. It's really just you thinking about this technique. So, when you do this technique by taking in a breath with each finger, it'll make you feel a different tone, a different pitch, a different feeling inside of you. Practice feeling these pitches, up, down, higher, or lower. Breathe through each touch of each finger as you're doing it in sequence. You're exercising your mind and allowing it to open up better in this reality. You're able to make your mind move into this reality to affect things on a greater level. For instance, if this were the matrix, in order to affect it, you would learn to think outside of it.

You need to be able to project emotions, so you're really training yourself to feel these subtle energies that, in the beginning, you almost can't feel. It's like reading Braille; a blind person who is first introduced to Braille might feel it, like any of us would; it just feels like a bunch of little bumps. We would feel that it's not much of a real pattern, except for the lines going up and down, and that it's too chaotic, at this point, for us to understand. But as you practice with it and you begin to recognize a pattern, eventually you would just rub your fingers over it and see words appearing in your mind. You learn to create a higher sensory within your brain, to communicate with what you're feeling. In this particular case, you're following patterns in such a way that it's teaching you to communicate better with your mind in this dimension. It's teaching you how to go into your mind to process information and to bypass the brain.

For instance, if you take your hands and put them out in front of you; put your thumbs on your pinkies, breathe in, and you would feel a certain vibration. At first, it's very subtle. Then move to the next finger, and then move to the third finger, and move to the fourth one. Usually people's index fingers are stronger. You work with them more; so they are going to have a higher, more meaningful connection. There will be a stronger feeling, if you really pay attention to it, rather than a subtle feeling. Look at this subtle feeling. It has profound use! Put your thumb to your pinky, and think about your heart chakra. Breathe in. You'll find it creates a more balanced, very calming effect. So it's really about experimenting with the different frequencies you can create. They do have a very specific connection to your emotional and your conscious self.

If you want to quickly and robustly build up your energy, like meditating on your chi chakra, or your lower chakra, take your index finger and thumb, put them together, and just breathe in, thinking about them. You will feel this, from about your solar plexus to your upper body. You will feel a very subtle change that's very shielding, very solidifying. Because it's such a subtle energy, in the beginning, practice by just sitting and then breathing on each one and focusing on how it makes your energy field feel. You're turning it inward. Everything is in conjunction with breathing, with this particular exercise.

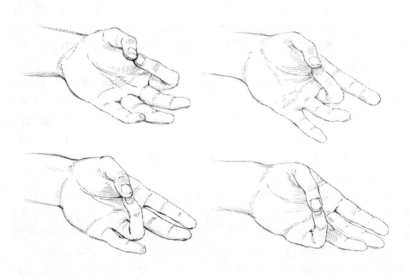

If you want to quickly build up your energy practice breathing in prana as you move through each finger mudra.

Many of your exercises with High Guard have a lot to do with breathing in and out. It's about pushing out, breathing out, and moving energy in, breathing in. Think about the visualizations and where you're pulling energy into when you're breathing. Don't really think about the breathing in, because breath is a giving and taking. Your mind works with the energy in the same way. It feels very natural, and it gives you a big advantage to pulling and moving energy in and out of you. Time everything with your breath. Now if you take your hands, clear your mind, have non-thought, and use your breathing, you will find that you can move your energy field in your body very well. It's almost like stretching before athletics. When you learn to work with your hands and this energy, it's a workout.

This brings us now to the Hand of Hands. The Hand of Hands is basically your index finger and your middle finger pointing straight out, your thumb pointing to its natural outward direction, and your pinky and ring finger folded down so they're basically touching the palm of your hand, as best they can. Once you can internalize this energy, raise this hand up, breathing in, and then project outward almost like its energy thrusts up, but it's very unique because it comes from your heart chakra. You will see some pictures of Christ doing this and, in certain circumstances; other spiritual people will utilize this, too. You can take this and dip the thumb down and rotate it, and as you rotate it you project out that everything is becoming brighter, like goodness, a higher vibration, a spiritual love. *It is a key to a frequency that can be released.* It's not that it's just coming from you. That is what's unique about it. It's as if, in a single moment, you take an entire room and you bring it to the same place you were when meditating individually. Instead of internalizing your meditation inward and being in that vibration, you take an environment around you and you shift it to that place. So it's profoundly powerful, but it's very difficult to do if you are not practiced with all of these other ways of working with your energy. In the right state of mind, in the most balanced state of mind, you can project this energy outward, upon an environment.

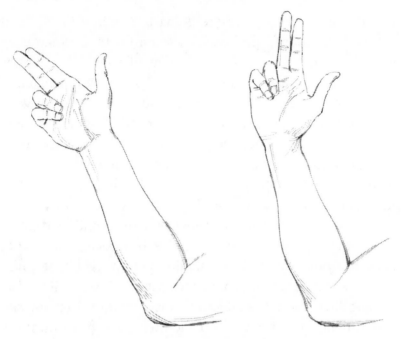

Using the Hand of Hands, raise your hand up, breathe in and release moving your hand down, projecting the energy inside of you out into the environment.

Is there a difference in using your right hand or left hand?

There isn't much difference in using your right or left hand rather, whichever your stronger or more dominant hand is, whichever you are naturally inclined to use. It is the position that is the most important part.

Why does your hand have to be in that specific position?

This particular position is probably very unfamiliar to your hand. It's the same position you would use if holding a gun. It's something that we don't necessarily reflect on. It's not something you're going to see in a lot of hand movements; there's probably a reason for that. When your hand is in this position, it's the feeling of the subtle energies with the thumb and finger touching. Somehow the shape of it reverse engineers into your consciousness, your nervous system. It has information that is encoded as a vibration. There is an inner knowledge. You're somehow responding to it on a much higher level. It's something else that reacts to you, when you react that way. It's like shouting to God, "I need you for a moment," and God is present. It's how you can create this energy in an entire environment, but it's extremely difficult compared to everything else. It takes a great deal of concentration. I suggest people don't jump right to it. Jump to it as a last resort after you have achieved everything else. It's not the McDonald's effect. It's not something that you can instantly figure out how to do and then receive gratification. It takes great skill and a disciplined state of mind in order to achieve the best results. I think if it's done extremely well, you can take a very dark room and actually raise the luminosity of light. It's as if the room becomes significantly brighter.

There's a tremendous amount of information here that can be expanded upon by just thinking about it. The possibilities are endless. Anybody who practices any of the material from *High Guard* is going to be infinitely more empowered in their life. It can be utilized in dozens and dozens of circumstances. It's an ultimate tool in the progression of spiritual freedom and enlightenment.

Now I'll lead you through a guided *High Guard* session. If you are sitting in a chair right now, or reading this book, that's fine. You don't need to be in a special place. Ideally, you will be in a place where you have some privacy, and feel comfortable closing your eyes and doing some simple motions without feeling like people will look strangely at you.

The Pyramid

Sit in position; half-lotus, Indian leg style, or chair.

Be aware of your body and surroundings such as clothing and temperature.

Take a slow, deep breath to relieve pressure and stress.

Focus on a white line forming in the center of your body.

Breathe in and imagine expanding the line to one inch from the body and exhale.

Now breathe in and make the line extend into the shape of a pyramid.

Exhale and surround your body with the pyramid by several feet in all directions.

Use another breath to make it impenetrable.

Fill your pyramid with energy and say, "So it is."

The Sword

Sit in a half-lotus, Indian-leg style position, or in a chair.

Clear your mind.

Hold your hands near the lower chakra as if you are holding the handle of a sword.

Visualize a sword extending out of your hands.

Move the sword around your body and cut all the connecting energy webbing around you. (In front of your head, behind your back, your sides and even under you.)

Bring the sword back to the starting position and see the sword disappear; its energy returning to you.

Let your hands return to a meditative posture.

While breathing out say, "I release,"

"It is complete."

The more that you choose to do these processes on your own, the better the results will be. The more time you take, the more detailed you can make the experience, the better results you will achieve.

I will stress to you the importance of the Pyramid and the Sword, although on both of these I just did a quick walk through. The more that you work with this, and again the more detail and emotion that you apply to this, the greater the results, and the more powerful the response is going to be to those effects.

With the Pyramid, a tip would be to use your heart chakra just before you complete your session, and surround it with a very positive feeling of love and happiness. Focus on your heart chakra, breathing in through your nose and emanating that energy out perhaps in a pink, white, or silver hue of positive energy, and then finishing at that point.

Chapter 5

THE AKASHIC RECORDS, A DUMMY AND YOU

I'M ALWAYS LOOKING for ways to help you to understand what I am teaching you so that you can reach a higher state of consciousness. Using different perspectives to explain something helps you to understand easier. When you read this the first time, you may not have grasped what I was talking about. However, when you read this now even though it hasn't been explained this way before, it will connect with all your other knowledge.

In order to reach enlightenment, you must be consistent with your knowledge. You must consistently think about it in order to remain aware of it. When you're not consistently thinking about it, and when you let the little things in life occupy all of your thoughts, you become a red cell. You become a product of the ordinary world, not the spiritual world. When you are constantly aware, knowledge becomes a state of mind. You don't think about it anymore, just like any other habit you pick up. This is a very good habit that you should start. Being constantly aware raises your consciousness towards enlightenment.

Many times, people ask me, "How do you know all of this information? Why is your knowledge so vast? How can you have something thrown at you and figure it out in seconds, as if you've always known it, even when you've never heard it before?" You can ask me a question and, automatically, I have the answer. How do I get the answer so quickly? I get the answers from the *Akashic Records*. What are the Akashic Records? It is the collective consciousness of the Earth.

Is there something beyond the Earth's collective consciousness?

Beyond the Earth is the collective consciousness of the solar system. It continues on, consecutively bigger and bigger until you reach the total consciousness of the Universe: God. This is vaster than most spiritually enlightened people can even begin to comprehend. There is a collective source of energy, which is one of the missing links in most spiritual teachings that generally give you the basic concepts. They tell you to do all of these steps, and eventually you might get there, but most people don't make it. If you can subdue your ego, you can open your mind to an ocean of knowledge. This ocean of awareness becomes you, but you have to learn to let your mind become fluidic, not to let your brain dominate.

Often when I read or hear something new, I come across little bits and pieces of valuable information. One particularly interesting article talks about people who have found a way to fool their brain to get incoming information from somewhere. They truly have tapped it; they just don't know what it is or where it's coming from. This article is about a ventriloquist who has a little wooden dummy. People who have these little dummies build a relationship with them; they really do. They don't think of their dummies as a toy; it's a way for them to express a multiple personality. The brain has the ability to divide into different personalities that exist inside of your consciousness. The limitations of the brain are beyond what most people can understand.

Have you ever heard of Edgar Bergen? I vaguely remember him. He was one of the first people who had a wooden dummy. He dressed him in a little tuxedo with a little, black top-hat. Bergen was an older man who would talk to his dummy and make jokes, and the dummy would tell him he was stupid. They were very famous a long time ago. It says in this article:

> "When I was a young child, my father was a comedy writer for a weekly radio show. He invited me to go with him to deliver a script to the ventriloquist Edgar Bergen. Bergen's chief dummy, Charlie McCarthy, was one of the best loved characters in radio comedy, and was featured in many movies as well. He was also my very dear friend, and when he was sitting on Bergen's knee he would have many spritely and mad-cap conversations. When Dad and I entered the open door of Bergen's hotel room, we found him sitting on the bed, with his back to us, talking very intently to Charlie and then listening with evident wonder and astonishment to Charlie's answers."

The guy didn't know that his script writer walked in with his daughter. Bergen had his back to them and was talking to his dummy inside the room by himself, not even aware that they were there. This wasn't about comedy. This was a serious conversation that he was having with his dummy!

> "Unlike in the radio programs, there was no flippancy here, no joke sarcasm. Indeed, one got the impression that Bergen was the student while Charlie was quite clearly the teacher."

Charlie, the wooden dummy, was talking to him.

> "I silently mouthed at my father, 'What are they doing?' He mouthed back, "Just rehearsing." As we listened to what Bergen and Charlie were saying, we soon realized that this was no rehearsal for any radio program that we ever knew about. For Bergen was asking his dummy ultimate questions like, 'What is the meaning of life? What is the nature of love? Is there any

truth to be found?' And Charlie was answering with the wisdom of millennia. It was as if all the great thinkers of all times and places were compressed inside this little wooden head and were pouring out their distilled knowledge through his little clacking jaws.

Bergen would get so excited by these remarkable answers that he would ask still more ultimate questions, 'But Charlie, can the mind be separate from the brain? Who created the Universe and how? Can we really ever know anything?' Charlie would continue to answer in his luminous way, pouring out pungent, beautifully crafted statements of deep wisdom. This rascally faced little dummy, dressed in a tuxedo, was expounding the kind of knowledge that could have come only from a lifetime of intense study, observation and interaction with equally high beings. After several minutes of listening spellbound to his wooden Socrates, my father remembered his theological position as an agnostic Baptist and coughed.

Bergen looked up, turned beet red and stammered a greeting, 'Hello Jack. Hi Jean, I see that you caught us.' My father said, 'Yeah, Ed. What in the world were you rehearsing? I sure didn't write that stuff.' 'No rehearsal, Jack. I was talking to Charlie. He's the wisest person I know.' My father exclaimed, 'But Ed, that's your voice and your mind coming out of that cock-eyed block of wood.' Bergen answered quietly, 'Yes, Jack, I suppose that it is.' Then he added with poignancy, 'And yet when he answers me, I have no idea where it's coming from or what he's going to say next. It's so much more than I know.'

Those words of Bergen changed my life, for I suddenly knew that we contain so much more than we think we do. In fact, it would seem that in ordinary waking reality, we live on the shelf in the attic of ourselves, leaving the other floors relatively uninhabited, and the basement locked except when it occasionally explodes. I also knew that I had no other choice except to pursue a path and career that would discover ways to tap into so much more of the deep knowledge that we all carry in the many lives of reality and nested Gnostics within ourselves."

Isn't that intriguing? As an intellectual person and spiritual teacher, I find that fascinating. I can imagine that you are equally moved by this article. It happened in the 1940's, which is really amazing because, at that time, channeling was an unfamiliar subject. Nobody really knew then about the way the forces of nature found a way to convey information through a person, even though Bergen had to speak in the second person in order to give him this knowledge.

We all have vast oceans of knowledge within us, but the way that we perceive our reality doesn't allow us to tap into that force of knowledge. It creates a fear inside of us that makes us doubt that higher knowing, that higher instinctual information.

This excerpt comes from a book by Ralph Abraham, Terence McKenna, and Rupert Sheldrake. Ralph Abraham is a very brilliant man and considered a genius. Terence McKenna is considered an esoteric genius and Rupert Sheldrake is a math genius and is highly respected. I find this article very interesting because I've never been exposed to any of these people. My knowledge is self-taught.

It's fascinating to compare what I know with these other people who have obtained a doctorate and have studied and traveled all over the world. I was in my twenties when I started teaching on a regular basis, but I really began to teach when I was 16 or 18 years old. So what does that say about what I'm offering, never having been exposed to higher education or outside knowledge? Rupert Sheldrake, one of the authors of this book, says:

"What I suggest is the existence of a kind of memory inherent in each organism in what I call a metaphotogenic or morphic field. As time goes on, each type of organism forms a specific kind of cumulative, collective memory. The regularities of nature are therefore habitual. Things are as they are because they were as they were. The Universe is an evolving system of habits."

As I have taught before, this is a cycle; it is a pattern. It learns from itself. The whole Universe is unfolding as an experiment, and God is learning. In *The Handbook of the Navigator,* I explain how the creation of God began in a system like this.

Returning to Sheldrake, what is he saying? Is he saying that the conversation via Charlie's knowledge comes from a memory capacity within our brains that we don't understand? Or is he saying that it's being pulled from the collective consciousness?

It's both. He's saying that there is a collective consciousness. Let's look at this a little differently. You are a universe within yourself, right? All the cells in your body are basically with you in that the cells respond to you. They function by your will from your low radiation impulses that tell the organs how to function. For as minute and simplistic as those cells are, they have already been designed to do their duty. They know what is expected of them; they just need to be told when to do it.

Where did those cells get that knowledge from on such a microscopic level? How do they know what they know? How do these living organisms in your body know what they know? It's ancestral knowledge. As one learns, they all learn from them because they all know the same information. How do they all know the same information? Does that mean that if you teach one of them something new, all of them will all know if they're all the same? We're going to get into that in a minute and it's very fascinating. The book says:

"For me, the key to unlocking what is going on with history, creativity, and progressive processes of all sorts is to see the state of completion at the end of a kind of higher dimensional object that cast an enormous and flickering shadow over the lower dimensions of organization of which this Universe is one."

That statement is from Terence McKenna. He is basically saying what I have been teaching for years. Instead of looking at the whole microscopic level and working your way up to understanding the following:

"The human is the microscopic level of the planet; the planets are the microscopic level of the solar system; the solar system is the microscopic level of the cosmos; the cosmos is the embodiment of the Universe, and so on until you get to the total body of God."

He's saying to just look at the body of God. Then reverse it and you will see all the lower levels. If I were to look at you, I would see your physical body. I would see that you're made up of a heart, lungs, kidneys, and all the rest of the organs that are inside of your body. If I were to select any one of those, I could go into the body structure, the different organisms and systems: the circulatory, respiratory, digestive, etc. all the way down to cells, atoms, electrons and the multi-universes within. McKenna is saying that you can look at it from a larger spectrum, but really, you should look at it from both sides of the equation.

Ralph Abraham says, *"There is another level, which I am calling chaos, or the Gaian unconscious. This contains not form, but the source of form, the energy of form, the form of form, the material that form is made of."*

His first statement was that of Gaia being unconscious. What does he mean by that? Well, I've never said that Gaia is aware. Gaia is similar to an amoeba right now. It hasn't found self-awareness yet, but its consciousness is rapidly changing. *That's why there is so much chaos in the world.* That's why there is such an intense focus on technology. The Darkside is approaching. It's getting ready for something to happen. Whenever anything happens, it's like giving birth. Is birth pleasant? It's beautiful, but it's also brutal and painful; yet something incredible is born as a result of it.

Everything in life has an intensity to come into being. There is a struggle. So is the current phase of the world, but the world is still unconscious. But it is now pursuing a direct course that will enable it to become conscious because neurons of information are moving rapidly from satellites, fiber-optics, cellular phones and other recent technology. This nervous system is reaching such a capacity that it's becoming one tonal. Gaia is becoming one life form of total awareness instead of just functioning.

> "Creativity and the imagination," says Rupert. "There's a profound crisis in the scientific world at the moment that is going to change science as we know it. Two of the most fundamental models of reality are in conflict. The existing world view of science is an unstable combination of two great tectonic plates of theory that are crashing into each other."

What are the tectonic plates? It's as if the entire continent of North America were moving and grinding over time. If Sheldrake is saying two tectonic plates, what exactly does he mean; what are the two plates? He says this isn't a minute problem, nor is it a medium problem. It's so huge that it's going to affect the whole world scientifically. This is a very serious and powerful statement that will bypass the consciousness of most people. He's saying the two schools of thought are going to crash into each other. That is absolutely huge!

"Where they meet, there are major theoretical earthquakes and disruptions of volcanoes of speculation."
So they argue about whose theory is the best one.

"One of these theories says that there is an unchanging permanence underlying everything that we know, see, experience, and feel. In Newtonian physics, that permanence is seen as twofold.

First of all, there's the permanence of the internal mathematical laws of nature considered by Newton and Descartes to be ideas in the mind of God, God being a mathematician. The image of God as a kind of transcendent, disembodied mathematician containing the mathematical laws of nature as internal ideas is a recurrently popular idea, at least among mathematicians. The sort of permanence is that the atoms of matter are in motion. All material objects are supposed to be permutations and combinations of these unchanging atoms. The movement they take part in is permanent and constant. These permutations are summed up in the principals of conservation of matter and energy. The total amount of matter is always the same, and so is the total amount of energy. Nothing really changes at the most fundamental levels, nor do the laws of nature change. This model of the eternal nature has been the basis of physics and chemistry and, to a large extent, is still the basis of physical and chemical thinking."

According to Newtonian physics, or everyday science, "Nothing evolves like we believe. Nothing changes. It's the same thing just weighed and measured." I disagree with this theory. I believe that the Earth is learning. The Universe is learning. It is adapting, changing, expanding and moving forward as It takes in more data from Its experiences. The Universe is refining what It knows to a higher level. This is what has made science move so methodically slow throughout time.

The other theoretical viewpoint is an evolutionary one that comes to us from a Judeo-Christian based heritage. According to the biblical account, there is a process in history of progressive development, but this process is confined to the human realm only, not to nature or to the Earth. Once again, religion is saying that God is focused only on humans. This is such an arrogant and ridiculous concept. The concept says that the Earth is not a progressive thing. It's not an organism. Everything is here because God put it here to serve man. It's just an outlandish concept.

"In the seventeenth century, this religious faith was secularized in the notion of human progress though science and technology. By the end of the eighteenth century, the idea of human progress was the predominant idea throughout Europe."

This is where Christian belief states that God created the Earth, and it's all about human beings and nothing else. It's a ludicrous idea in itself, but these are the two biggest players in all of this. Abraham writes:

"So how does this process happen? In my book, 'A New Science of Life,' I attempt to explain how the habits of nature can evolve. What I suggest is the existence of a kind of memory inherent in each organism."

Sheldrake says that the hundredth monkey theory is not exactly true. Whether or not it was done with monkeys is irrelevant. It's an example. There is a truth there and that is what is important. There is an evolution process throughout all the species of any kind of organism. They convey their knowledge to one another and progress. I've never had anybody come forward that really agrees with me on a scientific level, but I've always known this to be the absolute truth. I'll continue:

"What I suggest is the existence of a kind of memory inherent in each organism, in what I call a metaphotogenic or morphic field. As time goes on, each type of organism forms a specific kind of cumulative, collective memory. The regulators of nature are therefore habitual. Things are as they are because they were as they were. The Universe is an evolving system of habits. For example, when a crystal crystallizes, the form it takes depends on the way similar crystals were formed in the past. In the realm of animal behavior, if rats are trained to do something in San Francisco, for example, then rats of that breed all over the world should consequently be able to do the same activity more easily through an invisible influence."

They just somehow know because they're all the same thing. The Universe has habits for every specific thing. If there is a new thing that one's doing, they all must do the same thing because that's the law of the Universe. Everything is collectively, progressively moving forward. I think this is wonderful information!

"There's already evidence summarized in my books that these effects actually occur. This hypothesis also suggests that in human learning we all benefit from what other people have previously learned through a kind of collective human memory. This is an idea very much like that of Jung's collective unconscious."

So what are they really saying? What is the key word in all of this?

The collective consciousness.

What is the collective consciousness?

The Akashic Records.

The scientists from these articles are just going back to an ancient knowledge that has always been known; only they are now trying to find ways to prove it through experiments and testing plants. They're just beginning to scientifically conceive and understand these things.

That touches on something that I said a long time ago, "Everything I teach is the truth, but it will take science time to figure out these spiritual truths." In the end, they will come to the same conclusion.

"Could there be a kind of imagination working in nature that is similar to our own imaginations? Could our own imaginations be just one conscious aspect of an imagination working through the whole natural world, perhaps unconsciously, as it works underneath the surface of our dreams? Perhaps it could sometimes be conscious? Could such an ongoing imagination be the basis of evolutionary creativity in all of nature, just as it is in the human realm?"

Terence McKenna listens to these questions and statements, and concludes:

"For me, the key to unlocking what is going with history, creativity, and progressive processes of all sorts is to see the state of completion at the end as a kind of higher dimensional object that casts an enormous and flickering shadow over the lower dimensions of organization of which this Universe is one. For instance, in the human domain, history is an endless round of anticipation. The golden age is coming. The messiah is immediately around the corner. Great change is soon upon us. All of these intimations of change suggest a transcendental object that is the great attractor in many dimensions, throwing out images of itself that filter down through lower dimensional matrixes. These shadow images are the basis of nature's appetite for greater expression of form; the human soul's appetite for greater immersion in beauty; human history's appetite for greater expression of complexity."

What he's saying is actually brilliant. It's very interesting. I've said it in different ways, but God needs to motivate us to be stimulated to create, to think, and to add to God. What is a will or a desire on its part is broken and filtered down to the next level, the cosmos. The cosmos is filtered and broken down into 20 million rays of interest. Those rays break down into billions of smaller rays throughout the Universe and an infinite amount throughout the solar systems so they reach the planet where we receive it. All of a sudden, this ray hits all the nervous systems of the planet and we realize, *"Something is going to happen! Something is going to change. What will it be? There's a revelation of the messiah coming around the corner."*

There's a need. There's something inspiring all of us. It's God's way of communicating with the Universe through solar radiation. It's the inspiration and the instinct that we all feel; telling us that there is something more than us. It's the willfulness of it manipulating us as a species, as a collective consciousness, and as a nervous system to create consciousness, to create thought, and to become alive. Your heart doesn't pump just because it wants to pump. It pumps because something is telling it to pump. It's telling it to live. What is telling it to live? How does it know? Can it think on its own? Something from a higher place moves through this galactic Universe to constantly tell it, "Pump, breathe, live!" You want to live! It's the same for all the species, all the organisms, and for everything!

This is really what Terence McKenna is saying. It goes all the way back to the ventriloquist. Bergen is obviously tapping into a mirror of his own intellect.

Let's take another example. Bob is a mechanic. He is intelligent but otherwise just an ordinary guy. So, how could Bob begin to know these things that we have been talking about? How could Bob even dare to think that he could figure out the things that the greatest scientific minds are working on? What does he do to get around his negative thinking? He creates an *alter consciousness* that tells his brain, "It's okay. You can talk to me now because it's not you." Bob is really figuring it out, but he is tapping into something higher, even though he may not realize it. You have that same capacity. You have the same ability to do this.

Enlightenment is when you can walk *In-Between*. You may not know what *the In-Between* means yet, but if you don't, you will learn it in later lessons. You don't have to be at a level where you're seeing energy and walls turn into molecules. Just allow your mind to open. It's scary stuff because it's almost like you're going to lose your mind. Every instinct inside of you says, "Should I be doing this? Is this okay? Is this acceptable?" It's a little intimidating because you're afraid you're going to lose who you are. By allowing your mind to open, you reach the first stages of enlightenment.

Bergen found a way to let this *mindfulness* talk to him. It felt comfortable because he could receive the answers to the questions he asked. If the answers were wrong, it didn't matter because the answers were coming from the dummy; so he removed the fear of being wrong, and that's how the uncontaminated information came through. Fear is what screws things up. It's the same thing that I've done, in a sense. Instead of having a dummy, I've connected all of this information into my brain to become part of my identity because it's truly who I am.

There is an ancient and wise being inside of you. That ancient and wise being can surface and become who you are, because it is who you are. It's because you're too afraid to let this being come forward that you put limitations on it. You have to find a way to let the fluidity of this knowledge come forward to harmonize with this frequency, with this consciousness and feel comfortable with it. It's *elusive*. So, what does elusive mean?

Elusive means hard to control, difficult to capture; it's hard to hold or to describe.

In other words, if you grab it, it slips through your hands. If you trap it, it crawls out a backdoor. Somehow, you just can't manage to get your hands on it no matter how hard you try. It's elusive. It is a higher state of consciousness that exists inside of you that I call *the God-being*. It is the enlightened being part of you and it's elusive to you, so you have to find a way to get this elusive part to work through you.

A long time ago when I first started teaching, I shared this secret. I called it 'the box.' I said, "If you want to open the box, the harder you try, the more it will stay shut. But if you ever so gently, ever so calmly, ever so perfectly *WILL the box open* through compassion and love, it would open for you like a flower coming out of the ground opening to the heat of the sun. Nothing rips the flower up. Nothing peels it open. It does it willfully because it feels the presence of the sun." In the same way, you have to create this presence of being inside of you to awaken.

Can people that use their psychic abilities for negative purposes or selfish reasons affect reality in a dark way?

People who are doing this have tapped the *Darkside*. They are using a negative force of energy as a form of fuel; that's how they're doing it, but it can't compare to the power of *The Force*. The Darkside is, supposedly, the opposite of life, but it is more matter than matter itself. Matter is more energy and more illumination of light beyond your conception of light. It's just the opposite of what you think. Taking this further, the darkness is a mass of energy that is more solid. Even though we are solid, it's really a different kind of thinking. It's like quasi-thinking. It's metaphoric.

Therefore, it's not solid in the conventional sense?

That's right; it's a brain twister. Be careful! It will be painful if you go too far. Somehow, certain people have learned to tap into the Darkside and construct it into a way that it can make its presence and willfulness known. However, the truth to the matter is that there is just no comparison.

Would you say that time is a reciprocation of the Darkside? If the purpose of the Darkside is to suppress and destroy life, then doesn't time also serve this purpose in breaking down and dissolving matter?

Time is something that affects matter. It doesn't affect energy. Time is a measurement of existence. A mountain might be a mountain for a million years, but in time it deteriorates; then it becomes a desert or a jungle. Then the desert or jungle becomes an ocean. It's metaphoric in change. It is transformation, not true destruction. How long will it exist in its present structure is really the basis of how most people understand time.

What about time itself?

To me, there is no such thing as time. Time is really a measurement of distance. Time is a form of measuring. It's like a measuring cup. If energy cannot be destroyed, only recreated, how can you apply time to it? If you can no longer look at it as a form of matter, you have to look at it as a form of energy. Energy cannot be destroyed. It just exists. It doesn't dissipate, nor does it die. It just simply, consistently exists, as far as we understand it.

So then the Darkside doesn't exist in energy. Energy is just energy?

Yes, more or less.

The Darkside is more or less a part of lower tonals of energy and lower tonals of vibratory life?

You could say that it's tones of consciousness, which are affecting the energy in a different way.

You have a spectrum of high tonal that is intangible and then comes into tangibility. Does the Darkside then start to take form?

You can't quite put it that way but yes and no. First of all, the Darkside is an adverse reaction to energy. For every action, there is an equal and opposite reaction. Therefore, if the Big Bang was the presence of matter, which is energy, then where is the opposite and equal reaction to that? It is the presence and creation of an opposite form of energy for which we have no name or understanding. It does not work as a form of energy as we understand it. To specifically say what it is, we don't have any way of conceiving it.

**Through time everything recycles itself
and corrodes. But if it recycles itself,
how can you say when it began?**

You can't. So then time really is dismissed; therefore, time is not a factor. Time is only a factor if you put in the distance or ratio of the quantity of something. For the amount of time that it will exist before it metaphorically changes to something else, that something is still the same thing. Therefore, time does not really apply to it because it never changed. In a sense, it changed but it still is what it is. It never really stopped being what it was. It simply took on different forms.

In our terminology, would time be just a factor that contributes to lower tonals of matter or energy?

It is a way of gauging a form of matter, a form of energy that can only be used in this dimension. It can't be used in other dimensions because it can't equate correctly. If that's how you're looking at time, what you're searching for is not time. It is something else. *Time is only a label.* Time is something that we conceive something to be. Just because we conceive time to be a distance doesn't mean time is limited to that. It's just all that we understand so far about it.

So time has no relation to the Darkside at all?

Time is the neutral party. It is used to observe how the Darkside affects and destroys something. When the Darkside eradicates the existence of the entire Universe and all matter, then it has ultimately succeeded. When I say matter, I mean energy, in this instance, because this is all energy. If it destroys something, it is only destroyed as a useful object that is physically capable of being touched, felt, and moved by us in this dimension.

So time is a product of the yin and yang of the Light and Darkside?

It is really something that we can conceive. It's something that's important to us to gauge. It's a way of us recording and comprehending, like a language. It helps us to interpret moments; it helps us to comprehend change. If we don't have time, we don't understand change. That's thinking like a human being. That's thinking as a physical structure.

It's simply a tool for us to use as physical beings in this physical dimension so that we can comprehend. *Reality is what you perceive it to be.* For example, there are creatures that can't see color. Do they see and experience the same thing as you? If you were colorblind, would you see the world as everybody else sees it? How would that affect the decisions that you make? You could not feel structure if you had no sense of touch. How would it change the building? How would the carpet look? What would be the purpose of even having carpeting? Would we just have granules of dirt instead?

How would reality have changed for us? If you could not taste, would there be palates of food or would everything just be a substance of mashed potatoes to eat and sustain life? Reality to you is to what you can conceive it to be. Because you are a creature that can smell, touch, and hear, this is how you absorb data. You convert it to comprehend as an energy being inside of this body. So then, time is one of the tools to work with your senses. If you changed those senses, time would be irrelevant depending on which senses you change or how you would take in information.

Some people are able to eat different foods and conceive a structure that makes music in their head. It's a different form of sensory. How would that change their perceptions of math, reality, dimension, and time? They would have a whole different book of life.

What if time was not called time? What if it was called phonics that is really measured in sound? Time would not be measured by deterioration; it would be measured by how loud or how soft it sounds. So in the end, time is really just a tool that you use as a method of comprehending your reality. Your reality is what your senses choose to impart to you for information. Reality is different for all species on this planet. The planet collectively uses thoughts from us, but it also collectively uses thoughts from other creatures. It is much more ingenious in its form of collecting data than us! We have touch, smell, taste, hearing, and sight. It has black and white, sensory, and deprivation. It has intensities of light frequency that make the room look totally blue for light. Yet you can't even see through it. It has millions of forms of data collecting in its brain.

Time is a tool. It's no more a way of collecting data than it is to hear sound, smell, or taste. It's simply a way for you to put this information in your brain in a structural way. A computer uses zeroes and ones that means nothing to us, but look at what beauty comes from those zeroes and ones. You are using time as a way of making zeroes and ones in your head. It's a program. Time is a tool to help you conceive your reality. You're wrong to suggest that time is evil, but you're right to use it to comprehend evil. It's just a different road to get there. You have the tools. One person might have a rope and a pick to climb a mountain. Another might use a helicopter. Yet another might have hiking shoes and choose to take the path. You use the tools you have available to you. In the end, hopefully, you'll get the same thing. The only reason I know what I know is from living all my past lives as different creatures and species. I can conceive this but it's not something a normal person would probably think about.

Are there ways that we can all recall those things?

You have to start tapping into the Akashic Records. By being able to understand the questions you have, there are answers, but sometimes there are no words in English to decipher those things. There could be, but it might take you thirty years to decipher what could take five seconds of comprehension. No matter what kind of thinking you use, the method that you are using to achieve this knowledge is crude. That's the first thing you have to accept. Therefore, you must tap into the fluidity of letting the Universe explain it to you.

Bees all share information as if they're one honeycomb of singular thought. They all think alike. We also think alike but we're more complex in our methods. We all see the same color, feel, and touch the same. There are other creatures that feel and touch differently. Women experience pain differently than men; their tolerance for pain is higher because they have to deal with giving birth. You'll see a guy complain all day long because he's got a stomach ache, but a girl will tolerate that same amount of pain. She will just cope with it, which is really not easy for guys to do.

Each species of animals is different. How they touch, feel, store data, experience and hear is different. What if our hearing was ten times greater than it is now? Would that magnitude of hearing affect how we would build walls? Would that affect what we wear for clothing? We wouldn't wear anything that was scratchy. We would want everything extra soft because it would be annoying to us.

How would that affect our spaceships, our technology, and scientific discoveries? It would revolve around that kind of thinking because that's what's appropriate for our brain. Would we have come up with astronomical thinking if we were created with different kinds of senses? Would we be more advanced now because we might have researched and thought in different ways than we do now? Would we have gone in different directions in our evolution?

Perception is important. Time is not evil; it's a tool that a lot of species in this dimension, including human beings, use as a form of measure. But it's simply a tool to help us to comprehend. It's no more important that a pen and paper, or math, or using languages to communicate with.

In other languages, there are descriptions for things that we don't have in the English language, and there are words in other languages that don't have an English translation. There are terms and phrases in other languages that don't make sense to us, but it makes perfect sense in the other language. Does that mean we're limited? Yes, it does! Does it mean that they're limited if they don't have the same words? Yes, it does! So you must collectively work with as much data as you can to get to where you're going the fastest. Can we not have a word for shoe but one day come across it? Can they have a word for 'slipping your foot into a shoe?' Do we have a word for 'slipping into your shoe' other than using the words 'slipping into the shoe?' Maybe they have a word that is called 'footsa.' 'Footsa' might mean slipping into your shoe. The diversities are endless. Eventually we will all comprehend the same thing. The evolution of the entire Universe is much bigger than you can imagine.

How does one ever figure it all out? It seems so incomprehensible now. It seems so much more complicated. This is what's going to help you to comprehend it all. This creates fluidity in your brain. When you can understand this, you will able to let this information flow into you rather than trying to explain it through the concepts of crude human thinking. You're thinking in blocks. You have to think multi-dimensionally, in ways you never thought of before. It's not possible to just flip a switch and think comprehensively. It happens to you over time. The Universe starts telling you what you desire to know. It begins to make sense. That is working with the Akashic Records. Somehow, it overrides your brain and turns it into an answering machine so that you can construct and interpret data into a format that you can understand as long as you are in this physical body, comprehending in this system of communication that you are using.

Again, that's what the dummy was doing for Bergen. It was interpreting the incoming information into a format that he could explain to himself. In reality, it was the Force using his brain as a communication device. It's like sending radio signals into a radio, converting it into sound so we can appreciate it. He was using part of his brain as a second person to talk to him. He'd ask a question; it would be interpreted, and the dummy would do the talking for him. It would not have worked with any other method because he wouldn't be able to think of those things due to his perceived limitations. So he had to think on a level that would allow him to bypass all of that so he could give himself the answers.

The goal is for each of you to reach enlightenment. How do you get there? By beginning to think and see like a Master. When you begin to understand the same way as a Master, then you will be thinking like a Master. Sometime in the future, that switch is going to turn on in your head. Someday, somewhere, and somehow, you're going to ask all the right questions in your brain. You're doing everything that you're supposed to be doing. You're reading, learning, practicing, and by doing these things, you're opening up your mind. You're invoking new thoughts that might not have occurred until you were much older; but by then your body could have died and it would be all over.

In reality, you are taking in a form of consciousness from me that is *alive*. I have universal knowledge that is alive. It's living thought. I broadcast this knowledge to you. When you receive it, the knowledge becomes alive. It becomes a living thing inside of you. By thinking about it, you feed it. You keep it alive because you're reflecting on it. If you stop reflecting, it evaporates because it doesn't really belong there yet. You haven't created the generations of energy to sustain it so that it can stay there. You have to think about it all the time rather than just letting it function because you haven't learned to be enlightened in everything you do.

Teach other people. By talking about it and thinking about it, you're feeding it. As you feed it, it becomes stronger and it becomes you. By meditating, thinking about meditation, listening to music, and doing spiritual things, you're invoking the environment that it needs to exist in to take root. It is a frequency. Once your brain is used to this frequency, it will tap into a higher frequency to continue this flow. I may not have my students sitting down and doing aums because I don't think that's the best way to become enlightened. It's good for you and your energy though. Your brain might work a little better because you're taking in more oxygen. More oxygen breaks up more pathways. It gets the toxins out, but in the end, what's really going to make a difference is the moment you have a revelation in your mind and you say, "I understand!" Each one of you has had your little successes. You have been at that moment where you go, "Now that makes sense to me." You become a new person. You become more enlightened than you were the previous year, so something has profoundly changed.

When you learn this kind of knowledge, there is a passiveness inside of you. When you really start to take it in, you feel almost relaxed but you feel like you need more. Fluidity is alive inside of you. It's metaphorically changing you. Instead of having you do all these different mantras, yoga, and other things, I'm more interested in talking to your brain and giving you pure, undiluted, distilled knowledge. I like the word "distilled." What is distilled?

Pure, purified?

How is it purified?

It's filtered.

No, it's not filtered. Water has billions of minerals in it. It has chlorine, fluoride, and all sorts of stuff that you can't see with the eye. Distilling evaporates the water. The evaporated water goes very slowly through the air. You can't even see it but it is how rain is made. It gets caught up in some metal tubes until there are enough tiny molecules collecting to become a drop of water. Then it rolls down into the other bucket. When it's all done, what is left at the bottom looks like sand. All the minerals are now all bunched together. It looks like tiny bits of sand at the bottom. The other side is absolutely pure water. It's as pure as you can get. By saying the knowledge is distilled, I'm not putting the metaphysical, magical systems into it. I'm not saying that it's being channeled. I'm giving you absolutely distilled knowledge, as best as I can give it to you, so pure that eventually you will take so much of it, and it's just going to explode in your mind until everything makes sense to you one day.

That's what is changing your thoughts. It's because of this knowledge that's inside of you. You're already applying it to something that's starting to break down other concepts. You see the flaws and the holes. This is the highest form of knowledge, but it is without ritual. Ritual is good. You can apply everything you've learned from me in different methods of thinking. The more that you take on, the heavier you become. That is true spiritually as well.

What I'm teaching you is the latest knowledge, which means that it is of the highest evolution. All the other systems are old. They were the old way of thinking, but evolution has refined them. If you want to hang on to the old, it will always be there in a habitual cycle. Or you can become part of the latest product that's working its way down the ladder in order to affect all those other ones to bring them up. So what are you going to do to the old knowledge?

Distill it.

Distill it. We're going to distill their knowledge to get the real truth and the real quality out of it. That goes for Hinduism, Kundalini yoga, tantric, and martial arts. You have to distill all of it to get the real truth. That's really what I'm offering you. By listening, thinking, feeling, and hearing what I'm saying to you, in the end what's alive in your mind is going to free you. It's going to make you an enlightened being. You're already more enlightened than most human beings. To be sitting here reading this, you're already a white cell. There are other forms of white cells but what makes you enlightened is consciousness. It's not about walking through the air. It's not about the miracles you can do. All that stuff can come with time. What is really important is that you can conceive the Universe. If you can conceive the Universe, you're already vibrating at a much higher level than everyone else. By understanding the dynamic process of the Universe, you're already enlightened. I know that's hard to believe right now, but you're already alive in more ways that you can ever understand.

Do we already have an effect on the Akashic?

You are already part of the Akashic because you understand what the Akashic really is. You affect it now whether you realize it or not. You're part of it; you just haven't figured out how to talk to it yet. If you understand it, you are aware of its presence. Just the fact that you are aware of its presence means that you have to walk around it. You have to acknowledge it. It becomes a part of your reality. Those who have no idea that it's there can't affect you. Because you know it's there, even though you don't have profound things happening yet, it's affecting you already in the way you think and in the way you do things. You already know that it exists. That kind of knowledge is enlightenment. The more that you can understand it, the more it has the ability to affect you.

Ignorance is bliss, but in the end ignorance keeps you from moving forward. Since you can envision all these galaxies and universes as the total body of God, it affects you. Deep in your DNA, everything is written. The fact that you can comprehend and acknowledge that changes you. It changes who you are. Who you were before you met me is no longer the same person you are now. The information that I've given you is profound power. It is the power to change where you are. It is the power to walk through walls. It is the power to heal the sick. It is the power to do everything you ever imagined. It's just that you haven't reached that point of acceptance yet. You need to get everything to work in the right way, but you have the capability because you can conceive it in your mind. It is feasible and logical. It's not like a fictitious story in your head. It is workable. It's only a matter of allowing this knowledge to ferment and become something greater. In the end, it just happens. That is what I believe will happen with my students. That is my path.

I have looked at everybody else's teachings. I've looked at the strict, the feeble, the glorious, and the noble. In the end, they all live and they all die. Only a select, small portion will actually become enlightened. So maybe I'm not as strict as they are. Maybe I do not force this knowledge upon you as they do. In the end, I'm letting you grow the same way that God lets the forest grow and the ocean move with very little control. Some people consider that powerful control, but the knowledge that I've given you is really just letting you cultivate it. It is germinating it.

I'm curious to see what's going to happen down the road. You already know more than many teachers of spiritual knowledge. The only difference is that you haven't invoked it yet. You haven't sat down and invoked this chi energy, but you know how to do it. You even acknowledge that it exists. You may feel it, but you don't sit down and discipline yourselves enough to invoke it. You could heal the sick. You know exactly how to do it. You know how it's done. Yet you choose not to ferment this energy by going out and practicing it. You can move objects. You know how to do it. You haven't gone out to accumulate the energy. You know how to focus it, what to expect from it, and how you should manipulate it, but you just haven't chosen to set your mind to do it yet.

They say in Reiki, "We can heal someone from a distance." I bet that if you sat down, you could figure out a formula in your head that would work just fine. But you never really sat down to figure it out. You take in all of this knowledge, but that does little for anyone if you do not exercise it. I find that very interesting. You could do incredible things. You could walk through the wall. It's just a matter of exercising your beliefs. You still have doubt about walking through the wall, but you don't doubt that you could do other things. You haven't had the desire yet to go out and act on what you know. But you understand the dynamics of it. You just need to decide to apply yourself.

Spirituality exists extremely strong in everyone who learns from me, but you have to exercise it. Tai Chi makes perfect sense to you. The body movements make perfect sense to you. You can feel the emotions of Tai Chi, but you don't need to call it Tai Chi. You can sit there and just do it. You're *experiencing* what Tai Chi students need to imagine. You can *feel* this pure energy. Most of those students still need crude visualization skills while they're doing it. You already know how to do Tai Chi, how to heal, and how to reach different states of consciousness. If you just sat down for two days, you could perfect one technique. You already have all the techniques, awareness, and knowledge that you will need to do this. If you choose not to do it, perhaps you lack the confidence or you've lost some of your interest? You are looking at bigger opportunities. You're saying, "Why buy a Cadillac when in a week I'll have enough money to buy a Rolls Royce? So I'm not going to drive for a week."

Because of this sense of lethargy, many spiritual people are sleepers. It's amazing. Arm chair spiritualists! However, you are not skilled in just one thing; you are skilled in many things. That's a teacher. A teacher can take somebody and say, "What do you want learn? I'll teach you how it's done." Tell me that you can't do that. If somebody came to you and said, "I want to learn how to heal. How do I do it?" With this knowledge, you can explain how to do at least five different methods of healing from raising your energy, to pushing it out of your hand, to mentally evoking it. You already have all of the answers. Most people accumulate all of this information without willfully wanting to do it. I'm sure that there are areas that you could perfect, but I think you should pick one area and start focusing on it. Work on it. Become a Master in that one particular thing instead of just knowing how to do it. Kick the engine over, start it, and drive it around a little while.

I had a student who specifically wanted to do readings. He said, "I want to do this so that I can make money." I said, "Fine, you know how to do it. Jump into it. Don't be afraid. Act like you know what you're doing and it'll work out fine. Trust what you know." So he went and did extremely well. It's like anything else. If you want to heal, don't doubt yourself; just do it. Feel it. Become it. I'll tell you right now, it will work. If you want to do remote viewing, you know how to do it. Trust yourself and don't be afraid of being wrong. Sit down with it and give yourself trials and errors until you've perfected it. You already have the ability. You have to train your mind now to do what you want it to do. That will take a short period of time. You already have the answers. You are just holding out for something bigger. I know what you're holding out for. You want to be where I am. To be skilled in one thing, you just want some switch to click on in your brain so that you can do four things at one time.

I've never said this before, but I believe that when the time is right, when the circumstances arise, when you are put in a situation where you have to deal with a situation, *you'll know how to do it.* When you come across enormous challenges that you can't seem to defeat, you'll find a way of conquering that problem. That's how we live. That's what makes us alive. It challenges us and pushes us to be our best. At the right time and right place those things will occur, whether they are in Revelations of Biblical standards or whether they are in everyday life. I believe that your inner sense of knowing what to do will simply happen and you'll do what you have to do and you'll know how to do it.

Chapter 6

Thoughts on the Path

It is in our nature to help people because a white cell feels this need to give. I'll try to explain what I mean. It's a need to give to others: to help, support, nurture, love, and direct. It runs very deep in all of us, but there is a problem with having this need. We can give now to a few and it will take everything from us. We do not have as much to give as we think we do. Or we can take the time and energy that we spend giving to the few and focus it better. Then we can learn what we need to learn to become who we need to become. This will enrich us so we can grow stronger.

You can plant a seed, and when the grown tree bares one or two fruits, you can pick everything off robbing the tree of its strength. Or, you can have patience and let it grow stronger and larger with many leaves. Let it empower itself before you start weighing it with your demands. If you start using it right away, that diminishes its ability to grow to its full potential. If you pick the leaves because you need to do something with them, leaving only a few, you're taking the energy the tree needs to flourish. If you are patient and just wait, it will benefit so many others. It would give fruit to so many people by letting it grow.

Realize that in life, you're not always going to make everybody happy. You won't be able to help everybody, and you're not always going to be there for everyone. Do the best that you can, but also realize that people will try to sap your energy. Unfortunately, it's human nature to want, want, want.

It's less likely that we will receive in return, not that we have a problem with that. We are very giving people. We're very giving, but the point is, "Do you have the strength to step away from people so that you can become stronger to help more people?" You're better in the end and the need for the many outweighs the need for the few. You can look at this any way you want. You've got to build your life around your spirituality and not your spirituality around your life.

Make careful choices and don't burden yourself too much. I am very firm about this. There are certain things you should do for yourself in order to become self-sufficient. You've got to go to school to better educate yourself. You've got to go to work -- no one else is going to feed you. And you have to take care of your health because no one else is going to do that. The one person you should count on in life is *yourself.* That's being self-sufficient. That's being individually strong. It's okay to turn to people for nurturing and love, but even though they might have the best intention for you, something could happen to them so that they aren't able to help you. What if you have to take care of them? Making yourself strong and capable in life is very important.

Now let's have an open forum. You can ask me whatever questions you want.

I have a question about entities. To be able to see things dimensionally, you must obtain a certain tonal or vibration. Do entities need to change their tonal to affect this reality or is it a simple matter of concentration of their energy?

Your question is about seeing entities or willfully experiencing them, but the fact that you are choosing to seek them at all acknowledges that you have to raise your tonal. Do entities need to change their tonal in order to see us or to affect us? The answer is very simply, "What goes up must come down." An entity exists on another frequency. Just because we say a *higher frequency* or *lower frequency*, it's just the terminology of our perception. It's really not correct to say either a higher frequency or a lower frequency. It's correct to say it's a *different* frequency. So, in order for them to move into our frequency, the entity has to effectively will or control their consciousness so they can enter this dimension. This is very difficult to do. Just think about how difficult it is for us to reach another level. If it were easy to do, there would be so many entities moving through our reality that it would be profound.

This is why there are so few In-Between. This is another factor to take into consideration because only the most skilled people are able to move into those dimensions. The entities that come here seem to be pretty amazing. Well, of course they are because wherever they coming from, they are extraordinarily disciplined. However, there are always exceptions to the rule; you must remember this. There is no way to explain every circumstance that could possibly happen in an ordinary conversation. Whenever we have conversations like this, we're covering the basics so you can get a concept you can work with.

Sometimes entities are very powerful beings that should be in another dimension. They're energy beings; their consciousness should have shifted but because of their state of consciousness, they're stuck in this dimension. They're stuck in this frequency because of the thoughts they hold in some part of their psyche. For instance, people in an insane asylum are constantly seeing and hearing things. They have great difficulty relating to us in this realm. We think they're insane, but there is a very good chance they're stuck in that higher frequency. Somehow, because their physical body is here, they are trapped in it, and are considered dysfunctional people. They're acting insane. They're doing things that seem irrational to us; perhaps they're even frustrated or violent. Can you imagine being stuck in a place forever with people intruding on your privacy? You get a piece of their reality hitting you and it seems very difficult to cope with.

When I observe the entities that people call demons, smashing or kicking things, or acting violently, I realize that these are beings that should be in another frequency but are stuck in our frequency. They're reacting irrationally because they can't relate to our reality. From our frequency, we see them as insane, violent, evil, or aggressive beings. So, a passive-aggressive entity is not necessarily evil or bad. How much compassion do you have? If ever you get into a circumstance when you're dealing with an entity, don't always assume the entity is evil. Regardless, you do need to be careful.

There are times you talk about dimensional beings, but other times you say entities. Is there a difference?

I tend to use words that are vague and have almost gotten to the point where I've created my own language! Entities generally mean dimensional beings in our own reality that we consider here in the physical dimension. If someone used the word *entity* or *ghost*, ghost is usually referred to as an entity, so we use the word entity and naturally assume it is a being in this dimension. A dimensional being would be a being from another dimension. Now if we were in that dimension, we could call them an entity or if we were in that dimension, they could call us an entity.

It's not a description that you would find in Webster's Dictionary, but because we are talking about such a vast paranormal Universe that I work with and I give insight to, we sometimes have to coin our own little phrases to navigate through all of this information. Given that explanation, words sometimes take on multiple meanings.

If we go into their reality, would they be as surprised to see us as we would be to see them?

Sometimes entities or dimensional beings do react to us. They are usually surprised or shocked at our awareness of them and uncertain how to relate to us. When we move into other dimensions, they don't usually sense us. It's the same reason that we don't sense entities when they are here in this dimension. We think in very rudimentary terms of lanes 1, 2, 3, or 4. We assume, if we're in another dimension, that we can see everything there. But there could be a thousand little micro lanes and even though we're in that other dimension, we are not perfectly calibrated with it. We get there by moving our consciousness into that dimension, not that we're physically going there. Our physical body remains here. Until we've actually left our physical body behind, we're not one hundred percent in another dimension. It's still only a part of us. It's like being in two places at the same time. Everything on the planet is an organism, but when we send a satellite outside of the planet moving through our solar system collecting data, it's an extension that is sending back information.

Let's say that you're at a place somewhere and you reach out with your hand to touch something, but that it is not really where YOU are. Where you are is how the brain perceives where it thinks you are. Your hand is like a satellite; it is just hard-wired. And your eyes are really probes seeing at a distance. You're not physically there, but you have data coming back to you. Your ears can hear things from a distance. That creates an understanding in your head of what is there. So, are there other capabilities you possess that you're not even aware of yet?

When people talk about doing an astral projection and leaving their body, they're not really leaving their physical body. It's more accurate to say that they've created this other part of themselves that moves outside of their main source. When you go into these other dimensions, many of the beings existing there cannot detect or sense you. If they are sensitive enough to be aware of you, they might sense that you're there. It is the same thing in our reality when a psychic says, "I sense a presence," or "I can feel an entity."

There are a lot of variables and possibilities that can happen. Nobody in any one dimension can capture the full complexity of another dimension without actually being there. You can travel to Greece or Italy and spend a month there, but does that mean that during that time you've captured the essence of life in that culture the same as a person who has lived there all of their life?

As a teacher, people often assume that I must have everything exactly right. If I go back and change something because I think about it for a while, they think there must be a mistake somewhere. Few people realize the vast amount of subjects I talk about and how much paraphrasing I am doing in describing things in a way that you can easily understand. What is lost in conveying my thoughts on that place and what I know of it by putting it into English or human terms? This can dilute the explanation.

Is it possible for you to go into the aspect of moving into an astral projection?

There are certainly techniques to learn to do that. There are a good number of them. One of the main ones for astral projection is lucid dreaming. Lucid dreaming is when you are half asleep and half awake and you focus on a technique. There are various techniques where you're expanding and shrinking your body, getting smaller, getting bigger, and you go into a dream state of mind. Once you realize you're dreaming, it is believed that you are able to control where you're going. Presumably, you are not imagining it. You're actually moving in some other place or some other world.

There are many, many techniques that would be appropriate for this, but that's a whole other class.

During a previous class, you were talking about a time when you were in New York and were the victim of a psychic attack. You gave the analogy of the box and thinking in reverse. You never really explained what that meant. It was a term you used to project energy. Can you explain what you meant by that?

If I explain that, there's a good chance that you will be able to do things that I'm not sure you are ready to do. I'll give you a limited amount of information about it. To think in reverse leads to the assumption of just reversing thought. What you literally think that statement means may mean something completely different. You're already thinking in a process that seems logical to you but it's not in reverse. It's thinking in a normal process. This becomes a little bit of a brain twister; let me try a very simple way to explain this.

Imagine that you want to move an object with your mind. You sit there and think in the most logical terms, which is "move." Then you try to convince yourself that it's going to move. And if you truly believe it, it will move, but time passes and it doesn't move. Next you try to convince yourself that it has already moved and you begin again. You go through all these logical steps that don't really achieve a thing. What most people don't realize, and this is going to be a really amazing thought, is that when you're working on making it move, something happens in your environment that's unnatural. For instance, you'll be trying to make a pencil move and a cupboard will swing open, or the cat will run through the room all fluffed up, or a book will fall. Something will happen that seems unrelated to what you are doing, so you dismiss it.

Here is a helpful hint: If you think of moving an object that's in front of you and a cupboard door swings open, maybe you should think about the cupboard door swinging open. You might find the object you wanted to move, actually moves! Our brain tends to structure everything. It's how we think. It's how the brain is wired. Everything has its place, its function, and its own program that will affect you in this reality. You're not going to change that program. You're not strong enough to move the object yet, but there are ways to create glitches. You have to learn the programming language. *It's like computer coding, only this is coding reality.* If you can understand that and you can figure out all the glitches and allow them to create what you want to accomplish, then when you say move, it will move. In your mind, you will be doing the *right* combination not the *expected* combination. It makes sense in a bizarre way.

When you are in an altered state of consciousness, it is not just about sitting there and relaxing. You have to venture out, listen to the sound of the train in the distance, the sound of your feet scraping the ground, or the dog barking while you're walking by the neon signs. They appear to have nothing in common; unlike a dog barking that you expect to be in a fenced-in yard. But what if you are walking in a mall, looking at the neon lights? It seems like obscure detail so a part of you ignores it. Pay more attention to that, but let your other sensory give you the impact of the environment you're in. There's a conflict there. When that conflict happens, something In-Between happens to you and you go to this other place. Don't think about it; experience it. See it from that perspective. As long as you can stay there and see from that place, it moves you in a different state of consciousness.

You were asking me what was going on when I was psychically attacked. At the time, I knew that if I wanted something horrible to happen to that person, because they were doing something horrible to me, nothing would happen. That is thinking like a human. Only in thinking in a manner that I understood as *reality programming* was I able to defend myself, and that was the end of it. This is what I mean by thinking in reverse. If you're going to affect reality, you can't try to rewrite the rules. The rules are too well written. You have to look for loopholes or create a new language. Of course, it's not really creating a new language because it's already there. All the great mystics had an understanding of this. It's how every miracle you've ever heard of was done. They're in their groove, mentally. That's the only way I can explain it. To think outside the box literally takes on a new concept now.

Is it a matter of intelligence or a buildup of energy?

It's not a matter of intelligence, no matter how smart or intelligent you are. I don't think I was as intelligent as a child as I am now. If you handed me a guitar, I wouldn't be able to play it. If I gave it to somebody else, does it mean they are more intelligent than me because they are able to master it? No, it has nothing to do with intelligence. You either get it or you don't, but if you give yourself enough time, I think you can learn to do anything.

Sitting here reading this conversation is going to have an effect on you. It's like watching the chords being played on a guitar; eventually you're going to get something out of it. It's just a matter of putting yourself into the right situation. It means you have to expose yourself to the right environment and be observant of its affects. If you stand in the rain, you're going to get wet. If you stay out in the sun, you're going to get sunburned. If you study these classes, they are going to affect you. Sooner or later, you will start experiencing different things, and with that comes realization. You don't feel the intensity of the sun when you're at the beach, but when you go home you're sunburned.

What if I said that reverse technology is happening to you right now? You don't have an explanation of what it is, but you feel something going on. Your inner senses are saying something's happening. Eventually, that is what leads to a higher state of consciousness. You have a breakthrough, which I have heard many people call enlightenment. I would rather say this is profound knowledge, where someone else might say, "This must be enlightenment." If this is enlightenment, I've got news for you -- it gets a whole lot better!

A lot of spiritual teachings from "modern gurus," books, and ancient texts are putting some good stuff out there, but the people they're trying to reach are missing the context of their message. So, the teachers are over-complicating it, glossing it over. You can take a complex subject and make it very simple, and if you get it, you get it. You don't have to read the whole novel. You've just got to get the essence of what's being said. It's that simple! That's the premise I teach from. How could I possibly make this any simpler than that?

For example, the information that I just explained to you about reverse thinking may not be something new that you haven't heard before. It may not be something profound to another spiritual teacher, but I can guarantee that my explanation doesn't make your head spin with confusion. Other teachers may have extraordinary linguistic skills that make this all sound very complicated. You have to look up half the meanings in order to reflect on them. You will need time to chew on it given the ten to twenty different steps you must take, and then get back to the teacher to discuss it. After all of that, you're still going to be scratching your head unsure if you got it or not. This is how I put it out to you in the end. You got it, and you got it in ten minutes, or maybe twenty minutes. You don't have to be a rocket scientist to have enlightenment. Enlightenment is the path of the heart, not just the path of the brain.

There are a lot of similarities in the things that you teach with the lessons and books by Gurdjieff's or his students. A lot of topics are similar. One of them talks about when the astronauts were in

space; they saw the planet and realized that the planet was an organism. In one of the similarities, Gurdjieff also used the music scale when he was talking about vibration. Can you clarify this?

Before Gurdjieff used this knowledge, the Sufis used it. And a few hundred years before that, in the Middle East, you will discover where he learned it all. A lot of *new information* is from old teachings. It is reinvented and updated for our generation. The old teachings were very powerful, but they're only good if they're brought into a modern consciousness that will be understood in our reality. These are different times. We're not going to build houses out of mud and hay. It's not to say that doesn't still work. If you went back a few thousand years ago, a mud hut was the greatest thing since the cave dwellers.

As far as using different terminology, I'm always looking for better ways to say the simple truth; every spiritual teacher is. If someone else has found a way to simplify these teachings, of course, I want to borrow it. Why re-invent the wheel? If I were to quote every time I've gotten something and where I've gotten it from, we wouldn't have enough time to have a conversation. About ninety percent of everything I've ever taught comes from the distant past, long before I discovered it myself.

I remember when I found some books on Hinduism, Raja yoga and Gnani yoga that were written back in the early 1900's. I was in shock. I was reading it and thought, "This is the most brilliant man in the world. I agree with everything that he is saying!" I was a little upset. But this guy had been around a lot longer than me. Then I thought, "Maybe I don't know as much as I thought. Maybe this information is old stuff and I'm not the innovative person I thought I was in bringing it to other people." Then I realized something profound. This spiritual leader is unquestionably brilliant. If I'm already teaching this kind of information and he is confirming it, no matter how long ago it was taught, what does that say for somebody like me? It means that there's a Universal Truth in all of this.

There is a truth and my job isn't to reinvent the wheel. My job is to improve it. To take what's in there and encourage you, inspire you, and give my perspective on it. If I had found those books earlier on in my youth, I would have pushed them aside because I wasn't ready for them yet. There is a time when you're ready for something and there's a time when you're not. There are things that I resonated with along the way as I grew older. Being as vastly knowledgeable as I was becoming and looking back, I realized that I was naïve earlier on in my life. This stuff is phenomenal. I could see how important the information was back then, but I wouldn't have given it the time of day because I just wasn't ready for it. It wasn't that I couldn't understand it. The Universe has its way of directing you where you need to be, when you need to be there.

So, going back to your question, you will find that phrase in many books about the astronauts seeing the planet and all of them agreeing that it has one thing in common. There are just so many things one can talk about. I wouldn't be so bold or so arrogant to say there isn't knowledge that I teach that didn't come from others. Even though Gurdjieff used tones, I was talking about the tones and the frequencies long before I knew who Gurdjieff was. I was 15 years old when I started talking about the tones. When I discovered that Gurdjieff was too, then I knew he was a genius! That's why I encourage others to read about him. I freely share and identify valuable sources when I know them to be useful. I would never say I'm the one and only source of spiritual knowledge, but I'm alive. I'm here now, and I'm still breathing!

I think Gurdjieff was brilliant and he had a lot to offer. There are a few things I find questionable about his character, but that doesn't remove the fact of his genius. Anybody who's in a human body has issues of some sort; everybody does. Even Christ was upset when he lost his temper because of the money changers at the temple. Most spiritual people of today would probably say, "Man, he's got a temper," if they hadn't seen what happened that caused the outburst. For the most part, what I teach is largely inner-memory and the Gaia mind, which is the source of all information when you reach a state of advanced consciousness or enlightenment.

Most of the knowledge that spiritual masters have reflected upon now is part of the Gaia mind. So it only makes sense to come up with similar terminologies when you're trying to translate or give this knowledge to a newer generation. I don't always agree with everything that Gurdjieff, Ouspensky, or that entire group said.

Let us change course and talk about God. You once said, "God is not aware of Itself." I stopped and asked myself, "Does this statement mean that God is not aware of the individual components of Itself, or God is not self-aware?"

That is a very difficult question to fully explain because it's not like God is going to come down here and clarify all this for us. God is intelligent, but at the same time, I do not believe that we can gauge that intelligence. At least, humans cannot comprehend in their physical form how God thinks. It is so far beyond us and our limited human comprehension. Meditating and finding clarity in your life is one thing. It's another when you say you've moved to the higher dimensions of consciousness.

Understanding the higher levels of consciousness is literally a whole different frequency that goes far beyond this dimension of structure, visual things, and limited capabilities. Remember, there's a difference of perception when perceiving from the physical dimension. Everything we see is a new experience. Everything we touch, feel, or see has its own importance. It has its own feel, its content, and meaning. In a sense, what you are looking at around you is code -- computer code. It's data, and your perception of what that is. You must think outside of the box. Remember what I tried to teach you earlier? When you move into other dimensions, there are also different dimensions of consciousness. As a spiritual being, I see everything as a state of consciousness. I may relate to other beings, but that's like changing my perspective. It's like a prism. I'm bending it so that I see it this way and then I bend it the other way for a different perspective.

With perception, nothing has a single point of view. Everything is very complex, although simple if you just let it flow. It's hard to do that when you are thinking with a human brain that's chemically-based with its purpose of adapting to structured thinking. With that mechanism, how can you change the way you perceive reality? You do it by utilizing a consciousness of pure-electricity or thought. You begin to meditate. You harness the electrical part of your consciousness to use pure thought. When you achieve that, you get it! You understand it! It's amazing! Everything is light, but everything is data. Everything is knowledge. God is everything. I remember having trouble with reading when I was young, and suddenly getting it. It's like an epiphany when that happens. All of a sudden, it seemed so simple. Like another part of me finally kicked in, or another part of my brain connected the right parts together and I finally understood.

Let me step back and say that God is so vast that it's almost impossible in your present level of understanding to conceive it. It's hard for you to rationalize what I mean. On that same thought, try to imagine a child trying to perceive what you perceive. It is helpful to use comparisons to gauge something in this dimension. There are some things that I have to wait for, or to earnestly prepare myself to conceive. There's always room to question what I am saying. I simplify it to give you a basic sense of what I'm trying to convey to you.

In your body you have billions of living organisms all independently thinking and functioning. It's like a whole universe. Your body is a vast universe, and most of the individual cells will never begin to travel or ever move an inch within your body in its lifetime. Yet, out of all the billions of living organisms in your body, how many are you consciously aware of? How many? None! But don't you have an absolute love for your body, for your inner-universe when you really think about it? Do you not try to protect yourself, even though 'you' is not really you? It's actually billions of living organisms that the electricity of your energy, your spirit, symbiotically relates to and shares this space with in this dimension. Are you intelligent enough to be conscious of everything inside of you? Does intelligence have anything to do with your ability to do that?

So God is not aware of all the individual components of Itself?

That would be, more or less, true. It's not to say that there's not an awareness of every single individual because, on some other level in the recesses of your mind, you most certainly are aware of every single thing. Absolutely everything is functioning in unison in your body. It is in tune with you as much as you are in tune with it. If you weren't and the brain stopped functioning, then your heart would lose its rhythm, your kidney would stop functioning, and it would be a destructive process that would eventually fail.

If you were a spiritual teacher that mastered the body, such as a yoga instructor, you would have enough consciousness to slow your heart and your breathing down, to take in a limited amount of oxygen and extend it for a great amount of time. Now, does that mean that you are on a higher level of consciousness communicating with your inner-universe, and that you're aware of everything on a more intimate level? Yes. Everybody has that potential. It's just whether you can travel your inner-verse. As individuals, we can travel the outer-verse. We can find God, but we have to travel though our consciousness, which changes into energy. It changes into frequencies so that we can approach God.

Should we try to compare the way we think with the way that Gods thinks with his energy?

This is where it gets precarious because when I try to simplify things too much, we're skipping over a lot of important details. You must always remember that. Your body is very different than the Universe but, in some ways, there are a lot of similarities. Not being able to relate to every single thing of the inner-universe of your physical body is not to say the Universe operates the same way. It is to give you a concept to appreciate something that's very difficult to understand.

While you're thinking extra-verse, is it also important to think inner-verse?

The traditional approach, while you're thinking outer-verse, is to also think inner-verse. Without getting too deeply into this, there are teachings that instruct you to remove yourself from everything, to go back to the inner-core of who you are because everything came from the universe. This planet, your flesh, the molecules, all still came from one source. They believe that by traveling backwards, you will get back to the Source of which you were created, back to the Creator. I don't necessarily agree with that. It's not the best route to achieve your goal unless you've got time on your hands to waste. Stop and think about what is happening right at this very moment. Just by sitting and taking in this conversation, you can feel that gentle hum inside of you. Now that I'm pointing it out, you are thinking about it. There's a level of quietness right now as we're having this conversation. There are revelations going on at some higher level of yourself that you're not even fully understanding.

So, like being in the sun, you're going to get sunburned and if you stand in the rain you're going to get wet. You don't need to worry about whether you have to reflect forward or backward on this subject. If you get it, that's all that matters right now because the rest is just going to happen. Let it unfold like a flower in the sun. Whether or not you are aware of it, it's in the recesses of your mind because you are in constant motion. Over complicating things or thinking too much on it is like trying to force something to move; so I'm trying to steer away from it. If I suggest to you that you should or shouldn't do something, I'm actually misguiding you. That's why I'm steering away from it. There are certain parts of my consciousness that know if we discuss this too much, you're going to be stuck in what I call 'a place.' This is what happens to most people when they try to do spiritual work on themselves or when they are self-taught. They hit this wall where they're not finding anything and they're not happy.

You might know someone on the path who has meditated for ten years and they are into all these different methods of meditation. I recently spoke to a man who has meditated four to five hours a day for years. We started talking and come to find out; he's intrigued by what I have to say. He tells me he has never experienced anything in all his years of meditation. Keep in mind he has never done the meditation technique that I teach. He tells me it has given him a level of peace in his life, but he yearns for something more. Does the thought of wanting something more sound familiar to you?

He then admits that he feels as if he deserves to experience God or something that shows him that he is achieving something more than just peace. He asks, quite honestly, what I can do for him that he hasn't already tried to do after all these years and all of this work. I asked him to explain to me what he was getting out of it, what he thought it was, and to share that with me because one person always hears something different than the next. This is perception; this is how the mind works. When he was finished, I told him my recommendation. I suggested a few things for him to change. He said it was interesting and he would try it.

The very next day, we got a phone call from him. He called first thing in the morning, unable to wait to call later that night. He said he didn't know how to put what happened into words. He was afraid he would sound like a crazy person. Not only was he experiencing various things that he had only read about, but also they were profound experiences. It changed his perspective, his life, and reinvigorated his spiritual quest with a desire for spirituality on a whole new level. He felt undeserving of these things because it wasn't his time. After all those years, all that time, he felt it was about some universal decision. I explained to him that it's not about timing; it's just about getting it. If you're not getting it, you're either over-intellectualizing the concepts or you're just missing something. Keep it simple. He just couldn't believe what I recommended to him.

How you learn and what you learn is very important. That's why it is so important to have a good teacher or to have a good source of current knowledge. What most people are trying to understand is the old knowledge with a modern twist. You're a product of the 21st century. When you read the older stuff, the terminology is very different than what we use today. The context is lost. An old master would say to you, "Life is an illusion." I would say to you, "Life is the Matrix." Then you get it. It has more relevant information. That is how I teach everything. It's for this day and age. That's how you are going to achieve what you're trying to achieve. When you have older sources of knowledge, not only do you have to decipher what they are trying to say from that time period, now you've got to figure out what to do with it. It's twice as hard.

Sometimes when knowledge is shared, it can be so profound that it eludes this dimension. Gurdjieff often would speak of this. This kind of knowledge is almost meant to be forgotten. It's not really meant to be known. There is a point where we all scratch our heads and say, "Oh, what just happened? Why did we forget this?" It's not supposed to be read. It's too mind-altering.

My question is about an experience you had. You
traveled beyond God's body in this dimension
and looked back. How did it make you feel to see
the Force as a whole and globular shape as you
described it? Can you tell us about this experience?

First of all, you're in awe, but let's take this one step at a
time. That was done as a projection in this dimension. God
resides in multiple vast dimensions. What you see here is not
all of God. As long as you understand that, we can talk about
the experience in more practical terms.

Now, on those terms in this dimension -- moving out to the
rims of the expanding universe and heading out to infinitive
space, which is pure blackness, and then looking back is
like discovering or never knowing. Well, it's profound and it
moved me. It moved me in my spirit, in my heart, and in my
love for what I was a part of. When you look at God, you see a
reflection of yourself, and understand that this is what you are
part of. Every human being, every sentient being, and every
living being has that need because of the dimension we're in;
the idea that we are separate beings in many ways.

We're always looking to bond with someone else. We're
always looking to have somebody to connect with. So we
never fully realize that we are in the interior of something very
devoted to us. We almost need to extract ourselves from what
we are a part of, how our brain is designed in this dimension,
so that we can understand.

When I had this experience, it was profoundly beautiful.
Part of me finally understood what it really means to be a
part of something, to be within the womb of life. Nothing is
more satisfying or more beautiful. When you see a sunset,
it's a "*food.*" It moves something in you. When you see a
mountain or birds fly through a tree or a beautiful piece of
art work, there's a moment when you capture that *food*. It's
like a frequency inside of you that feeds some other parts of

your being. It's like eating food and you're gratified. Well, this experience contained that food.

When I saw the entire Universe and I knew it was God, I knew I never had to eat again. That's the only way that I can explain it. My spirit was fulfilled so deeply. It was that encompassing, that overwhelming, that gratifying, and it changes you profoundly, profoundly forever.

So, we were just discussing your meditations and you were saying that you had reached a certain level in your meditation. You went to a place you had never been before. I explained that's the place that I went to when I had this one experience. If you keep hanging out there, you're going to see a silver light, and it's going to be very profound. It's a good thing. You got there in a short period of time. You've been working at this for a little while, but that's a profound step you took. Most people never get there, by the way. Sometimes it takes years.

You should realize that you've done this in a short period of time, within months. You haven't even applied yourself as much as you did before, so the fact that this happened is truly amazing. If you were in a spiritual community, a lot of people would be taken aback that it happened so quickly. So appreciate that, and understand that the system I teach did that for you. It's more than just meditation. It's having this knowledge that helps you experience things like that. Again, it's standing in the rain. It's sitting reading, listening. You meditate; you don't have to think about anything. That part of you is going to take you there because that part of you gets it. Your physical self may not get it, but the dimensional self certainly does.

You will have profound experiences in your meditations when you get to that point. When your energy hits the frequency -- it's your moment. It will come to you because you're going to it. You're ready because you understand. It's your frequency. As you've worked, you've earned it. Most spiritual people think that you have to be acknowledged by something outside of yourself, and they're waiting. You don't wait; you earned it. You deserve to have that experience. God gave you a brain so you can find It, not so you can just simply contemplate what It is.

Therefore, everything that I teach is based on the concept that if you do your spiritual work and you take care of yourself, you should have profound experiences. The way you're going to have those experiences is based on goodness, love, and compassion because that is the frequency of your heart. That's what your spiritual work is doing. It's releasing a lot of lower negative energy. It's teaching you other methods to help you to achieve that. There's no fooling It. Your frequency is based on the level of your consciousness – right, wrong, indifferent. There's a Universal understanding for right and wrong and you have to do the work. You can't fool the Universe. You can't fool It. It's a frequency.

There's only so much light in this room. You can turn it up or you can turn it down, but there's a definite quantity. You can say, "My eyes only see so much. If the cones of my eyes were bigger, I could see more light." Then I would say that there are just so many photons in the room. You can't fake it to get to God. As you work on yourself, you earn your frequency by cleansing and purging yourself, by reflecting and understanding beauty. Even if you understand the beauty within your heart and say to God, "I get it! Isn't that pretty?" It isn't going to happen. It's a frequency, not a word. It's not a picture or a thing. It's a vibration. You have to absolutely get it or you're not going to move to that other frequency.

When you finally get that frequency, the whole room brightens, it just happens. You move into that space and share it, and it shares with you. So you earn it. If you practice a formula or technique and it doesn't do anything for you after a few months, that's giving it a long time. In my opinion, something's wrong. Something's profoundly wrong, so re-evaluate your situation.

Many people blame themselves. They think they aren't meditating enough. Maybe they are not reflecting enough. They're hanging on to anger too much or whatever the case may be. If you are working diligently at your spirituality, then anger is not an option. You don't have to remove it. It will just dissipate. Simply listen to what I'm teaching you and there won't be any misconceptions. If you have it constantly in the back your mind, it's always going to be there and it's going to affect your thoughts. When you need to remember is that it will come to you. It's just like eating the fruits and vegetables; you're going to eliminate what you really don't need. Your body's going to take in what it needs.

It's the same thing. You're building your vibrational bodies, your consciousness, based on the things that I'm evoking inside of you. You might scratch your head and think, "Well, I'm not doing this or that. I'm not meditating four hours a day. Why is it that I can feel all these things and see all these things when this other person is doing five hours of meditation a day and aren't able to experience these things?" It is not just about meditating. It's not about how smart you are or if you get it or don't get it. Apply yourself a little -- that's it, a little, not a lot. You'll know what you need to do. It will come to you, and you'll know that's where you need to be or that's what you need to do. You will know it because your dimensional body will tell you. It's like the feeling you get when you crave a certain food. "The banana over there looks really appetizing. I don't want the pizza; it's good, but that banana -- I know I need whatever is in that banana. I really want to have it." Your energy is going to know, when I'm talking to you, what it is that you need from this conversation. That's when you're going to get it. You do need to meditate so that you can progress rapidly, but it's how you reflect on things is going to create the breakthrough you are seeking.

You often talk about how the sixth sense is the missing link to awakening. This makes me wonder how much of a role the health of the physical body affects spiritual development or breakthroughs.

You are physically in this dimension. The most powerful part of being anchored and rooted in this dimension is the physical organic body and the way it is designed. What is its purpose and what is it designed to do? It's designed to experience. It's designed so you can take sound and create it into energy; so you, as an energy being can experience this dimension. Sight is transformed into energy so you can experience as an energy being. Taste, smell, touch, and everything is converted into electricity because you are an energy being.

Your sensory is highly acute, and when it is running improperly or affected negatively, it is still designed to go to your consciousness. Consciousness is your intelligence, your vibration, and your tonal. It's the deciding factor of where you're going to go beyond this life. If it is out of sync or if it is running poorly, it's going to distort the data so much that the rest of the information that has been waiting to come in can't be processed. It is not beneficial to you as an intelligent being.

It's important to be in the best health you can be for as long as possible. There are specific ways you can organically improve the sixth sense that affects you spiritually. For instance, B-12 or B complex vitamins are very important for me, psychically, spiritually, and mentally. When in this dimension, psychic abilities can be closely related to our physical five senses. I see them as a middle-level to access our spiritual growth. You have five senses, your normal consciousness that I call organic, and then the second-level of low radiation impulses of the brain, which I associate with your psychic-self. It's not a literal connection, but it's for the sake of bridging that communication gap to give you a better way of seeing it in your mind. The third-level is the finest and the best; it's purely energy.

Telepathy (to read one's mind) is a psychic ability. As an energy being, you're part of the matrix. You're part of something bigger than the matrix. You're part of the universal mind. Telepathy becomes a non-necessity, a non-issue because you can experience anything you really need to know. There are no hidden agendas; it's a different kind of communication. So telepathy is something that you really need in this dimension as a psychic ability, but more so for your five-sensory perceptions. The same thing goes for most psychic abilities.

Now stepping back, if I want to improve my telepathy using psychometry, photometry, psychic healing, or any of these things that I see in my middle-range area, diet is critical. Achieving these things involves not only meditating and drawing in energy, but also physical nutrition. Energy needs to bounce off minerals to carry electrical voltage. You can heal using a higher kind of energy, but you still have to lower that energy so that it communicates with cells that understand that particular frequency. So, take B-vitamins or lemon juice. Real lemon juice seems to have a great effect on physical health.

Everything in your body contributes to your psychical and spiritual health because when you're sick, it's more difficult to get your mind to beat the Babbler, to meditate, or to focus. Can you imagine having the flu and having this conversation right now? When I am really sick, I don't even want to watch TV. When you're ill or you've got a disease, imagine how difficult it would be to keep your concentration. So your health is very important. Every organ in your body is important. Just stay healthy; that's the trick. Walking is the best physical meditation you can do. It clears your mind. Walking helps air out your mental laundry. By the time you have a good walk, your mind is cleared.

After walking, it's a good time to meditate, to do some kind of spiritual practice, or to work on a different kind of project. Look at Vedic healing techniques, massage, or oriental medicine for information that is geared to the health of the body.

I heard a story recently about experiences some of your students had involving mind-keys. They were talking about Jedi mind tricks and how to use them. Are you willing to provide

that information in this conversation? Is there a specific key you are willing to share?

In ancient terminology, they gave you a thought that was like a Mandala, a certain phrase, or a secret terminology. And when you contemplated it, there would be an effect. That's the closest thing to a mind-key that I can think of. It's a kind of programming. It's reverse-thinking. Let's say you wanted to achieve something; a key is a way for me to let you know what that one little piece would be. I don't want to use negative terminology, but it's similar to a virus in a computer. There are good viruses and bad viruses.

I could give a key in one of two ways. I can evoke it through my mind into your mind and you wouldn't even know where it came from. All of a sudden, you would be feeling a certain way thinking that something's happening to you. Or I could verbalize it to you, and the fact that you heard it means that your brain would already be processing that thought and it would have an effect. You're going to react to it.

You do that all the time when you are talking to groups when you want something understood.

That's a very good observation. That's how I teach accelerated knowledge. It's concentrated knowledge. A lot of times, when I speak, people say it's as if they can hear things, or feel things in their mind. A different part of them is listening and learning information. It is like coded data in words that I'm sending to you. It's like micro-coding. You add water and it expands with more information. In some way, I'm using a different kind of communication. It's a whole different kind of vibration; it's very telepathic. I can see how people are looking at me, if they are in that zone. People listening to a recording should get in that zone too because it's that powerful, but those who are present feel it even stronger. That is the data unfolding. It is inspiration; it's something that is actually feeding you. I always remember something my father said to me once. We were eating some kind of cereal, Kellogg's Rally or whatever it was called then, and he told us, "You're going to eat these and this little bowlful will keep expanding in your stomach and you'll be full most of the day." It was an oat cereal and the oats would swell up. When I teach, I think about that.

It is like the urban legend that states that eating uncooked rice can be deadly to pigeons as it expands beyond what their stomach can handle.

Precisely, and that is another good analogy. Most teachings do that when you find a good source. When you leave with information that's really good, you mull it over for a long time, not just for a day, and it sticks with you. It becomes part of you. I have always said that what I am teaching you is alive. It is a living thing. What you are contemplating in your mind or beginning to understand and trying to piece together is creating something living inside of you. That's the only way that I can explain it. Consciousness is thought. Thought is the vibration of who you are. It's your other body. So when I say it's living, I literally mean that. You're creating a living thing inside of you that's really you. It is also a part of some higher vibration from another place.

It is very intriguing how you communicate because I see that there is almost a secret communication between you and your students. There are certain small phrases or words you use to set up a chain reaction. You could sit there and explain for a half hour what you wanted to tell them or you could set off this chain reaction like a set of domino's in their head and get the same reaction.

It is hard to explain because it is as though we have our own language that does not just use words. The word almost directs them to link up for a second. There is a lot of mental data going on. They have developed telepathy of sorts. It is a way of acknowledging something and them knowing what frequency to tune into, what station. That is what's really happening. In their mind, they set up the satellite dish to receive from me and then I am sending, in a blip, a volume of information to them. It is a form of telepathy. Most people think of telepathy in its crudest form. They think, "Can you read my mind? I am saying one, two, three. Say one, two, three and I'll know that you're reading my mind." Telepathy is a lot more complex than that. It has so many applicable formulas. The reason why a lot of telepathy does not work is because you're not using it in reverse engineering. If you could do it in reverse engineering, telepathy would work perfectly.

**We have talked a lot about non-thought
in meditation and in shifting. Is that how
you communicate telepathically with
people in images? Or do you communicate
telepathically with people in words?**

It depends on the person because, as much as you would like to send something to someone, they need the technology to receive it. If you didn't have a TV, could you get a signal for a television show? Somebody sends out a signal, there is data all over the place. Everywhere you go; the data that you can receive is determined by the apparatus that you have setup to receive it. There are students at many different levels that have worked to raise their tonals, sending higher volumes of data during a conversation. So, yes, it can be pictures. In many cases, it's imagery. It's also condensed information. Whenever I need them to know something, they just lean back for a second and I send it to them instead of speaking words. It's like an epiphany exploding in your brain. All these flashbulbs are going off and it's making absolute sense in your head. You don't know how you just figured it all out.

It's a form of telepathy. It's not like you sit down and think, "Can you hear me now?" That's like in the movies. Real telepathy is when you have a huge breakthrough and you think it's you, but it's really the teacher linking up to you. Every student figures this out sooner or later. They've got all of this stuff going on in their head and they're thinking, "Whoa." One day they sit down to teach somebody and they lock up and they can't get the information out. It's in them but they don't understand why it's not coming out. Then one day, when the student is ready, they will be able to teach. It takes time. I tell them, "Don't teach until you're ready to teach because understanding things yourself and passing on knowledge are two different things." They're taking in something very intense and they want to share it but the equipment isn't there. They have the machinery to receive it, but they don't have the equipment to send it.

So you've got to work on yourself. Eventually you'll get to a point when you're ready to share information with another person. It's a frequency you reach. You'll know when it happens; you will begin to project it. But you might have a hard time getting back there again because it takes time for you to learn to stay in that place. It's not really a formula. It's something that happens when you're ready. Wanting it to be ready and being ready are two different things.

I appreciate that. The last question I have is based on time speeding up. I'm curious of your opinion because I've heard you talking about that before.

Time is not something that I want to fully go into at this moment because we've covered a lot already. So I will keep this answer short. Yes, I do believe that time can speed up, but

I don't think it fits into our perception of how we understand physics at this point. Physics changes every year, according to what science understands at that particular moment in time. Science is improving with time but change is constant.

When quantum physics was introduced into the scientific field, scientists had to go beyond original thought in mathematics just to make sense of things, and it wasn't easily accepted. No one wanted to believe in quantum physics as a science. But they finally accepted it, and now there are different formulas for mathematics that are far beyond quantum physics.

Time speeding up can affect you in many ways but in other ways, time is not really relevant. There are so many more important things right now that you need to work on. It doesn't matter how many bags of rice you can stack in your closet today. That's how I feel about it. It has relevance if we think we're going to starve down the road. On the same token, right at the moment, there are more important things for people to be focusing on.

Someone told me that as time speeds up, like the mind, its ability to create matter is going to speed up. Do we need to carefully monitor thought because it will create faster?

Let me put it this way: forget the time context. If you're thinking with your organic brain, you're thinking at a certain speed. For those who are computer game literate, let's say that your computer works too slow. In an older version of computers, there used to be something called a turbo button. In the game, if the guy ran too fast, you'd press the turbo button to slow him down so that you could control the game a little bit better. Now just reverse this. You're thinking with your organic brain. You're moving at 33 mph all the time. That's what we're all moving at. It's like driving in a lane and the other cars are doing 33 mph and we're driving at the same speed. We can see what they're doing and they can see what we're doing, but you can't see what the people in the faster lanes are doing.

When you move your mind into the second stage, which I call low-radiation-impulse, you are moving at 66 miles per hour. So you're processing twice as much and you are able to do more at a faster rate. That makes you feel that time is slowing down. Is time really slowing down or are you just moving faster? When you finally move to the third state, which is pure electrical thought, and you stop all the chatter in your mind, you learn to think in a different way. You start moving at 99 mph. Does that mean that time is moving slower or are you just able to do a lot more because you're moving faster? When you're moving that fast, you don't realize it. Everything just seems slow to you. Does it mean that time is really slower or does it mean that time does not have the same meaning that you originally thought?

Look at it another way. Sometimes people who've had an accident will tell you that in the middle of the accident, they saw time fly by. Their whole life flashed before them. What does that mean? They saw their childhood, their life, their loved ones, and those they didn't love. I was in an accident many years ago. Some drunk drivers were in the middle of the road. I was moving about 60mph. I crashed into some people whose cars had smashed into others and my car flew into the air and landed on its roof. It slid way down the road and eventually smashed into the guardrails. What I remember most was that I was not in a higher state of consciousness at that moment. I focused on me being physically present. I remember the shock of the accident.

When you're filled with that much adrenaline and you can't move because you're in a car, there's not much that you can do. But your mind is working in hyper-speed. I was aware that I was upside down in the car, in the air in slow motion thinking how unusual it felt. I'd never been in a car upside down in the air before. Then it crashed. The window became brittle and then started to shatter. It was like a scene from a movie when they show all the scenes moving fast and then slow. I was wavering in between all these scenes. I was part of the accident that was happening to me, but I was also the observer in slow motion seeing everything happening.

The brain speeds up and responds faster electrically. I don't believe the biochemical part of the brain can produce chemicals as quickly in order to keep up with the thoughts in your mind. It goes back to railroading a higher stage of consciousness. It's forced on you for a moment. I'm thinking I'm going to die; this is it. This is my ticket out of here. I was thinking to myself that this really sucks. I don't want to die in a car accident. I want to have some really divine death. At the very least, let me die in bed with a bunch of my friends all around me. For the sake of my ego, I wanted someone to hold my hand, and say, "Oh Eric, don't leave us!" I remember thinking, "This bites!" Then it all changed. I comforted myself with the idea that I really wanted to get out of there anyway, so it didn't matter. But damn, I wish, I could talk to my friend Dan. There are so many things I should have said to him. Then I'm sitting there and I'm thinking, "God, this is taking a long time." The wind is coming through the windshield.

I had water and mud all over me, but I wasn't even aware of it until that moment. I'm looking around in the car, at my predicament, and it's crashing in slow motion. Sparks are flying everywhere. I started to wonder when it was actually going to crash. Then I started to try to figure out how it was going to happen. Is this metal shaft going to cut through me? Is something going to shoot through my head at any minute? How am I going to die? Then I saw movement and I was contemplating if the motor was ripping through. Sure enough, the motor started coming inside the car towards me in slow motion. Then I thought I was going to be squashed. This sucks. What am I going to do? I never got to say goodbye to my friends. Oh, they're going to be so sad. I want to tell them how much I love them, and on and on. All these thoughts were going through my head. I saw all these pictures in my mind, but then I stopped. Then I got impatient. When am I going to crash? I'm going to die already! What is the holdup? I started thinking, "This is taking a very long time." Then, finally, the car crashed and banged into the guardrails. I thought it must be in slow motion because I would be going over the cliff by now. I'm going to die.

Those were my thoughts. Then, finally, it all stopped moving and I realized I was in real time. I tried to get out of the car, but I couldn't. The window wouldn't roll down, the engine was squashed and the car was totaled. So I began to wiggle around and started thinking, "I'm not dead," but I was pissed because I was wet and it was cold outside. I wanted to be home already. I was alive, but now I really wanted to get off the Rock. I wanted to move into the next dimension. I figured I got a free ticket out of there and that was a disappointment to me. But I finally crawled out the window.

There was another car coming behind me that became part of the accident. They were trying to swerve out of the way, but instead of stopping they kept on going, which was really horrible. But now this other car was coming straight at me. And I thought, "Alright, this is it!" So I got out of the way and looked at the car. I was pissed because it was one of the first cars I ever bought.

So, these are the things that I was thinking. You might think that I should be glad to be alive. Well, I dusted my pants off, but I was mad because my clothing had dirt on it. I had a white shirt on. Then I straightened my clothes out a little bit and I realized there must be people in the other cars. I ran up to them and I started directing traffic, trying to see what I could do for those people. At one point, I went back to my car to get a blanket because I saw a girl on the ground bleeding. But the sheet metal from the car ripped it in half. It was in the seat behind me. I gave her the blanket and we used it for a pillow.

Finally, an ambulance came to the scene. They asked me how long had I been on the scene? I told them about twenty minutes. Then they asked what I knew about the people in the car. I walked them through the accident and I explained how I hit the car. They stopped and asked which car was mine. I pointed down the road where you could see two little lights hanging on the *guardrail*. They looked at each other and asked if I was okay and tried to get me into the ambulance. I told them I was fine and to help the other people. So they argued with me and we all walked down to my car. They looked at the car, and then looked at me and asked how I got out of the car. I told them I crawled through the window. They asked if I was driving the car because it was completely smashed and the engine was in the seat. I looked at the guy and I thought, "How in the hell did I get out of that?" I didn't have a scratch. Not a single scratch on me -- a little dirt maybe. I was mad about that. So I now think it's a wonderful thing that I didn't get hurt.

The reason for this whole conversation was about time. The neuron-synapses of the brain process faster when things like that happen. Did the accident happen in a few seconds or was that what it felt like to me? Is it because my mind was speeding up, and the reason I could do that was because I was conscious of myself? So, I gave the whole incident a great deal of thought. When you enter a state of consciousness with your energy elevated, you will perceive life in a different way. It's not a bad way. It's just different. This opens many, many doors for conversations about time. Most people don't understand time. They think time is just from A to Z; how long it is going to take you to walk from A to Z, as in distance. Time is something very different from what most people comprehend. When you move into the dimensional planes, it is also different there. It's very interesting.

I'll just throw something out to you and then we're going to wrap up this conversation. If you dream, is it a dream or is it an alternate reality that you visit? The time that you don't remember, could it possibly be that you were there for weeks or months or years, and then you came back to this dimension and experienced a different frequency of time? It's not to say that dreams aren't really dreams. For the most part, they are therapy for the brains. But there are also other dimensions and other places where one can exist and because you are a frequency of energy, what is a minute here is like a day in another place. Remember, you're sleeping in that state of mind for a couple of hours before it shifts into various states of mind. It would be great if you could decide where you want to go. You could take a little vacation every night!

Chapter 7

THE OPTIMIST

How MUCH OF a difference does optimism make on the outcome of one's life? It makes a huge difference. In the past, there have been several studies done on people who have a positive outlook on life. The results disclosed that optimistic people have marriages and personal relationships that last longer than most. And they tend to be wealthier, healthier, and better off than those who aren't as optimistic.

There was one particular study done on people around the age of fifty or sixty that were high school graduates. The results of the study revealed that those who were pessimistic had much higher divorce rates and more problems with their families. There was less success, less job opportunities, more struggles, and the pattern continued throughout their lives.

Your outlook on life is a projection of your consciousness. The people you deal with on a daily basis, whether white cells or red cells, are more receptive to your presence. They're going to respond to you in the same manner that you treat them. So, let's say there are people you don't even know that you are affecting, like people you meet in a grocery store or at the checkout counter. What about those people that you have business dealings with who may decide whether or not you get a promotion? Or the people who decide whether or not you get a good price when you are opening a new business or buying products?

People will respond back to you the same way that you treat them. I think that human nature is typically discerning, whether vocally or physically. For instance, there are people who can tell by scanning your facial features and your body language whether or not you're lying. How you perceive life and how you project yourself, whether you have an optimistic or pessimistic view, will have an effect on you. Look at this as a psychic wave that's emanating outward from you by several feet. You may be thinking, "Well, I'm not a very optimistic person. I'm more of a pessimist. But I want to be an optimist." To me, that is a lot more important. We're all struggling in this world full of challenges. I think the world in general is evolving faster technologically than biologically and it creates a lot of stress.

So, I think it's unusual to come across somebody who's more optimistic, outgoing, happy, and positive. It could be a flaw and they're just overly happy, but I think that it's their projection of happiness that is working for them. Ask yourself how you feel about these two kinds of people: one who is very positive around you and always happy versus someone who is pessimistic and gloomy? You already know what the answer is. You're going to choose the optimist. Everyone else feels the same way you do. It's a general, genetic, biological trait of all human beings to want to be happy.

So, what do you need to do to become an optimist? Well, the answer always seems to come back to meditation and mindfulness. Everybody forgets that mindfulness is to be mindful of your consciousness. Your consciousness is the portrayer of your emotion. So, if you are mindful, you are aware that you're either an optimist or a pessimist. If you aren't sure of what you are, you are not being mindful. If you were, you would immediately gain control over the emotions you project outward, but it can be very exhausting. It's tiring to be mindful all of the time.

I believe that you can train yourself to change a certain perspective or a bad habit. You will need to have a journal or a calendar to remind yourself of what you want to change. Otherwise you will forget. Like pebbles in a river flowing with the current, we're all being shaped constantly by the environment in which we exist. As much as we try to be a good person, to soften our rough edges, and to be certain things, inevitably the force of nature is constantly working against us. We call it the *Doe*. There is also a massive biological effect that is wearing on us. Agitation is agitation and we're going to react. How mindful can you be against that turbulence? How long can you endure it? Is there a breaking point?

Well, I think there are breaking points that are like storms that come and go. There are calm periods and there are stormy periods. Are you preparing yourself to weather the storm? And are you willing to set your course to get you through that storm? I think people who survive a crisis aren't always the people most physically fit. Rather, it's the person who's mentally willful with a survivor instinct inside of them, a desire to survive through anything that challenges them. They are the ones who are going to make it.

I think most people tire of it when they try to change the quality of their nature. It's the nature of a white cell and probably a red cell, to say, "I want to be a better person. I need to be a better person. I want God to help me to be a better person. I want to be more loving, more compassionate, and more understanding." I think we all secretly desire that in our heart; it's our nature. And the reason why we ask that of our nature is because it acknowledges the fact that we don't think we're as good as we could be. When you're acknowledging the One, you're also silently acknowledging yourself. That is the negative aura or negative field of energy you're emoting that you're not consciously paying attention to. You're not being mindful.

In order to change a bad habit, you must be consistent with it. Let's say you want to stop the habit of cussing all the time. Most people work on changing their habit for one or two days and then they forget all about it. It's like the Doe; they forget their commitment to change. If they just stick with it long enough, and stay in that mindset, they would change it. You should stick with your decision to change for a week or even a month in order to break the mental routine of unconsciously spitting out your habit like a piece of machinery. You've got to have the endurance for this.

You should be more disciplined to create that goal for at least seven days. Don't just say, "I'm going to change it." Do it! Set a goal and a marker to work towards. And if you can get yourself to that point, I believe that your chances of success are much greater. Now, you have to take in some other factors. You're thinking, "I've changed; I've stopped this habit, but in my environment everybody's cussing." It's a matter of time before you will start to cuss again. It's your biological nature. It's like moving to the south, after living in the north all of your life, and after a year you visit your old friends. Immediately your friends say to you, "Did you pick up an accent? You sound a little bit different." You don't sound like either a southerner or a northerner. You are already adapting to the environment you're living in.

You're constantly picking up stuff. So, to be mindful is to try to be aware of that. It's a very simple thing. It comes back to the rubber band that's on your wrist as a helpful reminder. Maybe it should just say mindfulness on it. You need to snap it and try to be conscious of the NOW. All the things that I've taught confirm this over and over again. What can you do to bring yourself back to the moment, to re-center yourself? That's mindfulness. It is self-awareness, self-consciousness and the main thing is not to be hard on you. It's very difficult to do this. Acknowledge your small successes because the monumental changes almost never happen. If you acknowledge your little successes, you'll find that you've made a lot of progress in the end, and you will recognize it.

Is it worth working on whatever triggers automation rather than just being mindful?

You may get lost when you worry too much about focusing on other areas. You have to get to the core of the problem and the core is not always what triggers you into automation. The core of the problem is forgetting. I don't think you're going to have a problem finding the trigger. I don't think you're going to have a problem pinpointing the source of it. The problem is that you can't maintain your focus long enough to resolve it. The forgetting part is the problem. While you're being mindful, strive to be more aware of when you go into automation because when you go into the unconscious state, you don't catch yourself doing it.

The problem with change is that it's a lot like dreaming. In the dream state, you can get a lot of information. When you first wake up, you can remember a lot of it but as the minutes pass by, you slowly lose it. It is the same with consciousness and trying to remain conscious of change.

I often tell people to write their dreams down the minute they awaken. Write down all of the details that you can remember. Even as you're writing it, the memory of the dream becomes vague and you feel as if you can't write fast enough to retain it. So, you start substituting with your imagination because you're trying to piece together what you just understood a moment ago. You're trying to figure out something you've already forgotten, which means you've already distorted the data.

So, create the opposite reaction. When you decide to work on something, write it in a journal. Write all of your daily successes and then date it, and later on go back and re-read your journal to see how you are doing.

Getting back to optimism and pessimism, can we talk about compromise, trading natural and negative thoughts for positive thoughts and using mindfulness or willpower?

Compromise is exactly what it says – to compromise. You might have a set of standards or perspectives of how you view something but the other person has a different viewpoint. So, it really isn't a compromise. There could be a compromise but there usually isn't if both people are on the same path. They both are in agreement and are working together for a more positive outcome. If another person has a difference of opinion, it can create friction and it's going to be a challenge.

Let me rephrase the question. If someone is a pessimist, and you say, "Look Joe. You need to change the way you think about that. You need to compromise so you can move into a more positive mind set." I find that extremely effective, what do you think?

If one person knows a pessimistic person who is very negative, confrontational, unforgiving, and non-bending, they could tell that other person, "If you want to find more peace in your life and you want to be happier, you have to be more forgiving. You have to compromise." Would it be that hard to just give in a little bit even though you think that you're right? Is this worth the argument? Arguing takes a lot of energy and that works on us emotionally.

In negotiating that compromise, you're letting that person feel as if they've gained some ground, and they're going to be more willing to work with you. The two of you can work together now because you're building trust with each other. And so it's something that's important because it does allow for self-growth. It creates a tool to remove the band of pressure. It's kind of a yin-yang thing.

Whenever you have a negative situation and you start to become cynical, you have to let that be a signal in your mind to remember to compromise. It's like a mental alarm to remember to compromise. It isn't always easy but the outcome is worth it.

Everybody's different. I think some people like to create an extreme situation in their lives and with other people; you won't be able to help them at all. You can't fix everybody. So the issue isn't whether or not they're extreme pessimists. The issue is you becoming exhausted because you so desperately want to help them. This is something that I struggled with for many, many years. People drained me because I always wanted to help them. I thought that there had to be a solution to every problem and that I should be able to find that solution, but you pay by losing your energy. What it really comes down to is that I either reserve my energy, improving myself so that I can help many people, or exhaust myself on a few people and burn myself out. The outcome is that I will achieve far less. There is a point when you realize, "I've done what I can for these people and now I have to let this go."

Each situation is different. In some situations, I may be able to listen and give a five second answer that completely frees them. With other people, it may be something that is not going to happen in this lifetime, as much as they won't want to hear that. You have to take into consideration that some people are biochemically depressed, and they need to deal with it on a different level.

Haven't I repeatedly said it's just like operating a vehicle? You are a soul that is perfect as the driver of that vehicle, but if the engine is whacked, it's whacked. You can only tune it up so much. You may have to take other precautions to fix it. Well, you may be trying to help someone who is extremely depressed or extremely pessimistic with your tools of better fuel, better spark plugs, and tune-ups. Maybe the issue is they're running on five pounds of air in their tire versus forty pounds, so you're trying to do the wrong thing. You have to be very careful about what you're trying to accomplish.

Most people know what their problem is. If you said to them, "Clear your mind right now; just clear it. Empty it all out. Take a nice deep breath -- in through the nose -- out through the mouth. And now I want you to answer a question for me.

I just want you to blurt it out as soon as I ask you. What is making you so resistant?" Nine times out of ten, they'll say it.

It's the same thing when someone gets married and ends up divorced, and they're angry. I can guarantee you they knew the person they married was a jerk the first time they met. So if you ask them what their first impression was when they first met them, they usually will say, "I thought he was a real jerk." They did not follow their intuition.

So, when it comes to people, it's not always that simple. There's not one fix that works for every situation. I hate it when people use this cliché, "Well, how can that be? Can't he just say that this is for everything?" I'm not saying that. There are some tools you can utilize that will work with most people, and this is one of them. Tell a person to clear their mind. Ask them the question and you ask them when their mind is clear, "What is the first thing that surfaces?" Usually their navigator will spit the problem right out. They'll know if it's their husband. They'll know if it's them or finances. They'll know if it's the house. They'll know if it's the way the furniture is set up. They'll know if it's their mother or their aunt. It will just come out. They'll know, and it sounds incredibly simple.

Sometimes the greatest truths come from the simplest places. You have to be very careful though because it can also become a distorted source of information. Then you might say, "Well, should I just start thinking that all my impulses are correct?" Once you know about it, you start polluting it because you create an 'I' that adapts to that situation. Then you cannot really trust it one-hundred percent unless you learn to keep your mind clear.

If you're going to use this tool with someone, they won't even see it coming. "Clear your mind, take a deep breath and just relax. Now, I'm going to ask you a question and I want you to tell me the first thing that comes into your mind. And I don't really want you to stop and think about it. Just talk to me. What is depressing you?" And they will say, "My mother's death." "Your mother died five years ago." "I don't know, that's the first thing that came to me."

Well, ten to one that is the problem. They might not think of it in a hundred years, but there is an issue there that they have not come to terms with yet. And it's in the fiber of their consciousness, in the fiber of their soul. So that's what you're after. You're after the first few things that come into their mind and what you can do to help them. What should you to do to help them? Help them to rebuild the negative memory and retrain the brain with a positive one instead for some kind of release. Everybody knows what their problem is. The problem is the Babbler. The human mind is so complex, so busy, and so demanding. If you just stop it and ask, it will surface. We're not psychiatrists; I'm just saying there are practical tools for you to use that are very useful and powerful.

In meditation, how do you help someone who has these third eye experiences and all these gut feelings, but they have strong reactions?

You've got to deal with this completely opposite from what you are thinking. You've got to bring them back down, have them meditating on their lower chakra, and have them touching physical things. You have to bring them back from 'way out there,' which is probably where they want to go anyway. They need to come down and re-adjust themselves so that they can re-approach the physical body in a calm manner. It's kind of like a spinning top. What happens when it starts wobbling? It quickly falls over. You have to make sure it stays upright. When you're feeling that somebody is all over the place, you've got to bring them back to square one.

Tell them, "Walk, breathe, and empty your mind. I don't want you to take in any data. I don't want you thinking about things. The second your mind starts going, I want you to put your hand on your lower chakra and breathe in through it. I want you to spend the whole week just meditating on the lower chakra. Don't even think about touching the heart.

Don't think about touching the mind. Touch the carpet, touch trees, and listen to people. Just use your five senses."

Even someone who has a higher sensory can get so plugged into it that they become topsy-turvy, and then you have to bring them back down. You've almost got to force them to listen to you. Once they calm down, you can re-approach them and they realize things make a lot more sense to them. That's how I would handle it, but each situation is very unique.

So, with pessimists -- it's all about them, and you know what the truth is? As much as you can tell them to clear their mind and to spit something out, you already know the answer, too. You already know what this person needs, that they're too out there. Their cup is so full of *new age* stuff. When people come to me with all that new age stuff, I tear it apart. I'm cruel to be kind because, if I don't clean that cup out, how do you expect me to work with it?

If you're a good surgeon, you can work on somebody without hurting them without the unnecessary bleeding. You can clean the wound out and stitch it, and they hardly know you did it. There is a difference in how you do things. A good teacher can disassemble someone, be stern about it, and rebuild them, versus a person who's just out destroying others. How do you know when a teacher is being destructive? It has nothing to do with the student. It's a bad teacher because they're letting their inner emotions abuse another person, just for self-gratification. Just because a teacher is a teacher does not mean they don't have their own issues. You have to be mindful as a teacher. You have to ask yourself, "Am I ready to do this and how much time am I willing to work on perfecting my skills?" You have to be stern, but you shouldn't ever be cruel.

I don't ever tell somebody, "Astrology is a bunch of crap and you're stupid for believing it." I approach it this way, "Well, they say there are twelve houses when in reality there's thirteen. That means that everything's off one house. It's based on the gravitational pull of the Earth." So, I use reason and never aggression. I simply give them something to chew on and let them come to their own conclusions. But I also make myself knowledgeable about the subject before I discuss something. Do you think I really want to know more about astrology? Absolutely not! But I need to know something about it if I am going to help somebody else. So, if you know somebody's into something and you know it's hokey, you should educate yourself first a little bit. You should not allow yourself to get into a battle over it. That's like getting into a battle with a religious person. You're on their turf. They're going to quote passages from religious sources. You need to be very logical, reasonable, and strategic in what you're communicating. Your job is to teach them, to inform them, to educate them, but your goal is to raise their consciousness to a higher tonal, not to judge them. Are there other questions?

Recently we were watching a show on TV about identical twins that were separated at birth. The show was to test how different their lives converged without contact. The similarities of the two lives seemed uncommonly familiar. They've both had husbands that were exactly the same, lived on the same kind of streets, same kind of job, married, and divorced almost the same exact time. It's really uncanny. What does it say about how the configuration of the brain designs our lives?

Well, I think there is a 50/50 chance that could happen. I think it's obvious that their brains are going to create similar situations in life. You could say they both married men that were in uniform: One married a fireman and the other one married a policeman. I think that is something that is probably genetically designed. You know what you're interested in. You know what you're not interested in or attracted to. The fact that they led similar lives goes back to people who are optimistic and those who are pessimistic in life. I'm not surprised at all that there are similarities between the two.

The design of the brain is a major influence on the frequency of your consciousness. Data is what builds, designs, and develops your soul. We are here to learn. So what you experience is what tunes you in. If your brain is designed with built-in features that help to advance you in life, then those are things you're going to naturally gravitate toward, but you're still going to draw data.

They both married men in uniforms, but one was a fireman and one was a policeman. There are big differences in those two occupations, yet they're very similar in many ways also. So, to me, it says something about the biological design. I think spiritually, their consciousness is resonating based on their experiences. There would be very similar tools to begin with, but I think you have to keep one thing in mind. When you watch shows like this, and I mean this in the politest way, this is ignorance on the viewer's part. We are watching a show that:

> *Its job is to entertain us because there are other people running shows that compete for your attention; therefore, it has to be entertaining.*
>
> *What is the show trying to show you? It's trying to show you how similar their lives are. So they're saying here are five or six amazing things that are the same. But if we spent time with them, you'd probably also find out they're uniquely different in so many other ways.*

So, if we just focus on what we want to see, that's all we're going to see. In this particular show, it is amazing to see the similarities between the two, but to me that is biological. I also think that if we were to look at other aspects of their life, their souls are individually, unique.

It's not really the soul that dictates their life's outcome as much as it is their biology, right?

No, twins are unique situations. There are plenty of twins who have been separated that have nothing in common at all. In fact, when they meet each other for the first time, sometimes they don't feel anything for each other. You generally don't hear about those cases as it's not as exciting or interesting. I've watched those same documentaries. We're dangerously focusing on one topic, creating antidotal answers that aren't actually truth.

How much of our biology dictates the outcome of our life, as opposed to chance, especially with just the arrangement of the brain?

Chance is probably a big part of it. It's hard to give the exact amounts, but I would say sixty five to seventy percent is biological; therefore, the reason why you meditate, the reason you try to raise your consciousness, and the reason you try to pop out of the cycle of the matrix machine. You're lowering that percentage. You're taking conscious control of your remote consciousness that is biochemically responding.

How you respond to things is sociologically taught to you, so it's imposed on your brain from youth. A lot of the genes that are receptors of the way you think biologically are part of the genetics of your family, so it's not unusual to view things like your parents.

But you also have your sociological background. You have your social circles surrounding you when growing up that adds to the twist of that psychological makeup. Also, you have to keep in mind that most people are red cells. They're biological functioning creatures based on their DNA as well as their sociological programming. A white cell is one that challenges everything and tries to disassemble it to allow a higher consciousness to surface and take greater control.

So, how much then would you say biology is linked to spirituality? Let's say that someone says they come from a long line of psychics or spiritual people, is their biology somewhat altered then?

If you're raised in a spiritual household, you were exposed to a greater belief in those things, which creates greater sensitivity. Biologically, I think the traits run deep. I think it's the same principle where you can look at somebody and say, "Boy, you sure can tell this is your kid." I think, biologically, some people's brains are a little bit more developed spiritually than others. So, it's a combination. Whether they do something with it or not is really the question.

Why is it important to strive to be happy? What does happiness really have to do with the development of consciousness?

Well, happiness is a flow of energy. Happiness is, in part, connected to a sense of freedom, liberty, flow; it's a sense of expansion. Ask yourself if you can feel the answer within you. Happiness is release. It is love. It is a sense of pleasure, but it's mostly peace. It is calmness and it's about being in balance with oneself.

So, what is the opposite of happiness? The opposite is control. The opposite is suppression. It's like holding something still and not letting it move. It's about non-creativeness. It's about non-flow in your heart, in your soul. It is death. It is despair. It is the tree that withers and crumbles. It is an inner sense that knows that when one chooses to be a pessimist, one chooses not to experience life to its fullest. It's as if to say that you are choosing to withdraw because you simply don't want to pursue anymore. You don't care. It doesn't matter. The Universe is expanding and growing; it wants to know more. It is human nature to have a quest. Ever since primitive times, we've migrated to search for better food sources, and that process made us learn because we were exposed to new things and we had to survive. We saw new things and created new ideas. It is in our nature to grow. It is in the nature of the Universe to experience. Happiness is gratification from acknowledging or experiencing things. Ask yourself what makes you happy. Nine times out of ten, it's from experiencing something new or something different. We go to the movies not to watch the same movie twice. We go to the movies to watch a new movie, to gain some new insight, and some new stimulation. We go to the state parks to get away from the same stimulation to find something new that's refreshing or reinvigorating. But there's this internal quest to expand ourselves, to improve ourselves. Happiness is gratification, hopefully in a positive way rather than in a destructive or controlling way.

Chapter 8

Navigation of Children

PEOPLE OFTEN ASK me how they should raise their kids as white cells living in a white cell family. Well, for starters, the best way to encourage your children to become more spiritual is to make them aware of sociological programming. They should understand how their behavior affects others, individually as well as in groups, beginning at an early age on a very basic level. TV is a major influence in their young lives, so be very careful choosing what they can access. You should understand the concept of monkey see, monkey do.

**Do you have any suggestions of
what to subject them to?**

The books that you choose for them should be about leadership, about moving to the beat of their own drum, and how to recognize the patterns that are imposed on them. Role models are very important. A policeman or fireman is a good role model for them as a public official. As human beings, we tend to organize our brains by tagging things, and that's a hard habit to obliterate. We are so inundated by this way of thinking that it is hard to think outside of the box.

You might give them box puzzles to figure out, wooden ones and three- dimensional ones. Explain the process of life to them starting with plants, trees, animals and nature, in general. Be honest with them about biological life. Don't tell them that storks or the birds and the bees are responsible for new life. Teach them honestly about sex education at an early age and simplify it. Help them to understand things earlier on because, for a white cell during their youth, they can be very frustrated. They want the truth not a made-up story. I think intelligent people are frustrated because they have an opinion that wants to be heard. They have something to say, but the elders only think of them as children. They say, "You're a kid. You don't know anything yet," and they suppress the child's spiritual growth by doing that. A lot of times when they do have intellectual questions, I don't think adults can understand the honesty of their question, so they practically punish the kid for asking it.

Nature and the Universe are natural teachers. Should we teach them about those things or wait for them to ask? Are they emotionally ready for those questions at a young age?

You must be consistently aware of how they react emotionally as much as you can. Having quiet moments sitting with your children reading a book, looking at a field, and looking at the stars at night will start them wondering about the vastness of the Universe and the micro life around them. Create things that show them the difference in micro and macro. *You don't want to ask the question. You want them to come to you with the question.* There is no real simple answer. But children are amazing and are not afraid to ask a question to learn the truth about something.

It seems like there is a lot of bullying going on in the schools today, also on Facebook

and other sources of media. How do I
approach this subject with my kids?

You know what I would teach my kids -- *what does it feel
like?* That's what I would teach them. When they do something
bad to somebody else, what does that feel like? If they steal
from somebody, what does it feel like to have something taken
from them? What does death feel like? What does life feel
like? What does that tree feel like? That's how you can help a
white cell to awaken at a very young age. To be conscious of
their choices, and to learn to be more aware of what they are
doing because that makes you a better person. I think that's
the ultimate answer.

If somebody asked me how I would help my child to be
more spiritual, I would say, "Teach them to ask themselves
questions, to feel inside of themselves, and to look at
something and say, 'How would that make me feel? How
does that feel?'" This way, they will learn not to harm other
people, because they can hurt others if they do not feel what
they are doing. They just feel what it's like to gain control or
power instead of what it feels like to be on the opposite side
of conflict. That's what makes us say, "Wow! I don't want to
feel like that. Why would I do that to someone else?" That's
what creates spiritual growth and a better person growing up
in this world.

Can children learn through their five senses to
internalize what they understand externally?
Would it be appropriate to teach them
positive experiences for spiritual growth?

I would teach them to use their five senses instead of
just letting them flounder and discover things on their own.
Everything we have in this dimension is externalized. Our

five senses are all externalized and that is why spirituality is about *internalizing* something *external*. What does it feel like to be in that person? If I can recreate it through my own awareness and understanding, only then can I understand something that my five senses can't necessarily show me. My mind, my sixth sense, and my consciousness have to create that in me so I can reflect on that thought. I think a lot of times we understand what it feels like to be hurt only when we get hurt. It might be funny to watch when somebody else gets hurt, but when you get hurt it's not so funny anymore. Get it?

I think that children see a lot of things that they know are not good. They know it's bad because they can relate to this feeling when they have learned it themselves. They have fallen from a bicycle before or somebody else has bullied them. So they are mimicking what they have learned by their own experiences. Therefore, if you can emphasize that it is good to reflect on things, you can turn this into a very powerful tool of self-growth for your children.

What kind of values and experiences should you push for in a child? What kinds of things should they be exposed to?

One of the biggest lessons is human values, like racism. I think reflecting on what it would feel like to be another race is a good beginning. How would you feel if you were black, yellow, brown, white, or any other color than what you are? What would you think? How would you cope with other peoples' judgment, hatred, anger, profiling, or what other people would say about you? Racism is projected in magazines and other forms of media. In order to grow spiritually, have an open heart toward others and do not judge another person for the color of their skin or the personality that they project as being the core of who they are. This sets a standard for your consciousness. You limit your capability to grow by immediately setting standards on the people around you.

It's no wonder that aliens don't want to come to visit us. There are so many different species that probably inter-breed and look different colors. We are barely getting over racism in our world. In India, they still have segregation of the different classes, and in the United States we struggle over same sex relationships. There is so much hatefulness for our own species rather than compassionate understanding for uniqueness of culture. How would it be possible to accept something alien, their biological environments, and how their societies are structured?

So with all of this in mind, I think the first thing that I would teach a child is to imagine what it would feel like to see the world from the eyes of a different culture? A child should recognize that there isn't one type of bad person, because that is stereotyping. There are no perfect humans. They all have their hatred and their malice. We first must learn to get along with all human beings as our brothers and sisters. So teach your kids how to communicate. Teach them how to get along with others, to be compassionate and kind. That will teach your child social skills and tolerance of others at a young age.

What about introducing them to culture and the arts?

You should introduce them to art, music, sound, and many other creative things. Expose them to musical instruments, explaining why this instrument is different from that instrument. Let them hear the sound of a violin playing, and string instruments, or wind instruments at a young age. There are several CD's now available, like Baby Einstein and various other classical pieces that can be played at an early age to teach them the feeling of music. They can feel the sound of an instrument reverberating off their skin, the vibration of the didgeridoo, how it makes them feel emotionally, the beat of a drum, and even the sound of a seashell from the ocean.

I would introduce different textures and have them feel the differences by comparing one with another. They may have textures in nature, but a child will always remember the moment they pick up a feather and feel its texture, its softness. They may not remember when they first felt the feather, but they will always remember the experience of it. How much better a child's life would be if you could introduce these things at an early age rather than coming upon them later on as they grew up. So, expose them to more things early on and talk about them.

What about communication skills learned through language, reading, self-expression, imagination, and learning how to articulate using stories, movies, or the computer?

The most powerful tool in our society is language. Communication is critically important, especially when teaching others. My communication skills are demonstrated by the choice of words and the tone that I use. So, in emphasizing what I said earlier about teaching children at an early age, I would want my child to learn by reading aloud. As I always say, "To be better speakers, read aloud." I would want to introduce books that have discussions at the end of each chapter to teach them how to articulate the stories. I would want to encourage those kinds of things so they can master those very important skills.

One of the problems of today is that people are lazy. People don't have the time, or maybe it's more that they don't take the time to do what is really important. It's just our busy world, work, and having to pay the bills. It's the demands of a bigger home and nicer things that everyone wants to have.

So, it's really hard to take the time to introduce these things to a child.

Computers are filling in to educate the kids of today, but I always call it surface knowledge. Surface knowledge is something told to you that you haven't personally experienced; but there is no greater knowledge than to experience. This is the reason that what I teach at Higher Balance shows you how to do these things yourself. In the end, you are experiencing for yourself because it is not just the knowledge that you want. You need to actually apply it and gain from it. You need to take it three dimensionally to fully absorb and digest the data. So, I think computer knowledge is good, but it's all surface knowledge. You need to spend time explaining and exposing children to certain things.

What about exposing children to energy? Or water sports? You spent a lot of time in the swimming pool as a child. Would that be beneficial in teaching a child how to learn about or feel energy?

Spending time in a swimming pool would definitely make a difference because they can learn different experiences from the water. For instance, I would teach my child to float. It may sound trivial to you; nonetheless, I would teach them to float like a log. They would float like a log and imagine themselves as a log floating in the water. They should already know how to swim if they are taught at an early age, so tell them, "Okay, now start swimming."

At this point, they are learning how to use their imagination to create different effects in the water. So explain to them, "When you float like a log, imagine that you can fly. Imagine yourself weightless. Imagine that you have no body. You are just floating in the air and there is no you and you are part of everything." That might freak them out a little bit, but it's also going to make them think a little more and learn to ask intelligent questions at a younger age. You just need to expose them to life, and to life experiences.

When I was young, I was naturally drawn to those types of things. But that may not be the case for most people. I spent hours in the swimming pool just floating. It wasn't because I wanted to float like a log. It was just that I enjoyed not feeling my body. My mind would move outside of itself. Those are the things you need to encourage a child to do.

Learn about energy. For me, energy is very real. It has texture. It has form. Your hand may not feel it, but it might feel it if you understand it. I believe that I learned how to move and work with energy at a young age from being in the swimming pool, from doing the *Phoenix Splash*, from causing whirlpools, and feeling water currents. I'd move my hands and then watch the ripples in the water. I could feel something inside of me. I'd pretend to project the wave outward, and I could see the ripple moving away from me, getting bigger and longer. Eventually, I could do it outside of the water. In the dark, I could see the ripple from my own energy. I'd pretend that I was in the pool and I could ripple the darkness and it was energy.

I didn't fully understand what I was doing, but this is how I taught myself. As a more enlightened person, it came to me intuitively the same way a thought comes to someone to pick up a feather, or to think up different ideas in their youth. I could unconsciously push it to higher levels to experience it.

You've taught us a lot about micro versus macro. What about using a microscope to study the different effects of liquids or solids?

When I was about eight or nine years old, I remember it was a rainy, gray day outside, and I watched the raindrops collecting on the window. I was just bored, staring at the window. I put my eye right up to the glass and stared at a raindrop. After staring at it for a while, I zoomed into it and I could see the micro life in that raindrop. It was like a microscope and I could see the living organisms in the water. Either the organisms were in my eye or they were in the water droplet. I spent a long time just looking at all of the little organisms in the water because I was mesmerized by it.

I once read an article in a science journal that said it's absolutely feasible for the eye to do that. I did countless things like that all of the time. Those are the things that made me understand things at a very young age. They were self-teaching, self-revealing in themselves. You don't need expensive equipment to learn about nature, energy, and the Force. Go work in a pool and you will have those types of experiences.

Can you tell us about some of the experiences you had as a youth? Were you into video games at all?

Well, a child has nothing better to do with their time so they can engross themselves with certain things of a more bountiful nature to gain knowledge and experience. As we grow older, we don't have the patience, the endurance, or the time to do these things so we can refine and perfect ourselves.

I remember playing Asteroids and having a lot of time to kill. I played Asteroids so many times that I could virtually fly through the game at Mach speed. Once you to a certain point in the game, it just starts again from the beginning. I had learned all the programs and all the possibilities. I just knew where and when everything was going to happen.

One day, there was a kid named Vic who said, "I will kick anybody's ass at Asteroids." So, we bet about five dollars on it. They all were shocked that I could just go on and on and didn't think anything of it. For me, it was just about the patterns. Once I learned the patterns, I knew when the asteroids would break off. I knew which way the game would go, and I knew how many, I could virtually just go on and on and on. That is what burned me out on video games because all I can see now is the patterns in all the video games. It doesn't matter how complex they have become. It's simply the same game dressed up in different graphics. It's all zeros and ones. It's the same battle over and over again. They are just making it harder and weakening you. Once you build up your strength, and the other players are weaker, then they just re-vamp them, change their uniform and it's the same thing again.

These are the things that I learned very early on. Maybe it is because of the experience I had out on that little pond that heightened my sensitivity. I remember just reflecting, and thinking about it.

You mentioned about taking your friends astral projecting. We were talking about floating and flying just now. Is there any correlation in that?

It was exactly the same time when I lived in an apartment complex. It had a big swimming pool and they were friends that I had back then.

Do you think we should use water and movement as an energy source for parents to encourage their children?

Anyone who wants their children to be spiritual should encourage them to play with water. There's a huge connection. When I was three or four, we had an above ground swimming pool. I was fearless of water. One time, when I was about four, I should have drowned. I remember being in this pool and the whole family was in there. My grandmother had on a bathing suit with a little skirt on it. It was flowery, old school stuff.

Everybody was in the pool. I remember walking around the bottom of the pool looking at everybody's legs and seeing a reverse reality. It seemed so surreal to me. When you're that small, seeing people walking around on the outside of the pool, it seemed so unusual. I was really amused by it all. I remember being underwater, not thinking about air, breathing, or anything. Somebody eventually pulled me out of the water.

I always loved the water. I loved the feeling of being detached from my physical body. It felt more natural than when my body was weighed down by gravity. It was a spiritual thing. That doesn't mean you should run out and get a deprivation tank. I have mixed feelings about deprivation tanks. There is no substitute for a good swimming pool when it comes to doing certain exercises because it gives you a reaction that you can observe. It's a representation of energy so that you can understand how a concept works.

In order to be able to do something, you have to understand how it works. That's why I use so many analogies. Even if something doesn't work exactly how you expect, it's enough for your brain to grasp it. Your brain will make it work. You need to get past the Governor, that barrier in your head that's struggling to control whatever you are doing. When I'm pushing energy, I see it and feel it in my mind. I am certain it's going to happen because of my experiences in the pool observing the ripples in the water. I know that if I move the water one way, the wave will fan out from one direction, from smaller to wider. It won't make a big full circle. It will make a wave in a certain direction that will only get so many feet apart. I know that if I do a full body circle, it's going to do a certain thing. I know that if I implode it, it pops back up and it creates energy. So, I know how it works.

Ironically, when I think about energy, my hands move the same way that I move water. When I move energy around my body, it's because I am able to move it in the pool. I can move water towards me. I can feel it rush over my skin and that has taught me how to move the energy inside my body. So, I learned a lot from those experiences. When most people swim, they just swim. They just enjoy it, but not me. I feel and I work with the texture and the pressure of the water. It's so minute, yet it tunes you because you get so used to the minute textures.

Are the methods for working with weather patterns similar to working with moving water?

That's what taught me how to manipulate the weather. A lot of times when I work with air and wind, it's the same thing. I can feel it like a body that I relate to, like water, and I work with it the same way. I understand it so I can pull and move it. When you move a body of water, you can move and project it across the pool. So, I learned to project energy great distances because of how it perpetuates. There is no limit. The only limit was the pool wall. If you are moving something bigger than that, like clouds in the sky or energy, there are no limitations. It's just how much of a burst or how much energy you put into it.

When kids reach a certain age, the Governor kicks in and the brain starts to develop some conventional tools. What do you recommend to prolong the open mindedness that children have at an early age?

I think it's all about their environment. If you start their development off right, that is the main concern. It starts in the womb with your emotions, your vibe, and your consciousness. Up to the age of seven, it's critical you're mindful of what you project to your child. After that, you're going to understand perpetual motion. Again, I am thinking about the example of the water movement. Where is it going? How big is it going to get? How will it ripple? What is it going to touch?

The brain reacts based on what you communicate to it. It functions a certain way in the early years up to the teenage years. It will learn all of the necessities for integrating into our environment, but you should also continue to be supportive of your child's creativity. Hopefully, they will move in a positive direction as they mature.

When would you start promoting experiences of a metaphysical nature?

You have to be very careful with that. I experienced a bit of resentment after being exposed to entities and spirits when I was very young. I don't think that's a bad thing but I was a unique case. It was horrifying for me so that's where my father made a critical mistake. He should have been a bit more careful and he should have spent more time explaining and personally training me, which he didn't do. He wanted to entertain his friends so he had me doing things to appease his own interest, rather than helping me to understand what I was doing. Therefore, I was left to interpret and understand a lot of things on my own. There were a lot of entities and other things that I could see that were never explained to me.

It was simply an ability that was far beyond his comprehension. I don't believe he was aware of what he was doing or my true capabilities. They are certainly far beyond who and what he is. So, I don't blame him in that aspect. I just wish he was a little bit more careful with the Ouija board exposure, the table rapping, the séances, and those kinds of things. Fortunately, I was intelligent and could figure things out on my own. Yet, there were still some things that were very frightening to me. It exposed me to advanced level sensing and feeling things I wasn't fully prepared to understand.

So, I would help my children to understand that entities don't necessarily pose a threat. They are like dogs. Don't go out and pet them, but they generally won't bother you if you don't bother them. Grumpy entities are a lot like dogs. Their bark is a lot worse than their bite. They make a lot of noise and put on a big show, but they really aren't going to do anything because they just don't have enough energy. Most entities seem fearful because of their desperation to talk to you because they can't talk to anyone else. It sounds complicated, but at the same time, other things in life can be just as complicated. You just have to spend the time to understand. Kids need to feel safe and secure. To me, the most important thing is that they are allowed to safely explore on their own, and they need a safe place to do it.

This is a tough world and we live in extreme times. How do you protect your child from the dangers that seem to lurk everywhere? Children feel invincible, often unaware of unexpected influences.

When you send your children outside to play when they are toddlers, they don't usually go running off, although I did when I was very young. There is a false sense of safety when you are a child. You can wander around in your backyard and the world seems huge. People will say to you, "Who knows what is out there in the woods?"

This is a very tough subject because fear builds up sensory. I was constantly in fear, but that is what built my amazing sensory. I constantly worried about what was in the woods. I felt all of those entities. If I had a better mentor to explain things to me, my spiritual awakening would have been a more peaceful transition. Be patient, compassionate, and loving to your child. If you accomplish that, they will do very well. I don't think there is a simple answer for raising a white cell child. Just do the best you can.

Chapter 9

WATER OF LIFE

THE *WATER OF Life* technique is more of a process or ritual rather than an everyday practice. I would like to see it used in a ritual format. This technique is specifically designed to raise tonal, energy, and consciousness; the most important is tonal. Tonal is the vibration of your soul, your essence. It decides the level of your energy, and it decides the actions of the Karma you will take on. It is the vibration that the forces of the Universe respond to. The lower your tonal, the lower your energy; and the higher your tonal, the higher your energy. Higher tonal is more spiritual, more ethereal, and closer to a level of God consciousness than lower tonal, which is associated with feelings of being extracted from that consciousness.

The higher you raise your tonal, the higher your consciousness becomes. Your high, spiritual vibration is sent forth and people will feel something from you and be drawn towards you; as all creatures and all people are drawn on a psychic level to a person with very high tonal. That is the purpose for the *Water of Life*. If you follow this technique, you will raise your tonal, your consciousness. If you don't, then that's your prerogative. I believe in the frequency of Karma. Either you're ready for this kind of knowledge, or you're not.

Now I'm going to take you through the basic sequence. It's very important that you understand the process. The first thing you need is a glass of water. This glass of water should be about four to six ounces; the water should be pure. You cannot use soda or juice or other forms of liquids. Water is the only thing that's acceptable. This water should be room temperature, or the same temperature as tap water. The glass of water will be energized: when the liquid is being poured into the glass, focus and think of Prana. Think of the water as being pure energy, pure life force. Feel Prana moving within the water that's being poured into the glass. It is the spiritual concept of a ritual that you are following. Visualize Prana filling this glass of water.

With non-thought, as water is being poured into the glass, focus and think of Prana moving into the water. See and feel it glowing with life force.

When you are pouring water into the glass, it's very important to try to attain non-thought, other than the fact that you are visualizing Prana or energy going into this glass of water. You don't want to program an essence or an emotion within this liquid if you can help it. Not that it's easy to do, but it's something to keep in mind. The water will be placed down in front of you within reach when you sit down in a half-lotus position. I will go through the complete technique in a moment; for now I will discuss the process and then apply it later, step-by-step. Once you have the water and are sitting down, pick up the glass and hold it above your head outstretched at a roughly seventy-degree angle; just above your forehead.

As you do this, visualize Prana coming into this glass of water. Visualize it drawing in Prana and illuminating with Prana energy, glowing with life force. Next, say aloud, "I take the *Water of Life* within," meaning that this water will nourish your physical body but the essence of the Prana that is in this water is going to fill your spiritual body, your spiritual soul. As you begin drinking the water, visualize this liquid going into your body, almost like liquid silver or liquid white illumination, nourishing your body with Prana. It's nourishing your body with water which is the vital essence of life on this planet essentially. Hold the intention that you want to give yourself this water to nourish your body and feed your spirit. This water is literally a purifier; it's a purifier because it's water and it's pure, but it's also a purifier because it's Prana. It's pure Prana that you're taking into your body. The more that you clearly focus on the Prana, the more that Prana has an effect on you. Let nothing else enter your mind. Continuously think about the effect of the Prana coming into your body and the connection of the Prana to God.

1. Sitting half-lotus, place the water in front of you, within reach.
2. Hold the water above you, roughly forty-five degrees. Visualize drawing Prana into the glass and illuminating with life force.
3. Begin drinking, visualizing white glowing liquid flowing through you as you begin to illuminate.

Some people may want to use this exercise in an outdoor environment. If so, you're more than welcome to use bottled water or whatever you like. Don't have a sports cap that you have to squeeze the water into your mouth because then it takes away from the fluidity of the liquid flowing into your mouth. When you drink this water, focus on the thickness of the fluid coming into you. Roll your tongue up so that the water goes underneath. Think about absorbing Prana underneath your tongue. There are a lot of ancient teachings that suggest that the main glands or the area of the body that absorbs the majority of Prana is actually located under your tongue. Then, thinking about the water, experiencing the Prana, slowly drink it. Experience it as it's flowing down through your body into your stomach. Visualize it nurturing and filling every single nerve, bone, and muscle. The more complex you get, the better. Experience a very blissful, beautiful harmony within yourself that you've just raised your first level of tonal because you're thinking of Prana. It's very good to have your consciousness on Prana.

You might want to do some stretching exercises before you actually sit down and begin the *Water of Life*. First, find a quiet location to do this. Before you get your water, make sure you have a space and the time to complete it. If you are going to be meditating indoors, then it's good to use the same spot consistently. The reason for this is that energy saturates whatever area it is regularly projected into. It saturates the area that you sit in consistently, like a sponge with water. Keeping this in mind, when we meditate we are reaching a higher level of consciousness, producing an excellent form of energy. We're saturating the environment that we are in or the spot that we are sitting in and whatever's close to us with this energy. If we sit there again in the future, it's going to have a much better effect on our meditation, which is exactly what we want to have done.

When you go outdoors to meditate, spend time searching for the right place. Listen to your inner emotions. Listen to your inner feelings. Clear your mind and let your hands fall loose at your sides. Open your palms to feel the air, the temperature and the wind movements. Use your mind to feel and look around with your eyes as to what is calling out to you. What area is saying, "Meditate with me," or, "Meditate under me; I'm a tree; just choose this spot," or next to this body of water or this spring making a nice soothing, relaxing sound. Not every spot is an excellent spot: some places are better than others. You just can't walk to any spot, plop down, and say, "Okay, this is going to be a great spot." You have to feel for it. It's like looking for diamonds or for gold. Look for an energy spot that's attracting your frequency because in your mind you know what you want. You know what you are seeking! You're going to find the right place if you keep your mind clear and free from heavy thoughts. Having a spot to meditate in is a process of choice, and searching.

When you find your spot, sit down in the half-lotus position keeping your back straight. The straighter your back, the better; energy flows up and down the spine. You do not have to have a perfectly straight back; you don't want to exhaust the muscles in your back; just have a straight posture. It's very important to have your head straight, because if your head or your chin is drooping down, the energy flow is not quite as good as having your head facing straight up, and having your body firmly straight in a sitting position.

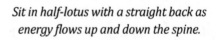

Sit in half-lotus with a straight back as energy flows up and down the spine.

A half-lotus is when one foot is underneath the leg and the other foot is lifted up and placed on top of the opposite leg. Some people have problems with this because one knee is sticking up and the other one goes down. That's really not much of a problem; just work with what you have. If you have to sit Indian-leg style, that's okay. I prefer that you sit in a half-lotus if you can. It does take a certain amount of time, but you can allow your legs to rest, and as they are resting, and you practice the half lotus, you will find that your muscles in your legs get used to stretching which is very good. You'll be able to do a half-lotus after several weeks of practicing. If you have a bad back or a problem sitting, use a chair. Do not cross your legs when you sit in a chair. Make sure the chair has a straight back on it so that you do not slouch.

While you are sitting in half-lotus, rest one palm on top of the other, so that your palms are facing up in your lap. It circulates the energy much better.

Now, during the *Water of Life,* we will seek to achieve non-thought. That is to shut off the Babbler which is a process in your head that goes, "Gee, how long is this going to go for?" Or, "Boy, I have to do laundry tonight," and, "Oh, wait a minute, shut up, I'm trying to meditate." You're trying to have absolute non-thought. The brain is the machinery of the body, the computer that's programmed by society. The mind is the closest thing to the soul; it's the actual spirit that runs the body and the brain. Over time, the mind has become submissive to the brain. This makes the mind very weak. In meditation, you're raising the power of the mind versus the brain. We want to silence the Babbler to achieve a higher state of consciousness.

During the exercise, there are periods where you should hold non-thought for one minute. Try not to think about how long you've achieved this or how long you haven't had non-thought. The best way to do this is to set up a timer; otherwise you will be counting in your head. Make sure it is only one minute, not longer. It isn't a competition. During that minute, you must focus on having non-thought and nothing more. You can do this one of two ways: find a spot and stare at the spot with a soft gaze while you have non-thought with your eyes open, or close your eyes and maintain non-thought with your eyes closed. I will leave it at your discretion. I would suggest staring at a spot with non-thought. It can be a little more difficult in the beginning to have non-thought with your eyes closed in silence.

Now, let's talk about breath. Breath is very important. Set your breathing to match the beat of your heart, so you may want to get your pulse from your arm. If you don't know how to get it from your arm, then put your finger on your neck and find it there. Practice now before you start the technique. Count six beats of your pulse, then count three beats. That's the rhythm you'll follow. So breathe in for six beats, and then breathe out for three. Then immediately go back to the inhale for six beats. Perhaps you want to correspond your breathing to the rhythms of your heart so you can set a sequence. Stay in rhythm.

Do not let yourself get caught up in listening to your heartbeat. Put your hand on your pulse the first few times you do this technique. After that, try to automate it. If you don't, you're going to find that you're saying numbers in your head which breaks non-thought. Set the rhythm and move on. The rhythm doesn't have to be perfect. Don't get over-fixated with the concept of following that rhythm. Let yourself flow and go with the practical rhythm that you have figured out.

We will do a set of ten of those and then go back to your normal breathing pattern. Always remember to sit firmly, straight, and keep your mind as clear as you can.

The next thing that we'll do is to have a session of Aums. An Aum is exactly that: "Aaaauuumm." Focus on that sound; clear your mind. Keep it clear and feel the relaxation and the power that comes from that state of mind, that state of thought, that vibration because it's really not a thought. We'll do a series of seven Aums.

If you're out in public keep in mind that some people may be watching you. Take pride in what you do. Don't be self-conscious or defensive because many people are simply curious. If you were walking out in the park and heard somebody doing Aums, wouldn't you be intrigued? Wouldn't you want to talk to that person or at least get a look? When someone is in a meditative state of mind, it raises their consciousness and others will pick up on the vibration. It's different. It sticks out. You may come across people who are intrigued, and who are searching. You may be able to give them some guidance, especially when you're in a higher state of consciousness and very peaceful in your mind; you may find it very rewarding. So, take pride in those Aums. Let everybody hear them. If other people are willing to play their religious music or sing in church, you too should take pride in what you're doing.

Next are hand postures; hands are a direct route to your mind. It is a reverse process of thinking. It is like when Italians make their hands move around a lot in the air as they're talking or using their hands to express emotion. The Universal symbol to stop, by placing your hand firmly out with the palm up and fingers out pointing upward, has an effect on people's minds. It's a way of expressing ourselves subliminally without verbally speaking. We can apply this trick by using hand gestures to alter our consciousness.

One particular hand gesture that is considered universal for a high state of mind is done by placing your middle finger onto your thumb and placing your hand about heart level. When you put those two fingers together that is telling your consciousness, "Perfection, perfection, absolute perfection."

Place your middle finger on your thumb, holding it heart level, and feel the frequency of, "Absolute perfection".

If you very carefully listen to your consciousness right now and clear your mind, you can place your thumb on your pinkie and think about how it makes you feel. It has a certain vibration. It's like playing a piano. If you bring your thumb to your ring finger, you'll find it has a different feeling. Skipping your middle finger, go to your index finger and placing your index finger on your thumb, you will find an energy feeling. It helps to control your energy. But the middle finger makes you feel very proud and certain of your spirituality; it's a superior and well-tuned energy. It helps to redefine and redirect your energy body.

Only use one hand; allow the other hand to rest down; eyes open or closed. To avoid distraction, eyes closed might be best. Have a sense of pride and power, when you do that.

While you are doing the exercise, keep in the back of your mind as an intention that you want to raise your Prana, raise your energy, and get closer to God.

Near the end of the session, when you feel more vibrant and spiritually aware, outstretch both your arms towards the sky but the intention is towards the Universe. Like people do when they say, "Hallelujah," and really mean it. It is a grateful embrace, a liberating surrender. Outstretch both your arms like the letter T, with your hands diagonally up and palms out, head facing the sky. Verbally say out loud, which is more respectful than mentally saying it because you're conquering your fears, "I accept the power of the Force within me," or, "I accept the Force within me."

*Near the end of the session outstretch both your arms towards the
Universe. It is a grateful embrace, a liberating surrender. Say, "I accept the
power of the Force within me."*

It's a way of signifying that you are accepting this tonal,
this energy that you've risen to, which is a very spiritual, very
beautiful, very kind vibration. Then bring your arms down
and literally just bow. Bow to the ground saying, "Thank you;
I'm minuscule to the Universe; I'm nothing compared to the
Universe, but as long as the Force resides within me, I am
completely one with the Universe and that's all-powerful." All
is one.

Keep in mind that the purpose of this is to raise your
consciousness, to raise your tonal. Your tonal is the essence
of your energy. The higher your tonal, the more powerful, the
more spiritual, and the more ethereal your essence of being
is. Your tonal will enable you to heal the sick. Your tonal will
enable you to do miracles. It will enable you to become a
spiritual being on this Earth. It will help you to awaken. It will
help you to become one with whom and what you may be,
which is beyond what you realize that you are. In this process,
a lot of things may happen. When your tonal is very high, you
will become aware of things that you may never have been
aware of: sounds and sights become more intense, colors
become more brilliant, and the world takes on a different

level of experience. You will find that plants and trees, having no negative vibration whatsoever, become more receptive to you.

These are feelings you want to enjoy and project outside of yourself. Allow these feelings and energy to flow. Always keep in mind that when you are in this state of tonal, this endless depth of love of vibration, nothing can touch you. Nothing's going to affect you in this state. Watch how life becomes richer, more fulfilling, and more rewarding to you. Everything around you becomes fantastic; that's walking and living in a higher level of tonal.

These are the things that we are trying to achieve. Each Water of Life session takes approximately twenty minutes in its totality. Practice this technique at different times, or different locations. Shorten or lengthen the session, whatever is good for you.

Before you begin your first session, get a cup the size of a regular drinking glass, filled about halfway with water. Make sure you have a place picked out where you can remain undisturbed. When you sit down to start, place the glass on the ground in front of you.

Water of Life

Exercise Walkthrough

Fill a 4-8oz glass with room-temperature water.

As you fill this glass of water, *focus* on the water being *energized. Concentrate* on the water being *saturated* with Prana.

Relax. Do some stretching to limber up. Clear your mind.

Sit down in a half lotus. Set the water in front of you.

Take three deep long breaths in through your nose, visualizing Prana. Exhale through your mouth releasing all negative energy.

Allow one minute of non-thought.

Inhale *slowly* through your nose, drawing in the Prana. Exhale through your mouth releasing all negative energy.

Center your concentration on the glass. With both hands, raise the glass to a 45 degree angle above your head.

Visualize the energy from your body *infusing* the glass of water. *Envision* the Prana from the environment around you permeating the water as well.

Say aloud, "I take the *water of life* within."

Bring the Glass to your lips and drink. *Feel* the water underneath your tongue absorbing the Prana. Then place the glass back down beside you to the right or left.

Allow one minute of non-thought.

Feel your tonal increasing.

Now, inhale through your nose, visualizing Prana, and exhale all your *breath* in half the time you spent inhaling. (Repeat 19 times)

Relax and return to normal breathing.

Allow one minute of non-thought.

Take a long deep breath in through your nose absorbing Prana energy. Exhale through your mouth, releasing all negative energy.

Complete seven Aums out loud; followed by allowing one minute of non-thought.

Take a long deep breath in through your nose absorbing Prana energy. Exhale through your mouth, releasing all negative energy.

Take your right hand and place your middle finger to your thumb. Extend your hand about a foot in front of your face and *center your focus* on how that hand position feels to you.

Now, breathe in through your nose, focusing on your energy vibrating at a *perfect* tonal, *absorbing* perfect Prana, and exhale as a master.

Now inhale through your nose, visualizing Prana, and exhale all your *breath* in half the time you spent inhaling.
(Repeat 11 times)

Return to normal breathing.
As your energy *tonalizes*, raise your mind to the *Love of God*, the *Love of Spirit*, *Soul*, and *Universe*.

THE NEXT STEP IS YOURS

THANK YOU FOR joining me on this journey. My hope is that you take what you have learned from this book and apply it to your spiritual path. Higher Balance is a dedicated, grass-roots organization. We rely on the power of people to spread our mission and knowledge.

If I could ask one thing of you: share this book with one other person who might be interested or leave a short, honest review at Amazon.com. Help fuel the growth of spiritual knowledge. Let consciousness prosper.

What happens next depends on where you are in your journey and what can serve you best.

What are you waiting for? Continue Your Journey

Further reading is available in the following books:

The Handbook of the Navigator
www.navigatorhandbook.com

Meditation within Eternity: The Modern Mystics Guide to Gaining Unlimited Spiritual Energy, Accessing Higher Consciousness and Meditation Techniques for Spiritual Growth
www.meditationwithineternity.com

Bending God: A Memoir by Eric Robison
www.bendinggod.com

ADD TO YOUR EXPERIENCE
READERS ONLY FREE MATERIAL

Readers of this book receive special reader-only material that you can download for free. This extra material expands on the knowledge you have gained here.

To receive your free downloads, visit
www.ignitingthesixthsense.com
then click on the Readers-Only option. Follow the directions to enter a password from this book to login.

Beyond this Book

To discover techniques and knowledge to experience awakening yourself beyond what has been discussed in this book, please visit us at: www.higherbalance.com.

Higher Balance Institute's programs were created with the purpose of stimulating and activating the dormant sixth sense, the missing link to spiritual awakening.

Higher Balance programs are provided as books, at-home audio courses, or a self-paced online system, that comes with everything you need to accomplish your goals. It is the most unique and powerful program of its kind in the world. Join us and the thousands of others worldwide who have been transformed through the Higher Balance experience.

Higher Balance Institute
515 NW Saltzman Road #726
Portland, Oregon 97229

www.higherbalance.com

Sit vis vobiscum.

CPSIA information can be obtained at www.ICGtesting.com
Printed in the USA
LVOW13s1328200813

348766LV00006B/11/P